To
Claire and Sara,
who put up with a great deal.

Icons of the New Economy

- Rocket scientists
Often the unsung heroes, without the rocket scientists the Internet and the Web would not exist as we know it today. Laboring behind the scenes, the rocket scientists have pioneered many of the technologies that we now take for granted.

- Money men
Every revolution has its financiers. The money men stoke the fires of the new economy by providing the risk capital that makes it all possible. In doing so they have created a new industry – Venture Capital – virtually from scratch.

- Wunderkinder
Breathing new life into the new business revolution, wunderkinder are carrying the e-business torch for the digital generation. Fearsomely bright, computing is their second language; some were programming computers before they were into their teens.

- Mavericks
The firebrands of the e-business revolution the mavericks are harnessing the power of the Internet to challenge establishment thought and put a match to the temple of tradition.

- Incumbents
  There at the start, they may well be there at the finish. Many of the incumbents started the original digital revolution. They're not about to let the new kids on the block railroad them into a quiet retirement.

- Dreamers/visionaries
  Just as Ancient Greece had its Delphic Oracle, so the e-business revolution has its own cyber visionaries and seers. The visionaries look further than the next quarterly set of economic figures or corporate results – something Wall Street could learn from. They tell us how the new technologies will impact on society and business at a fundamental level.

- Chroniclers
  When history looks back at the Internet-inspired business revolution it will do so through the eyes of the chroniclers. A new voice for a new era the chroniclers capture the zeitgeist and disseminate it across the globe.

- Alchemists
  The rocket scientists may have invented the Internet but the alchemists have turned it into commercial gold. The alchemists cast their spells over traditional business models to conjure up some of the most innovative e-businesses imaginable. Only time will tell which spells will last.

Contents

Acknowledgements

We would like to thank all those who have chronicled the Internet business revolution; their endeavors made our task infinitely easier. We would also like to thank Mark Allin and Richard Burton at Capstone Publishing for their indulgence, and Stuart Crainer at Suntop Media, for his encouragement and moral support. A big thank you, too, to Sparks and the guys at Carbon8 for their eleventh-hour icons.

Introduction

The Internet is all-pervasive. Its influence and power extend ever further into every aspect of our private and professional lives. We routinely use it as a source of reference, a medium for discussion, and, increasingly, as a place to conduct business. The 'e' in *e-business* is now so ubiquitous that it is easy to forget that just a matter of years – indeed months – ago, the world looked very different. The business world in particular has been turned upside down by the Net. The word *revolution* has been used so liberally that its meaning has become devalued. Yet, the reverberations in the world of commerce that have resulted from the Net constitute nothing less than a revolution. Every revolution needs its architects. Without Lenin, Trotsky and others, nothing would have happened in Russia in 1917. Without an intelligentsia and people to take new ideas and make them a reality, nothing changes. So who are the architects of this business revolution?

Some connected up the information pipelines that make the Internet what it is today: people like Tim Berners-Lee, who created the World Wide Web; Vinton Cerf, who first introduced the ideas underpinning the Internet at UCLA; and Jon Postel, whom *The Economist* described as the closest thing to an Internet god. These largely unsung heroes are the true architects of the Internet – the rocket scientists who invented the technology to make it all possible. Then there are others, whose names are more familiar to businesspeople. They saw the Internet, understood its potential, and created business models to exploit the commercial opportunity. Technologically competent, but primarily business pioneers, they are people like Jeff Bezos, founder of Amazon.com, and Jay Walker of Priceline, who 'got it' and got on with it. Others combine technological brilliance with commercial savvy. Among them David Filo and Jerry Yang who founded Yahoo!, and Marc Andreessen, co-founder of Netscape, who was just 23 when he led a team of programmers that created the Web browser Netscape Navigator.

The list goes on. History will confirm that since the mid-1990s, these and other remarkable individuals have been busy revolutionizing the business world. This is already having a major impact on big business. Unthinkable just a few years ago, the Fortune 500 – a mere nine percent of the US economy – is no longer where it's at. It's more than just a changing of the old guard, it's a palace coup on a grand scale. By definition, that's a revolution. OK, so there have been one or two hiccups along the way. It's par for the course.

In recent months, the pure play dot-coms have been assailed by the slings and arrows of outrageous fortune. Many of these companies, and the individuals behind them, have been on a rollercoaster ride which has taken them (and their companies' share prices) to dizzying heights only to fall to earth. It was ever thus for those gathered up in the whirlwind of technological change. But how significant is the advent of the Internet, really?

History's perspective

Caught up in the vortex of hyperbole, it's hard to put the Internet revolution in perspective. We know that the business world is changing, but is it a revolution to end all revolutions? Opinion varies on this point. Writing in *Fortune* in November 1999, Justin Fox offers some badly needed perspective. He argues that what we are experiencing is just the latest in a string of technology-driven shifts. Far from being unique, he says, there are remarkable parallels with earlier technological advances:

> "The historians' input is crucial because despite the prophets of the Digital Age who depict it as unprecedented, it's not. Just take a quick look at business history."

Once you look back at the early days of the factory, the railroad, the automobile, and especially the harnessing of electricity, a lot of what seems new about the Internet starts to look familiar. The true commercial revolution took place in Western Europe some 500 or so years ago, says Fox. A complete break with the past, it paved the way for subsequent technology-led revolutions. It was built on one of the key realizations of the age. Summed up by the economist Adam Smith in his book *Wealth of Nations* (1776), it asserted that the true wealth of a nation is measured not by how much gold it possesses, but by what it can produce.

Productivity was crowned king and has reigned supreme ever since. This laid the foundation for a series of technology-related revolutions – of which the Internet is the most recent. But what about the explosion of entrepreneurial activity ignited by the Web? Well, it seems that the advent of almost every new technology during the past 150 years has spawned a free-for-all for entrepreneurs. There were, for example, 150 companies making automobiles between 1910 and 1920. Wild investor enthusiasm is another common feature. Net stocks may be up today and down tomorrow, but the phenomenon is nothing new. Investors have repeatedly gone gaga over the next big thing – from canals to railroads.

For example, Thomas Edison invented the light bulb in 1879. Three years later, electricity stocks were selling like crazy, with 16 new electrical companies floated in a single two-week period in June 1882. More sobering still is the impact of IT on productivity over the past 20 years. On this test, the computer's track record isn't all it's cracked up to be. Despite corporate enthusiasm for information technology, the much vaunted productivity gains have so far largely failed to materialize. IT currently accounts for more than half of capital spending by US companies. But in manufacturing the productivity needle has barely moved. The words of MIT Nobel economist Robert Solow still haunt us: "We see the computers everywhere but in the productivity statistics."

Why should the Internet be any different? The simple answer is because it connects us in units of one. Interconnectivity, once we get to grips with it, has the potential to create huge productivity gains. We may indeed see a new economy, but we are only at its threshold. The mistake with e-commerce is to regard the first clumsy attempts to leverage the power of the Internet as anything more than that. What we are seeing, to borrow from Winston Churchill's famous wartime speech, is not the end, not even the beginning of the end, but, perhaps, the end of the beginning.

Technological leaps have punctuated the evolution of humans. The history of business, too, is littered with technological breakthroughs which redefined the economics of commerce, triggering massive redistributions of wealth and employment. Although the most recent manifestation is the world of the Internet and e-commerce, this isn't the most important phenomenon in the history of business. Money, the wheel, writing, electricity, mass production, the microchip, arguably, these all had a bigger impact.

What can be said, however, is that the Internet is one of the most significant technological breakthroughs of our time.

Truly astonishing are the following:

- the rate of growth of the Internet;
- the wealth it has already generated; and
- the claims made on its behalf.

Table 1 Number of people online March 2000

Area	Nos. in millions	Annual % increase
Africa	2.6	136
Asia/Pacific	68.9	155
Europe	83.4	108
Middle East	1.9	111
Canada and the US	136.9	41
South America	10.7	102

Source: US Department of Commerce, June 2000

Let's put this in context. The pager took 41 years to gain 10 million consumers; the telephone 36 years to reach the same level of use. It took radio over 30 years to reach 60 million people, and television 15 years. The VCR took nine years to reach 10 million consumers. The Internet took just two years to pass 10 million, and has now hit 300 million.[1]

Consider this: the total US Internet economy more than doubled between 1996 and 1997, from $15.5 billion to $38.8 billion. By 2001, the total US Internet economy is projected to be over $350 billion. Business-to-business e-commerce is expected to account for the largest share, $186 billion. Consumer retail activity is expected to emerge more slowly, possibly totaling $18.4 billion in 2001.[2]

Wealth creation

Despite its non-profit making origins, millions and sometimes billions of dollars have been made on the back of the Internet. John Doerr, a partner at the VC firm Kleiner Perkins Caulfield & Byers, has described it as "the largest legal accumulation of wealth in history." A glance at Tables 2 and 3 confirms the point.

Table 2 Worth of Internet billionaires

Name	Company	Ranking	Worth ($ billions)
Bill Gates	Microsoft	(1)	60
Larry Ellison	Oracle	(2)	47
Paul Allen	Microsoft	(3)	28
Masayoshi Son	Softbank	(6)	19.4
Michael Dell	Dell	(7)	19.1
Steve Ballmer	Microsoft	(=9)	15.5
David Filo	Yahoo!	(=36)	6.6
Jerry Yang	Yahoo!	(=38)	6.4
Jeff Bezos	Amazon	(=41)	6.1
Pierre Omidyar	eBay	(=49)	5.0

Based on *Forbes* World's Richest, April 2000

Table 3 Revenues of high-ranking, high-tech companies

Company	Revenue $ millions	Ranking
MCI World Com (Cerf)	37,120	(25)
Intel (Grove, Moore)	29,389	(39)
Dell	25,265	(56)
Microsoft (Gates, Allen, Ballmer)	19,747	(84)
Xerox	19,228	(87)
Cisco Systems (Chambers)	12,154	(146)
Sun Microsystems (McNealy)	11,726	(150)
Oracle (Ellison)	8,827	(195)
EMC (Egan)	6,715	(260)
Apple (Jobs, Wozniak)	6,134	(285)
AOL (Case)	4,777	(337)

Based on *Fortune* 1000, April 2000

The claims made

The claims made on behalf of the Internet are mind-boggling. Some are just plain outrageous. Others are logical but are hard to imagine. Take some examples. A quarter of a century from now, says Deloitte Consulting, manufacturers won't so much be pushing products on consumers as customers will be pulling products onto the market.

According to Deloitte:

"In the year 2025, the world will be dominated by customer-centric notions. Consumer buying-power and the pure raw horsepower of the Net and other communication technologies will have made the individual consumer absolutely dominant."

Global B2B e-commerce will reach $7.29 trillion by 2004 and 37 percent of this will be facilitated by B2B e-markets, according to the research company the Gartner Group.

The first wave

The first wave of the e-commerce assault was a landgrab. The name of the game was to occupy empty territory. Companies that succeeded, most notably Amazon.com, relied on speed, innovation, and 'cyber savvy' to snatch online market space from under the noses of existing businesses. In many cases, they left more traditional rivals standing, as they charged up the virtual beaches and raised their flags. The first battle may be over, but the war is only just beginning in earnest. Yet, despite the astronomical valuations some of the new arrivals achieved and the inevitable knock backs that followed, many of the new stars are just as confused about the next phase of the war.

The second wave – or generation – of B2C e-commerce will be shaped more by strategy than by the tactical use of speed and experimentation. According to Philip Evans & Thomas S. Wurster of the Boston Consulting Group, the key players – branded-goods suppliers, physical retailers, electronic retailers, and what they call pure navigators – will shift their focus from claiming territory to defending or capturing it. The future belongs to the strategists not the tacticians.

Successful strategies will focus on ways to achieve competitive advantage – which can ultimately be turned into profits. Victory will go to the businesses that get closest to customers – the ones that help customers navigate their way through the Web to deliver real value. Indeed, navigation, Evans and Wurster say, is the battlefield on which the fight for competitive advantage will be won or lost. There are three dimensions to navigation: reach, affiliation, and richness.

Reach is about access and connection. This is where the greatest gains have been made so far by the cyber insurgents. Affiliation is about whose interests the business represents – companies will form their lines around serving customers' interests, or those of suppliers. Finally,

The Net effect

The Internet Economy supported an additional 650,000 jobs in 1999 as revenues soared to over half a trillion dollars, according to the University of Texas at Austin's Center for Research in Electronic Commerce.

The Internet Economy now directly supports 2.476 million workers, more than the insurance, communications and public utilities industries and twice as many as the airline, chemical and allied products, legal and real estate industries.

These figures – the Internet Economy Revenues Indicator™ (IERI), the Internet Economy Jobs Indicator™ (IEJI) and the growth rate – are the principal findings of the third report on measuring the Internet Economy commissioned by Cisco Systems. The University of Texas study also found the Internet Economy grew to $523.9 billion in 1999 and could grow to $850 billion in 2000 if current growth conditions continue.

It also indicates that Internet Economy Employees are *very* productive. Revenue per employee continued to rise as companies leveraged the Internet to increase operational efficiencies and worker productivity. As a whole, revenue per employee jumped 19 percent from year-end 1998 to year-end 1999. The most dramatic gains occurred in the service- and goods-based layers. For example, revenue per employee at the E-commerce and Intermediary layers grew respectively 37 percent and 30 percent from 1998 to 1999, suggesting huge productivity gains.

The report concludes: "Starting around 1994, the Internet Economy has grown at a much faster pace than the Industrial Revolution that began in the 18th century. Perhaps more importantly, the potential scope, size and overall economic impact of this economic system are much larger than what we can comprehend today."

richness is the depth of the information that a business supplies or collects about its customers. Navigators such as Yahoo!, and e-retailers such as Amazon.com, are likely to be stronger in reach and affiliation; while traditional product suppliers and retailers have the inside track on richness. These relative advantages suggest different strategic opportunities and threats.

Clicks & bricks

We have now entered the next era of e commerce, or so it is widely believed. It is the era of clicks & bricks – or clicks & mortar if you prefer. As the commotion about online insurgents stealing markets from traditional companies begins to die down, there is a growing consensus that the most successful companies in the new economy will combine clicks-&-bricks strategies to bridge the physical and virtual worlds. But in putting their Internet plans in place, incumbents face a crucial decision: whether to integrate the online business with the traditional operation, or keep them separate. To date, many of the incumbents that have embraced the Internet have done so at arm's length. These companies have sought to create separate online operations. In a *Harvard Business Review* article (May–June 2000), Ranjay Gulati and Jason Garino argue that integrating online and offline activities offers huge potential benefits to B2C (business-to-consumer) companies.

"Our most important finding is a simple one: the benefits of integration are almost always too great to abandon entirely," say Gulati and Garino, respectively associate professor and student at Northwestern University's Kellogg School of Management. The question should be: what degree of integration makes sense for a particular company?

In planning their online strategy, Gulati and Garino suggest, companies should examine the benefits of integration across four dimensions: brand; management; operations; and equity (whether to own or spin-off). Useful as their insights are, however, no road map through the clicks-&-bricks minefield exists. Companies will have to feel their way. Whatever lessons the architects of the first and second waves of the Internet business revolution teach, the reality is that the architects of the future will have to draw up their own plans, based on a future they believe they can make. The business models of the future remain to be discovered.

The future of e-commerce

Projected figures for e-commerce are impressive, but predictions are notoriously unreliable. So what does the Internet really hold for the future of business? If nothing else, the last few years should have taught us that what lies ahead is impossible to foresee. Futurists, people who have made a career out of extrapolating the present to tell the future, are

B2B

Fascinating as B2C is, many predict that the biggest area of growth in the next few years will be B2B (business-to-business), especially digital marketplaces. Over 750 networked marketplaces had already been developed worldwide, reported *The Economist* in March 2000.

- In the B2B world, the number of online digital marketplaces, exchanges, and vertical portals will rise from about 500 to nearly 10,000 worldwide. Among the newcomers will be consumer crossovers Yahoo!, AOL, and others.
- In 2000, B2B transactions will account for 77 percent of worldwide e-commerce.[3]
- Worldwide demand for Internet services was $16.2 billion in 1999 and is expected to grow to $99.1 billion by 2004.[4]
- 79 percent of the Global 500 used their Websites for recruitment compared with 29 percent in 1998.[5]
- 45 percent of online consumers access the Internet for health information.[6]

struggling. The business world is moving so fast that gazing at a distant point on the horizon is no longer tenable.

Today, the best that futurists can hope to do is peer round the next corner. Peter Schwartz is one such man:

> "The new technology of knowledge-intensive networks is insinuating itself into every significant economic, social and political relationship. It is a universal solvent that is destroying geography and time; speeding things up; enriching, informing and transforming old ways of doing things and creating wholly new things and ways of being."[7]

The new technology is the engine that is now driving the new economy, he says. But because it is so new, we are unsure of its destiny. Behind the purple prose lurks the kernel of the problem. No one really knows what is going to happen next. No one know whether the Internet will lead to an increase in wealth in less developed countries, or even if wealth creation in the US can be sustained. Schwartz outlines three alternative theories for the future of the new economy.

- *Theory 1*

  This says the new economy is all about greater efficiency. Doing things cheaper and better. This view suggests we are moving towards a globally liquid economy, where geographical location is less important, and will ultimately become irrelevant. Anyone anywhere in the world will be able to compete with anyone else. Transactions will be instantaneous, and frictionless. Under this model, e-Bay's auction business model, Schwartz says, is the paradigm. The world economy gets a major boost as the supply curve shifts to the right, ushering in a period of rising standards of living. The parallel is the long consumer boom in America in the 1950s.

- *Theory 2*

  This postulates that although a new economy is emerging, it will be a much slower process. This theory views the impact of the Internet and other dimensions of the new economy as having a profound and lasting impact, it argues that the incumbent companies and the old rules of business will slow things down. This, Schwartz says, is illustrated by the difference between the pure plays and the clicks-&-bricks players. So, for example, a pure play company like eToys will have to build its infrastructure and brand very rapidly, while a clicks & bricks outfit like Toys 'R' Us has the basics in place and can pursue its online strategy with much less expense. In this scenario the future favors incumbents who can adopt the new technology, making the transition cheaper, and faster than a new company starting from scratch.

- *Theory 3*

  This is the skeptical view. It says that the new economy and the Internet business revolution is mostly hype. The fundamentals have not changed. Profits are still the best measure of a company's future viability. This theory is derived from two basic arguments. First, it invokes Solow's famous observation that productivity gains have manifestly failed to materialize, and that those that have pertain primarily to the IT industry itself. The second argument is that far from improving the efficiency of knowledge workers, the new technology simply enables them to work longer and harder than previously. There is evidence to support this. When it comes to working hours Americans work the longest hours in the industrialized world. The average American worker clocks up nearly 2000 hours at work every year – two weeks more than his or her Japanese counterpart. Despite the speed of technological innovation, American working hours have actually increased by 4 percent since 1980. In Europe the general trend is downwards. The US leads the rankings in terms of GDP per person, but plummets to ninth if measured by GDP per hour. "Americans have more money because they have less leisure," MIT's Lester Thurow has simply noted. This puts the US economic miracle in a different light.

As theory 3 indicates, there will always be skeptics. This is healthy. But there are signs that the productivity needle is now moving. As *The Economist* noted recently: "American productivity in the second quarter of 2000 grew at an annual rate of 5.3 percent, its fastest increase for 17 years. Despite rising wages, unit-labor costs declined, giving some credence to proponents of the 'new economy.'"

We can speculate endlessly about the impact of the Internet on business, and the real or imagined existence of the new economy. The plain fact is that today more than 300 million people as far apart as Bangalore, India, Palo Alto, California, and Beijing, China, start their day by logging on, collecting their email, and surfing the Web. They are being joined each day by tens of thousands more. The Internet is already changing our lives. That is an incontrovertible reality.

Architects of the business revolution

This is not the final word on the Internet business revolution. How could it be when that revolution is only just beginning? Nor is it a definitive listing of its most important players to date. Rather, it is our personal choice based on our readings around the subject and canvassing of numerous experts. The people and companies featured in the book have been selected because they exemplify the opportunities, challenges and above all the infinite possibilities that the Internet presents. We hope the 50 we have selected are an eclectic and interesting mix. They are people who have contributed materially to the story of the Internet so far.

Happily, many of those we feature would be included if our selection were based on financial criteria alone.

Des Dearlove and Stephen Coomber, 2000

Sources

1. *E-Biz Business Week*, May 8, 2000.
2. Source: http://www.business.gov July 1999.
3. Source: *IDC Predictions 2000 Bulletin* #W21342, December 1999 – IT Research.
4. Source: Worldwide Internet Services Market Forecast and Analysis, 1999–2004, March 2000 – IT Research.
5. *Global 500 Web Site Recruiting 2000 Survey*, recruitsoft.com and iLogos Research.
6. 13 Jupiter Communications.
7. Peter Schwartz, "The future of the new economy," *Red Herring*, September 2000.

1958–1980	Some milestones of the business revolution	Companies founded
1957		Fairchild Semiconductors
1958	The US Dept of Defense (DoD) founds the Advanced Research Project Agency (ARPA).	
1968		Intel
1969	DoD commission ARPANET to research networking.	
1970		Xerox PARC Arthur Rock & Assoc.
1971	15 nodes, 23 hosts (systems with registered IP addresses) established: including MIT, Harvard, RAND and NASA. NASDAQ introduced.	
1972	Ray Tomlinson introduces email on ARPANET and chooses the @ sign.	Kleiner Perkins
1973	Vint Cerf and Bob Kahn present the basic concept of Internet protocols at the University of Sussex, Brighton, England. Bob Metcalfe at Xerox PARC – the ethernet.	
1975		Microsoft
1977		Oracle

1980s	Milestones of the Business Revolution	Founded companies
1981		Softbank
1982		Sun Microsystems
		E★Trade
1984	Domain Name System (DNS) introduced.	Dell, Cisco
1985	First dot-com – Symbolics.com – registered.	
	Nicholas Negroponte starts MIT Media Lab.	AOL
1986		CMGI
1988	Jon Postel appointed director of Internet Assigned Numbers Authority (IANA).	
1989	159,000 hosts.	

1990s	Milestones of the Business Revolution	Companies Founded
1991	Tim Berners-Lee – World-Wide Web . Philip Zimmerman – Pretty Good Privacy (PGP). NASDAQ hits 500. Linus Torvalds working on Linux.	
1992	1,136,000 hosts. *Wired* magazine launched.	Palm Computers
1993	Marc Andreessen – Mosaic browser. *Red Herring* magazine launched.	Red Hat
1994	Top Domains: com, edu, uk, gov, de, ca, mil, au, org, net.	Amazon Netscape RealNetworks
1995	Charges introduced for domain name registration. Netscape – IPO. Fast Company magazine launched.	Yahoo! eBay Healtheon
1996	AOL down for 19 hrs due to demand.	Hotmail buy.com Double Click
1997	business.com sold for US$150,000.	MP3.com
1998		Priceline
1999	business.com sold for US$7.5million! The Melissa virus.	
2000	Denial of service attack affects Yahoo!, Amazon and eBay. +1 billion indexable pages Inktomi. NASDAQ hits 5000.	

MARC ANDREESSEN

– *Netscape & Loudcloud*

T oday the Internet is so pervasive that it's hard to believe that pre-1993 it was relatively inaccessible to the majority of ordinary computer users, let alone the unwired masses. Two key events changed that: the creation of the World Wide Web by Tim Berners-Lee; and the invention of the Mosaic point-and-click graphical browser for the Web invented by a team of students led by Marc Andreessen.

In 1993, Andreessen (born 1971), was still an undergraduate student at the University of Illinois' National Center for Supercomputing Applications (NSCA) – a federally funded research center. The NSCA had been in place for over eight years and had a budget amounting to several million dollars a year. It also had a large number of staff who in Andreessen's words had "frankly not enough to do." If the staff were a tad underemployed at the time, it was probably because the micro-computing meteor had collided with the world of supercomputers, leaving the latter somewhat confused about its future.

Fortunately for Andreessen, and the rest of us, the NCSA had a fairly *laissez faire* attitude to the research interests of its students. As Andreessen recalled: "The NCSA is not a place where there are necessarily a whole lot of well-defined directions or goals. A lot of the interesting things that have happened there – in fact, most of the interesting things that have happened there – have been because one or more people decided to do something interesting … and then did it."[1]

It was in this spirit that Andreessen led a team of students, Eric Bina among them, on a project to develop a graphical browser client application for Tim Berners-Lee's World Wide Web. The result, released in February 1993, was "Mosaic for X" a point-and-click graphical browser for the Web designed to run on a UNIX platform. The team followed up with free versions for Macintosh and Windows operating systems in the fall of 1993. In much the same way as the Windows OS with its Graphical User Interface had previously opened up the use of PCs to the layman, Mosaic was to change the face of the World Wide Web for ever. With built-in support for Windows and Macintosh systems, non-techies could finally access the Web and navigate by pointing and clicking. Better still the browser implemented the HTML <img> tag so browsers could see in-line images as well as text.

This was a major breakthrough. But the success of Mosaic caused problems at the NSCA, which wasn't set up as a commercial venture. The research center licensed its inventions to commercial enterprises. The inventors weren't the ones who got rich on the back of the technology. Commercial exploitation was not what it was about. This did not suit Andreessen, so he left. His logic was that the NSCA wasn't the best or most appropriate place to be developing great software. As he explained: "It [the NSCA] wasn't a company, so it didn't have a clear, well-defined mission to be able to create and maintain great software ... And so, as a result of not having those attributes, it also wasn't, in any sense of the word, 'managed' in a way that I think you'd want to have it be, if you were trying to create and maintain great software. We basically reached the end of what we were able to do at NCSA. It got popular and, after that, there's basically no way for an organization of that nature to maintain it."[2]

When Andreessen left NCSA in December 1993, naturally enough he headed for Silicon Valley, settling in Mountain View, California close to Palo Alto. He took a job with a small software company called Terisa Systems, which was a subsidiary of Enterprise Integration Technologies (EIT) – another research organization funded principally with government money from Advanced Research Project Agency (ARPA) grants. For a short while Andreessen put Mosaic to the back of his mind and worked on security products for transacting commerce on the Web.

But it wasn't long before the man *Business Week Online* described as a "hamburger-chomping moon-faced boy" received an email that was to change his life. "You may not know me," it began, "but I'm the founder of Silicon Graphics ..." It was from Jim Clark, and like most other people in the industry Andreessen knew exactly who Clark was. In Silicon Valley Clark was already a legend. Having sold stock in the company, he had left Silicon Graphics in January 1994 with a stack of cash. When he saw the Mosaic browser he knew exactly what he wanted to do next. He contacted Andreessen, and together they flew to Champagne-Urbana, the home of the NSCA, and signed up seven of the original Mosaic team – including Eric Bina. The new employees were to get good salaries as well as one percent of the stock of a new

---

Insight

It's possible to summarize Andreessen's success as the right product at the right time. But life was made much more complicated by having to compete with the Microsoft-adapted version of Mosaic, which Andreessen had himself helped create. The lesson? Beware of your own genius – it might come back and bite you.

---

company called Mosaic Communications Corp., which subsequently became Netscape.

The rest, to use that well-thumbed cliché, is history. In a race against time Netscape rushed to get its new browser, Navigator, out before the rival Mosaic browser – by this time licensed to a company called Spyglass – could get an unbreakable grip on the market. What was significant was the strategy Clark and Andreessen adopted. When Netscape released Navigator it redefined the business model in the software industry by giving the browser away as a loss leader – and making money selling server software to go with it. When the company was floated on Wall Street in August 1995, the stock price headed skyward and Andreessen became a multi-millionaire overnight.

A short time later, it dawned on Microsoft just how important a piece of technology the browser was. Taking the shortest route to market, the Redmond-based company went to Spyglass to source its own browser. It used Mosaic technology as the basis for Internet Explorer, firing the first shots in what became known as "the browser wars." After a bruising battle with Microsoft and its Internet Explorer, Netscape was eventually swallowed up by America Online Inc. for $4.2 billion.

Andreessen spent six months as chief technology officer (CTO) at AOL before finally leaving to set up a new venture called Loudcloud in Sunnyvale, CA, with fellow Netscapee Ben Horowitz. Loudcloud helps start-ups by building their back-end computer systems from scratch. This allows the client company to concentrate on its core business, leaving Loudcloud and its team of experts to worry about the technology.

"Nobody in their right mind would call this sexy, but it's critically important," observes Ted Schadler, an analyst at Forrester Research Inc. "They're like the people who built the roads and the power grid and the banking system."[3]

Play to your strengths

With one successful start-up behind him – Netscape – you might forgive Andreessen for thinking he has enough smarts to run the next one pretty much on his own. But he knows the value of delegation: "I may not be the best person to build the business day-to-day, but I do think in terms of how to do that and what it's going to be like," says Andreessen.

He is only too happy to bring in the right people with the necessary skills to execute his vision – people like Jim Clark, James Barksdale and Ben Horowitz.

Andreessen, has set high standards for Loudcloud. The company guarantees a 100 percent service, offering refunds should the service fail. If all goes well, he reasons, the customer will return, swelling the Loudcloud coffers by purchasing additional services.

It's a lucrative market space. Worth around $2.7 billion today, Researcher Dataquest Inc predicts it will be worth around $22 billion by 2003. No surprise, then, to find it's a competitive market with both start-ups and major players like AT&T moving in. Loudcloud will have to stay on its toes. But at least this time Andreessen won't have go head-to-head with the mighty Microsoft. Indeed, the former enemy supplies Loudcloud with software.

With his considerable experience in the industry Andreessen knows only too well that you're only as good as your last start-up. And it's some act to follow. He comments:

> "This is a different business. Hopefully it will be a success, but it will be a different kind of success. One thing I've learned is nothing is duplicated, nothing is the same. I guess you could say it's just like having kids. Is your next kid going to be better than your first kid?"[4]

It would be a brave man or woman to bet against the innovative Andreessen pulling off another success.

Links

www.loudcloud.com

Notes

1. 1995, interview with Thom Stark – www.dnai.com.
2. *Ibid.*
3. *Bweekonline*, February 2000.
4. *The Standard Online*, February 2000.

TIM BERNERS-LEE

Surfing the Mine or the Mesh doesn't have quite the same ring to it does it? But if Tim Berners-Lee hadn't discarded "Mine of Information," and "Information Mesh" – both potential names for the Internet application he developed in the late 1980s, that's what we might all be doing today. Perhaps the surfing metaphor would have been replaced with something more in keeping. Who knows? Fortunately, however, he came up with a name that not only encapsulated the nature of the application he had written, but was a little more catchy – the World Wide Web was spun.

Berners-Lee came from a numerical family. His parents were both mathematicians. They met at the computer company Ferranti. Berners-Lee's mother has been described as the first commercial computer programmer because of her work on the Manchester University Mark 1, sold by Ferranti, and one of the first commercial computers. Unsurprisingly, young Tim had a flair for computers and computer programming. In 1976, while still at University, he built his first computer using a soldering iron, an M6800 processor and an old television. What no one could have predicted is that he would go on to create an application for the Internet that would revolutionize business and transform the world of computing.

Berners-Lee (born 1955) graduated from Queen's College, Oxford University in 1976, with a degree in Physics. With little indication of what lay ahead, Berners-Lee started working life at the engineering company Plessey Telecommunications in Poole, in Dorset, UK. There he worked on distributed transaction systems, message relays, and bar-code technology. He soon moved on – not to Silicon Valley but just down the road to Ferndown, Dorset, where he worked for DG Nash Ltd, writing typesetting software for intelligent printers, and working on a multitasking operating system.

Eventually, however, Berners-Lee set up as an independent consultant. And in June 1980, he started a six-month stint as consultant software engineer at the European Particle Physics Laboratory in Geneva, Switzerland – part of the European Center for Nuclear Research CERN. CERN (Conseil Europeenne pour la Recherche Nucleaire) conducts research into the nature of sub-atomic particles. Using a massive underground particle accelerator situated under Geneva, particles are accelerated close to the speed of light and then smashed into other particles. The results are carefully monitored. Whilst there, Berners-Lee wrote a program for sharing information, which used random associations. Named "Enquire," and never published, this program formed the conceptual basis for the future development of the Web. The motivation behind this program was a desire to access data stored in different places on different machines and databases from one point. At the time CERN ran several different proprietary systems for information retrieval and storage with little or no interconnectivity. Berners-Lee found that with his personal information scattered around the various systems, management was a laborious and frustrating task.

"I needed something to organize myself," he later explained in an interview. "I needed to be able to keep track of things, and nothing out there – none of the computer programs that you could get, the spreadsheets and the databases, would really let you make this random association between absolutely anything and absolutely anything."

A lesser man would have bought a filofax, they were popular at the time, or designed a personal organizer. But Berners-Lee was looking for something more radical. "Enquire" – short for "Enquire-Within-Upon-Everything" – was inspired by a Victorian how-to book of the same name, and became Berners-Lee's personal answer to the problem. Enquire acted as a memory prompt where words in a particular document could lead to other documents for further explanation. It was similar to an application written for the Apple Mac called "hypercard". Although it remained unpublished, Enquire sowed the seeds for something greater. Shortly after this, however, Berners-Lee left CERN for a time.

From 1981 until 1984, he returned to England and worked at Image Computer Systems Ltd, where he was responsible for technical design. Work here included real-time control firmware, graphics and communications software, and a generic macro language. Seeking a change from life in England, Berners-Lee then returned to CERN in September 1984, where he took up a fellowship to work on distributed real-time systems for scientific data acquisition and system control. The pieces of a monumental jigsaw puzzle were beginning to fall into place.

Back at CERN, Berners-Lee once more confronted the challenge to organize and retrieve information more efficiently. In a forerunner of the knowledge management initiatives launched by countless companies since, he highlighted the problems in an early research proposal. He noted:

> "A problem is the high turnover of people. When two years is a typical length of stay, information is constantly being lost. The introduction of the new people demands a fair amount of their time and that of others before they have any idea of what goes on. The technical details of past projects are sometimes lost for ever, or only recovered after a detective investigation in an emergency. Often, the information has been recorded, it just cannot be found."

More jigsaw pieces were now in place. In Berners-Lee's absence, CERN had implemented the Internet TCP/IP protocols and by 1989 was the largest Internet site in Europe. Berners-Lee looked for a way to solve CERN's information problems utilizing the Internet.

In 1989 he wrote a proposal entitled *Hypertext and CERN* and circulated it among his colleagues for comment. Partly inspired by the work of Ted Nelson on the Xanadu project, his proposals incorporated three new technologies: HTML (Hypertext Markup Language) which is now used to write Web documents; HTTP (Hyper Text Transfer Protocol) the protocol to deliver the page; and a Web browser client World Wide Web, which allowed the Web page to be viewed and edited.

In the introduction to his proposal Berners-Lee said: "The actual observed working structure of the organization is a multiply connected 'web' whose interconnections evolve with time."

The proposal requested four software engineers and a programmer. The development time for each phase was projected to be three months. Although the proposal didn't receive unconditional support at this point, it was subsequently reformulated and recirculated among the CERN fraternity in October 1990, this time with Robert Cailliau as co-author. This time it received a green-light and Berners-Lee set about building his vision – with the help of object-oriented programming, courtesy of the new NeXT workstation – another forward-looking product from a company inspired by the visionary Steve Jobs.

Insight

Making money and making history do not always go together. Genius brings its own rewards. The Web remains, at heart, an egalitarian, rather than commercial medium. Companies can and do make money from their applications. But Berners-Lee and others have left an indelible legacy that should not be underestimated. Companies ignore Internet history at their peril. The open-platform movement is part of this tradition, and may yet prize Microsoft's grip from its most potent commercial pressure points.

The World Wide Web, as Berners-Lee envisaged it, was to be based on the client-server model of computing. Networked computers called servers hold information – other client programs (browsers) access this information. Prior to Berners-Lee, the Internet, whilst being egalitarian in principle – non-commercial, free to use, the majority of applications given away by enthusiasts and so on – was elitist in practice. To use it assumed a level of technical knowledge beyond most people. What Berners-Lee did was provide an application for the Net that broadened its appeal beyond the IT community. He invented an interface between the unseen myriad of servers containing information and the user. In doing so he brought it to life for millions of non-IT-literate people around the world. What had begun as a knowledge management system for a molecular particle accelerator laboratory gave rise to a very different sort of particle accelerator – one that would shake the business world to its core.

But building a World Wide Web of this kind presents problems. Take the European Union as an example – a collection of disparate nations bound together by treaty. The politicians know only too well that to operate successfully it needs to be a true Union – hence the drive for standardization and harmonization, the introduction of a single currency and the prospect of a common language. In the same way if the Web was to be a success Berners-Lee understood that all machines servers/clients, wherever they were physically located and whatever applications they ran internally must be able to communicate with each other through accepted common standards.

This realization drove him to develop a set of protocols to govern activity on the Web. The "address" of any machine connected to the Net was expressed as a URL or Uniform Resource locator. Information exchange between machines was governed by HyperText Transfer Protocol (HTTP). And documents were to be written in hypertext Mark-up Language or HTML.

With the establishment of these protocols Berners-Lee had in one single stroke created a comprehensive and persuasive application that was to pervade the Internet. The breadth of Berners-Lee's vision was mind-boggling. The creation of the WWW took just over one year.

By May 1991, an information-sharing system, incorporating the three new technologies – HTML, HTTP and the Web browser client World Wide Web – was implemented on the multi-platform network at CERN. The files were made available outside of CERN in August 1991 by the first Web-server – the main file-storage computer at CERN

This is where the story takes a curious turn. Instead of going on to make $millions out of the commercial potential of his invention, Berners-Lee joined the Laboratory for Computer Science (LCS) at the Massachusetts Institute of Technology (MIT) in 1994. He didn't abandon development of the Web, however, becoming Director of the World Wide Web consortium that oversees and co-ordinates the global development if the Web.

Links

www.w3c.org

JEFF BEZOS

– *Amazon.com*

J eff Bezos, the founder and CEO of Amazon.com, is the most
famous son of the e-commerce revolution. The company he created became a business phenomenon. Amazon is the best-known
online brand in the world.

If nothing else, he has proved that you can sell a lot of stuff over the
World Wide Web. Turning that into profits, however, has proved more
problematic. The truth is that Bezos pulled off one of the greatest PR
coups in history. He promoted Amazon.com to the point where it is now
synonymous with e-commerce.

Bezos himself has come a long way in a very short time. Back in
1994, he was a young senior vice-president at a thriving Wall Street
hedge fund. That's when the explosive growth of the World Wide
Web grabbed his attention. Surfing the Net one day he came upon a
fascinating statistic – Web usage was growing at a rate of 2300 percent
a month. Online commerce, he realized, was a natural next step. Part
Wall Street insider and part computer nerd, Bezos was perfectly placed
to cash in.

He drew up a shortlist of 20 products he thought could be successfully sold over the Web. The list included music, magazines, PC software
and hardware – and books. The list was shortened to books and music.
In the end, books won for two simple reasons. First, he reasoned that
with more than 1.3 million books in print versus 300,000 music titles,
there were more to sell.

Second, and perhaps more importantly, the big publishers seemed
less intimidating. They didn't appear to have the same sort of stranglehold on the business as the six major record companies that dominated

music. The biggest book chain Barnes & Noble accounted for less than 12 percent of the industry's $25 billion in annual sales.

"There are no 800-pound gorillas in book publishing or distribution," Bezos observed. The decision made, Bezos, followed the advice to earlier pioneers to 'Go West young man'. He quit his job and packed his bags, telling the removals company that he would be in touch once he'd chosen between four locations Boulder, Colorado; Portland, Oregon; Lake Tahoe, Nevada; and Seattle, Washington as his new home.

According to Amazon.com folklore, his wife MacKenzie drove them cross country in a Chevy Blazer, while Bezos sat in the passenger seat pounding out a business plan on a laptop computer and negotiating seed capital on his mobile phone. "I will change the economics of the book industry as a whole," he is reputed to have told one venture capitalist. Ironically, fund raising was also carried out in the coffee shop of his local Barnes & Noble bookstore.

He knew he needed to base his operation in a state without a state tax, and settled on the Seattle area because of the richness of high-tech talent and the presence of a major book distributor – Ingram's warehouse – down the road in Roseberg, Oregon. In classic high-tech start-up style, Bezos and his first three employees set up computers in the garage of their rented suburban home. They were already busy writing the software that would support the new business model before the furniture even caught up with them. The rest, you might think, is history. Not quite.

Bezos originally decided to call his new company Cadabra, with the magical incantation in mind. But friends talked him out of it, explaining that it sounded a bit like cadaver. Reasoning that it would carry many more books than conventional stores, he opted for Amazon, after the world's largest river.

According to Amazon itself, the company "opened its virtual doors in July 1995 with a mission to use the Internet to transform book buying into the fastest, easiest, and most enjoyable shopping experience possible." Book buying was only a start. The Website proclaims: "Today, Amazon.com is the place to find and discover anything you want to buy online. We're very proud that 17 million people in more than 160 countries have made us the leading online shopping site."

Launched as a Website in July 1995, by the beginning of 1999 Amazon.com Inc. had a market capitalization of $6 billion – more than the combined value of Barnes and Noble, and Borders, its two biggest bookstore competitors online and off. In the fourth quarter of 1998, net sales were $252.9 million, an increase of 283 percent over the same period in 1997. With so much cash flowing into the coffers, analysts and e-commerce commentators seemed unperturbed by the absence of profits. For the longest time, they were content to trust Bezos's instincts. He predicted that Amazon would reach $1 billion in sales by 2000 (and he was right – net sales for just six months to June 30, 2000 amounted to $1.1 billion). Cannily, too, he kept his own counsel about when he expected the company to make a profit. Amazon, he said in 1999, was in "an investment phase," as befits a firm that has only just celebrated its fourth birthday. The "harvesting cycle" would come later.

David Gardner, author of *The Motley Fool Investment Guide*, observed if Bezos wanted Amazon to be profitable, it would be but it would only be a small company. But even Gardner, a Bezos fan, admitted that if Amazon did not make a profit in the next couple of years it would be in trouble. The day of reckoning seems to have been closer than either he or Bezos thought.

Bezos appeared to have done everything right. He had invented a new business model, successfully hyped the hell out of it, and still managed to stay firmly in control of his creation. But in e-commerce, first mover advantage does not provide a safe sinecure for life. The success of the new business model also contains the seeds of its own ruin. Bezos succeeded in demonstrating that the new model works, and traditional suppliers have followed in his shoes, creating their own direct channel to the customer.

But Amazon.com no longer has the market for online book sales all to itself. The competition, comfortable and lethargic as it was when he started, has had a nasty shock. Barnes & Noble in particular is now mounting a serious challenge to Amazon.com's online business. In the next few years, customer loyalty will be the battleground.

The key question will be whether the value-added component of the Amazon formula is sufficient to ensure customer loyalty. Whether he is remembered as the architect of a lasting and profitable Internet empire, or simply one of the pioneers in the colonization of cyberspace remains to be seen. The tricky bit for e-CEOs is that the share price of the business often relies on something even more ethereal than cyberspace itself – namely the confidence of analysts that they have a bright future. But then no one said that being an e-CEO made it easy to sleep at night. Few people can be so well-suited – or well qualified – for the role as Bezos. "I always run through the office," he says, "I mean physically I'm a little bit hyperkinetic. That's why I like this environment." Maybe it's smart to keep moving. For a while the company's market capitalization was in excess of $30 billion and it still hadn't turned a single penny in profits.

But by June 2000, the wolves on Wall Street were baying. NASDAQ got the jitters in April 2000. As investor confidence in dot-coms faltered,

Insight

Dotting the coms

To this day, many insist that Amazon.com remains the most-promising success story on the Internet. Whatever the final outcome, Bezos has demonstrated that he understands the new paradigm in a way that others don't. In three key areas he has proved prescient. First, he anticipated the rapid and exponential growth of the Web when few commentators believed it would catch fire. Second, he successfully converted commercial potential into a business reality, albeit without profits. Third, and perhaps most significantly, he understands that explosive growth is vital to the new business model. Without it, his company could well have already succumbed to the threat of the larger traditional bookstores imitating his web-based business model.

From 1996 to 2000, Amazon was the brightest star in the dot-com firmament. Bezos was the toast of Wall Street. But by mid-2000 some were saying his company would soon be toast. The vultures were circling over Amazon. Bezos' place in business history now looks uncertain. But regardless of the denouement, his achievement is considerable.

The Web has the power to change whole industries. It can be leveraged by companies at three different levels:

- as an information platform;
- as a transaction platform; and
- as a tool to build and manage the customer relationship.

While most companies were primarily using the Web as an information platform, Bezos jumped straight to the second level. In doing so, he managed to overcome the issue of security of payment, which many people believed would prevent e-tail from taking off. He has proved beyond doubt that this is a workable model. The question now is whether Amazon.com can successfully migrate to the third level – using its brand to justify higher margins and create profits for shareholders.

Amazon's currency – always based on a multiple of hope rather than logic – started to become devalued. A string of analysts became increasingly disillusioned about the long-term prospects of the company. Even the Amazon faithful, who have accompanied Bezos on a long sojourn across cyberspace to find the source of the promised profits, began turning back.

In June 2000, Holly Becker, the Lehman Brothers e-commerce analyst and long-time Amazon believer, greeted the company's results by switching her recommendation from a buy to a neutral. She was, she said, "throwing in the towel on Amazon." One of a number of Amazon aficionados on Wall Street to do so, some saw Becker's change of heart as a turning point in the company's fortunes.

Today Jeff Bezos looks increasingly likely to be hoist with his own petard. He promoted his brand to the point where it is now synonymous with the whole dot-com phenomenon. He successfully resisted pressure to post profits, preferring to plough the money Amazon generated into growing the business. How long he could sustain this remarkable juggling act was always going to depend on two crucial factors: the continuing bull market for all things Internet; and confidence that he, and Amazon.com, would deliver in the long-run. Both look increasingly shaky.

For Jeff Bezos, the hardest test is yet to come. But like Bill Gates at Microsoft, his restlessness and competitive nature may be enough to give him an edge.

Links

www.amazon.com

SABEER BHATIA

– *Hotmail & Arzoo*

"I did not want to do just another job; I wanted to create something which would change the world." The words of Sabeer Bhatia resonate in the new economy. Bhatia changed the face of email by co-founding the first Web-based email company, Hotmail Corporation, in 1996. The company instantly became the market leader with Bhatia at its helm as CEO and president. In 1998 Hotmail was bought by Microsoft, making Bhatia several hundred million dollars richer. Today, Hotmail is still the largest Internet-based email service provider with over 50 million registered users. And Bhatia has moved onto his next Internet start-up Arzoo.

Sabeer Bhatia was born in Chandigarh, India in 1968. He had a middle-class upbringing. His early education took place at the Bishop Cotton's School in Pune, where his father was posted as a captain in the Indian army. Later the family moved to Bangalore where Bhatia's father took a position as a senior official in the Defense Research and Development Organization (DRDO) and his mother worked as a senior manager at a bank. In 1986 Bhatia attended the Birla Institute of Technology (BITS), in Pilani. Then, in what was to be a providential move, Bhatia gave up his studies in India and traveled to America to take up a transfer scholarship at the California Institute of Technology. The ink was barely dry on the offer letter.

The decision is characteristic of Bhatia's approach to life and business. He arrived at Los Angeles after a 22-hour flight. He was in a strange country where he knew no one, he was 19 and had the princely sum of $250 in his pockets. It was a big risk that could have gone badly wrong but Bhatia was not averse to risks.

"The best piece of advice someone gave to me was that the biggest risk in life is not to take a risk at all," Bhatia told one interviewer – a theme he has often repeated. His decision to relocate to California was evidence of the self-belief Bhatia had even then. That confidence helped him make his way in the US. "In the long run, it boils down to a simple fact," he says. "How much faith does one have in oneself."

Bhatia moved on from Caltech to Stanford University, graduating with a Master's degree in Electrical Engineering in 1992. At Stanford, Bhatia's imagination was fired up by the words of visiting entrepreneurs like Scott McNealy and Steve Jobs. These icons of the business reformation spread the Silicon Valley gospel that anyone could make it big with the right idea, a bit of luck and a lot of hard work. After Stanford, Bhatia worked first at Apple and then on the hardware engineering side at a small start-up, Firepower Systems. He also struck up a friendship with Jack Smith, a friendship that proved highly profitable.

Bhatia was already caught up in the entrepreneurial spirit of the time. He had determined, despite making good money working for someone else, that the path to even greater riches lay in starting up his own business. And when he received a phone call from an excited Smith one evening, he knew they had hit upon the Holy Grail of all start-ups "the killer app." Bhatia stayed up all night writing a business plan and next day showed it to co-worker Smith at work.

The killer idea was a universally accessible email service. Users would set up their own email accounts accessible remotely via the Internet from anywhere in the world. Bhatia and Smith called their service Hotmail. Initially, the idea was to capitalize HTML thus – HoTMaiL – alluding to the link with HTML the Internet's standard language. But the linkage soon fell by the wayside. All they needed now to put their brilliant idea into action was money. Quite a lot of money – maybe $500,000.

If they had been anywhere else on the planet it might have been an impossible proposition. But in the Silicon Valley of the nineties all things were possible. Only there could two wet-behind-the-ears 27-year-old hardware engineers with nothing but an idea hope to raise hundreds of thousands of dollars to start a business. And that's exactly what they did.

Scared that some unscrupulous would-be investor might steal their big idea, Bhatia and Smith hawked a Net-based software database concept called Javasoft around the VCs with their secret weapon – the email idea – concealed. They were waiting for the right moment and the right person. The moment came in the offices of Draper Fisher Jurvetson. When Steve Jurvetson showed little interest in JavaSoft, Bhatia hit him with the Hotmail idea. Jurvetson was knocked out by it – so much so that Draper Fisher Jurvetson offered Bhatia $300,000 for a

30 percent share on a valuation of $1 million. Bhatia might have been expected to gratefully accept, especially as he had already been turned down by some 15 or 20 VCs. But he had other ideas.

At this point in the financing process Bhatia revealed what was to become another defining characteristic – an uncanny ability for negotiation. Possibly driven by his innate self-belief, or possibly by a stubborn streak, Bhatia held out for a $2 million valuation giving Draper Fisher Jurvetson 15 percent equity. Although they balked at the proposition at first, eventually the surprised VCs conceded.

Bhatia then delivered on his end of the deal. As he later pointed out: "We have also been the first of the companies funded by our venture capital firm to deliver a finished product on the exact day we promised to finish it – on July 4, 1996. We intended to keep up this professionalism."

Following the launch of Hotmail on that day, the subscriber base grew at an astronomical rate, faster in fact than any company in history. Part of the reason was the simple convenience of the service: it was a great idea because it was a really useful service that no one else was providing. Another reason for the success was the way the product was marketed. Today viral marketing is part of every e-marketer's arsenal, but back in 1996 it was gunpowder waiting for the invention of the gun. Every email sent by Hotmail contained within it an exhortation to sign up via a hyperlink to the Hotmail service and so the product spread like a ... well, like a virus.

It took almost a year before any significant competition surfaced in the form of Four11's Rocket Mail. By the time Microsoft had woken up to the possibilities, Hotmail had 8 million subscribers. Today it has over 50 million. Microsoft might have been slow on the uptake but it quickly realized that buying Hotmail was the best way to catch up. The deal for close to $400 million was announced on New Year's Eve 1997.

It was a triumphant vindication of Bhatia's vision and reward for the faith shown by Draper Fisher Jurvetson. It was also another testimony to Bhatia's fearsome negotiating skills. He had spurned Microsoft's early offers, holding out for a price that he felt adequately reflected the value of the business he had created. Not bad, considering the resources at Microsoft's disposal and the fact that it had its own formidable negotiating team. Long-standing employees were pleased with the Microsoft deal as well. Bhatia's persuasive skills convinced the first 12 Hotmail employees to forgo their salaries in favor of stock.

Suddenly Bhatia was no longer an entrepreneur leading his own start-up to ever-dizzier heights. Instead he was part of a software giant.

Insight

Tough negotiating skills

Sabeer Bhatia knows how to negotiate. He could have sold Hotmail to Microsoft for tens of millions. Microsoft came to the table with a team of six. Bhatia elected to negotiate alone, this way he could avoid divide and rule tactics. The Microsoft team returned every fortnight for two months. Then Bill Gates invited Bhatia to Redmond for a chat.

Microsoft offered tens of millions. Bhatia asked for $700 million. Microsoft offered $200 million. Bhatia said no. Microsoft offered $300 million. Bhatia said no. Microsoft offered $350 million. Bhatia's staff at Hotmail quietly suggested he should secure their future by accepting. Bhatia's management team said he should accept. Bhatia said no.

When the deal was done at an undisclosed price – 2,769,148 of Microsoft shares were exchanged for ownership – a value of $400 million at the time of the deal. Some might question whether it was great negotiating, stubbornness or plain foolhardiness. In the end the outcome justifies the means. One of the golden rules of deal-making is: don't underestimate the value of what you are offering.

After overseeing the process of merging Hotmail with the Microsoft online empire, Bhatia became a manager for MSN.com with responsibility for strategic business development.

But it wasn't long before Bhatia grew restless at Microsoft. As he explained:

> "There were really no disappointments at Microsoft. The only drawback for me was that I am a start-up kind of guy who enjoys a high-energy, fast paced dynamic environment that Microsoft was unable to provide me with. It is because Microsoft is not a two-person company and so probably does not have the edge of being a high-energy, fast paced start-up."[1]

Bhatia moved on to become one of a growing band of second-generation serial Internet entrepreneurs, joining the likes of Jim Clark and Marc Andreessen. His latest venture is Arzoo (an Indian word meaning passion or heart's desire). Arzoo.com is an e-commerce company using new technologies to improve the experiences currently available to online shoppers. Armed with prodigious self-belief and the experience of building a "best of breed" Internet company, Bhatia is well placed to succeed again.

Bhatia's achievements have been widely recognized. *Upside* magazine, for example, named him as one of its "Elite 100," trendsetters who have made the greatest impact on the Internet industry. And he remains relatively unfazed by his success. His interests extend beyond the tunnel vision of many valley techies. Golf, tennis, camping and skiing number among his diverse pastimes. He's also passionate about cricket. Despite his millions, Bhatia has managed to keep his feet firmly on the ground. When asked why with all his wealth he was still living in a modest apartment and hadn't bought a house, he replied: "They're just all so overpriced. I think I'll save a little money if I wait until they come down."

Links

www.arzoo.com

Notes

1.   *Rediff on the Net,* April 1999.

SCOTT BLUM

– *Buy.com*

Buy.com is the online company that aims to make money from losing money. The company, based in Aliso Viejo, California, loss-leads on products, selling them at or below cost. So where do the profits come from? Buy.com hopes they will come from the sale of advertising space and other services like warranties and the leasing of equipment. It's one of the most radical business models to emerge in the new economy, and one that is championed by Scott Blum, the company's outspoken chairman and founder.

Blum likes a challenge. An accomplished swimmer, he started aged five, and became national champion at eight. Swimming was the reason Blum's parents moved form San Jose to Orange County, LA. The move meant Blum, a national team prospect, could join a top club – the Mission Viejo Nadadores. Aged 14, Blum won four gold medals, two silvers and a bronze at the US Junior Olympics. Tellingly, he did this despite being smaller than the other competitors in his age group.

But at 16 his competitive swimming came to an end, and Blum went off the rails. Until that point, his life had been governed by the discipline of swimming – training, competitions and the like. "After quitting swimming, I completely lost my mind. I did it all," he has been quoted as saying. *All* turned out to be a bit too much for his high school, and after driving the principal's golf cart into the swimming pool he was asked to leave.

At around this time, he also moved out of the family home. He went to live in Denver with friends of the family, where he graduated from another high school. On his return to Newport Beach he worked parking cars at the Ritz for a while, until finally getting a job at a Nordstrom store. Nordstrom channeled Blum's energy in a positive direction. In a matter of months Blum was the No 1 shoe salesman in the store. He was still working at Nordstrom when he launched his first start-up – Microbanks. The company sold memory modules and was a great success. Blum had been fortunate enough to lock into a contract just before the price of memory rocketed. Microbanks sold memory chips at mark-ups of over 600 percent and still remained competitive. By the time he was 21, Blum had sold Microbanks to a company called Sentron Technology for $2.5 million in cash.

Encouraged by his success, Blum's next business venture was Pinnacle Micro. The company designed and sold optical disk drives and was run by his father William Blum, who was CEO. This time things didn't run as smoothly for young Scott. Despite strong revenues, the company got into difficulties that provoked the resignation of its auditors in 1995. The upshot was that Scott Blum resigned from Pinnacle in late 1995 after an investigation by the SEC into the company's accounting practice. Pinnacle continued to trade, run by William Blum.

In hindsight, leaving Pinnacle may have been a good move for Blum junior. His next venture was a company selling cut-price computer equipment – buycomp.com. After the acquisition of the online book and video retailer SpeedServ, Blum changed the company name to buy.com

The business model is staggeringly simple.
1. Buy.com sells a product at a cheaper price than its competitors.
2. That's it.
Just in case this needed reinforcement, the company's war cry is: "The lowest prices on Earth." And well they might be, but the obvious question is how does buy.com make any money?

Blum says the answer is with 'eyeballs'. Customers' eyeballs, he claims, are worth money. Advertising revenues and to some degree warranties on the products will bring in the profits. This remains to be seen.

Gray hairs

The idea might sound a bit crazy but Blum has still managed to convince a number of senior executives to join the company to help him realize his dream of $10 billion revenues by 2003, with one percent gross margins.

The board of buy.com includes five older men, all with experience running a large company or division. Experienced executives such as Donald Kendall (ex CEO at PepsiCo), Bill Richion (ex-VP global

Insight

In the Internet economy, Scott Blum argues, you don't have to make money to make money. Maybe it's not as radical or wacky as it appears at first sight. One way to view the buy.com business model is like a newspaper or magazine, where profits accrue from advertising revenues based on the number of readers, rather than from the cover price.

accounts Hewlett-Packard) and John Sculley (ex-CEO of Apple Computers) add gravitas to the reputation of buy.com. Blum also brought in a senior executive Gregory Hawkins from Ingram Micro to replace himself as CEO. Blum remains as chairman.

The success of Blum's business relies on a number of factors. The most crucial of these is attracting the customers to the Website. To do this, buy.com has spent large sums of money on branding. Distinctive attention-grabbing advertising communicates buy's cheapest-retailer-on-the-planet message.

To keep the customers hooked, order fulfillment must be satisfying enough to prevent consumers going elsewhere despite the price difference. To some degree this is a weak link in the chain, because in order to keep costs at a minimum, goods are dispatched direct from the wholesaler; buy.com holds no inventory. This leaves the company at the mercy of the wholesaler's distribution, unlike say Amazon.com, which retains control over the process from order to delivery.

Finally Blum must give consumers what he has promised – the lowest prices. Buy.com's proprietary technology may sniff out the competitors' prices and keep prices low. Customers also have price guarantees. However with the increasing proliferation of shopping bots – automated software programs – the sophisticated surfer may in the future control the shopping process from their hard drive remotely. This means they will not consciously visit a particular Website to make a transaction. Instead, a personalized intelligent agent will be dispatched to trawl the Web and carry out the transaction from start to finish on their behalf. This would also involve flexible pricing, where a Website's own agent would negotiate price with the shopping agent in the virtual equivalent of bartering.

This technology may be little way off yet, but it is coming – already research labs, like the MIT Media Lab, are working on this type of software. So where would that leave buy.com? In the world of the intelligent agent, branded e-tailers would be reduced. If buy.com is not able to offer the absolute lowest price then it becomes just another e-tailer – albeit an efficiently managed one. This has ominous implications for all online retailers who rely predominately on pricing to pull in customers and advertising to raise revenue. The issue for clicks and mortar business is somewhat different as the intelligent agent shopping model is confined to the Internet.

This scenario is still some way off. In the meantime buy.com has enough cash to last a while yet, despite its policy of selling at less than cost. Softbank Technology Ventures pitched in with $20 million for 10.25 percent of the company in buy.com's early days plus another $40 million from Softbank Technology's parent company (9.9 percent stake).

If anyone can make the buy.com business model a success it's probably Scott Blum. Back in his car-park attendant days, Blum had his eye on some of the ocean front property in Ritz Cove, south of Laguna Beach. To the amusement of his fellow attendants, Blum would tell them that he was going to live in one of the exclusive developments there. In fact Blum went one better. He didn't buy one of the houses – he had a house built there to his own specifications.

Links

www.buy.com

SERGEY BRIN & LARRY PAGE

– *Google.com*

Most people have heard of Excite, AltaVista, Yahoo!, and Lycos. They made their names by offering search engines that allowed Internet users to find what they wanted on the Web. But over time, their role as natural portals – doorways into the Internet – encouraged them to diversify. As the number of users grew, these portals sprouted add-ons – shopping malls, personal pages and a whole host of other content. Many believe that these additional services detract from their original purpose – helping to navigate the Web. In answer to these concerns Google.com offers a pure search facility.

Google is a throwback to the old days; stripped of the glitz it's a lean mean searching machine. And the Mountain View company of the same name plans to use its technological punching power to full effect.

Founded in 1998 by Sergey Brin and Larry Page, Google is a search engine with a difference. What makes Google so good? The answer is its patented PageRank search technology. The mathematical analysis behind the engine is dazzling, as you might expect from two mathematics students. But for the less mathematically inclined, Google offers important benefits. It analyses each Web page for ranking purposes by looking at all the content on the page. By differentiating between headings and font sizes is offers a more precise search engine, taking searches to new heights of sophistication. It also takes a peek at the text of nearby pages to get an idea of context, as well as looking at hypertext links. Then it weighs all the evidence and makes a ranking judgment.

The upshot is that, because Google is drawing on more information to make a decision, you get good results from a search even when you are searching for something fairly obscure. The search engine covers a staggering billion pages – almost the entire estimated content of the Web – of which 560 million or so are fully text-indexed. A search can be made in 10 different languages, including French, German, Italian and Spanish – Japanese, Chinese and Korean are on their way. It's fast as well, generating search results in less than 0.25 seconds on most occasions.

According to Larry Page, Google CEO and co-founder, in a company statement: "Google's new gigantic index means that you can search the equivalent of a stack of paper more than 70 miles high in less than half a second. This unprecedented power enables millions of Google users worldwide to communicate, learn, and entertain like never before."

The story of Google's success reads like the archetypal West Coast tech start-up made good. And, yes, there's a garage in there somewhere. Brin and Page can sensibly be described as whiz-kids. Page was born to be a computer programmer – his father was a Computer Science professor. He took a science and engineering first degree at the University of Michigan and then started a PhD at Stanford University. Brin, who hails from Moscow, Russia, graduated with a Bachelor of Science degree in mathematics and computer science from the University of Maryland at College Park. His knowledge of data extraction and search engine technology is way beyond the ken of most mortals. The name Google is a play on the term 'googol'. A googol represents a one followed by 100 zeros and was coined by Milton Sirotta (someone has to think of names for these things). Google uses the association with googol to suggest the mind-boggling amount of information available on the Internet.

Brin and Page met at Stanford – where else – as PhD students in computer science. By all accounts they didn't hit it off straight away, in fact they have been reported as saying they found each other obnoxious. Technology overcame their mutual dislike however as the two ended up working on a project conducting research into creating a better, more perfect search engine than those currently available. The project became part of their doctoral thesis and then a major part of their lives.

By mid 1998 the two had abandoned their doctorates and were working on search engines full time in a friend's garage. Eventually they outgrew the garage and were forced to look for funding. Persuading the VCs to part with their money didn't prove too difficult. In fact they have received funding from angel investors such as Andy Bechtolsheim, Sun Microsystems cofounder, as well as Kleiner Perkins Caufield & Byers and Sequoia Capital – two "A" list VC firms. John Doerr of KPCB and Michael Moritz of Sequoia, both leading lights of the VC industry, are on Google's board of directors. The money has been put to good use, to

Insight

The right atmosphere

Like many other employees in tech start-ups, the Google crowd work hard and long. Brin and Page however have introduced a few little extras that make working life more pleasant. "This is a fun place to be, and I've worked hard to make it that way," says Brin. "At Google we really do work to improve the overall quality of the work environment."[1]

Perks include:

- gourmet chefs on the staff;
- professional masseuses; and
- activities such as roller hockey, skiing and scavenger hunts.

Forget about the mahogany desks, and antique books, among Google's office furnishings are pianos, a Ping-Pong table, a pool table, shuffle-board, a disco ball and, rumor has it, a bed – for those who are completely Googled.

acquire premises, fund R&D and hire a raft of PhD scientists including one bona fide rocket scientist from NASA.

The Google search engine may be a technological masterpiece, but that's no guarantee of success. In the fast-moving marketplace of the Internet, public companies with billion-dollar valuations, spend millions of dollars a month on promotion and advertising. The Google team has, however, shown great marketing savvy. Google has not suddenly erupted onto the scene in a blaze of costly publicity. Instead, momentum has built through word-of-mouth and strategic deals. Nary a penny has been spent on advertising or PR. Instead the media latched onto the tech wizardry, the Stanford background and the sparse simplicity of the Website. The Google vibe soon spread through the Net until Google assumed cult status.

Commercially, Google has made some astute moves. In mid-1999 Netscape agreed to use Google's search engine for its search facility. In November 1999, Google signed its first deal in the UK with Virgin Net – a deal that made it the main search tool for the ISP's base of over 150,000 users. And in July 2000 Google's rivals were sent reeling from what may prove to be a knockout blow as it announced a deal with

Yahoo! to supply the leading portal's main search capability, ousting the incumbent Inktomi.

It's all very well being the No. 1 search engine but what's the business model? In common with others, Google's search service for the public is free. But for the corporates, who want the trendy Google logo adding cache to their sites, it costs. Prices vary. There are several packages on offer. Take the Silver WebSearch for example which covers four million queries a year for $1999 a month, and $8 per 1000 over the limit. With the Google search engine propagating itself throughout the Web, Google should turn some kind of a profit fairly swiftly, particularly as it is unburdened by the costs of advertising on a large scale.

Brin and Page profess a desire to complete their doctorates at Stanford. It may be that, for them, the business world holds less appeal than the more arcane and esoteric world of research. Remember, both are scientists at heart. Nevertheless like two famous *wunderkinder* before them, Messrs Yang and Filo of Yahoo! fame, the desire to complete their studies may remain unfulfilled as the monster they have created continues to grow.

In the meantime, surfers everywhere can breathe a sigh of relief as they discover a search engine that unearths information they want, on or near the first page of search results and not the twentieth and, equally attractive, a search page that is an oasis of quiet amid the cacophony of visual noise that constitutes most of the Net. Expect to see a lot more of Google in the future.

Links

www.google.com

Notes

1. *The Dartmouth*, April 2000.

STEVE CASE

– *America Online*

For the uninitiated, the Internet can be a daunting experience. Television manufacturers worked it out a long time ago. Press the button and there it is – and there it stays barring a power cut. Broadcasters, too, have made their offerings easy to use. All you have to choose between are some content specific channels. For the average non-computer user getting onto and navigating the Internet, is, by comparison, like taking a degree in quantum physics. Enter Steve Case, CEO and co-founder of America Online (AOL), a leading ISP (Internet Service Provider). If the Internet was "the next big thing," thought Case, there might be some money to be made from making it a simple user-friendly experience. He was right. By January 2000 AOL boasted revenues of over $5 billion, and had the muscle to merge with the multi-media giant Time-Warner.

Steve Case (born 1958) is a world apart from the Marc Andreessens (Netscape) and David Filos (Yahoo!) of the New Economy. Not for him the geekster's path to billionaire status – studying computer sciences or engineering in some West Coast tech hotspot like Stanford or Berkeley. Case took a degree in political science at Williams College, Massachusetts and got a job in marketing and sales. It was only after spells at Proctor & Gamble (hair-care products), and PepsiCo (the Pizza Hut division) that Case turned his attentions to the Internet.

Case recalls the first time he logged on: "I thought it was magical then, I still think it's magical today. The center of my world is consumers," he has observed. "Every day, I wake up and say, 'How can we make America Online more interesting, more useful, more fun, more affordable, so that it will attract a broader audience?' Because I still remember that excitement 13 years ago when I first connected to an online service."[1]

A video games service company followed. The company wasn't a great success but it did introduce Case to Jim Kinsey and Mark Seriff. It was a good combination: Seriff was a techie – he had worked on Arpanet, the forerunner of the Internet; Kinsey was the finance man; and Case provided the sales and marketing know-how. The trio formed Quantum Computers. They started by offering online services to users of the soon-to-be-defunct Commodore computer. Commodore passed away, but America Online (AOL) as the Quantum business was re-named in 1989 went from strength to strength.

Case instinctively knew what the customer wanted. He pitched the product at the average person and, possibly driven by his non-tech background, aimed to make it as simple an experience as possible for users to enjoy. "Our strategy has always been crystal clear," Case said in a 1998 interview. "Consumers want one place where they can find good Internet content and meet interesting people. And they want someone to make it easy for them."

From the outset AOL was a content-driven offering. In 1992 the company went public. By then its membership was up to 150,000. On the back of an innovative marketing strategy, which involved shipping out AOL CDs offering a free trial, customers flocked to the company; 4.6 million had signed up by 1996. There were even discs on the wall of the company's marketing guru Jan Brandt bearing the message, "Resistance is futile." Swelling the ranks of the AOL subscribers were converts from Prodigy, a rival service provider. Prodigy's strategy of moving from a flat fee structure and raising its charges had backfired badly. AOL capitalized on the situation by cutting prices and targeting Prodigy users in an ad campaign.

With AOL dominating its main rivals CompuServe and Prodigy, and with Microsoft's MSN a distant threat, Case might have been forgiven for thinking the game was won. But success also brought its problems. AOL replaced usage charges with a flat fee structure and found, as UK companies discovered with unmetered usage several years later, that usage figures went through the roof. People spent more time online, the systems couldn't cope, and the service caved in under the pressure.

Case meanwhile was struggling to find someone to take over the day-to-day running of the company, someone who knew how to deal with a corporation the size of AOL. In an inspired move he hired Bob Pittman, co-founder of MTV, a media man who understood content delivery.

Making money out of the subscriptions, however, proved a tough nut to crack. The more users AOL signed up, the more AOL spent on infrastructure and maintaining quality of service. Together Case and Pittman focused on a business model where content sucked in subscribers who then spent money. If they had a captive audience, advertisers would fight to get onto AOL's service. Businesses would compete to be the preferred suppliers. That's what they hoped, and they were right.

Pittman attacked costs and in particular drove down customer acquisition costs from close to $400 dollars per new subscriber to below $100. AOL sold concessions; 1-800-Flowers bought the flower concession for $25 million; and N2K paid $18 million to become the sole music retailer. Amazon paid $19 million to be the exclusive bookseller on the external aol.com Website. Barnes & Noble went one better paying $40 million to be the exclusive bookseller inside.

Today, there are so many Websites offering space that advertising revenue is one of the most precarious revenue streams. AOL however has taken steps to beef up content provision sufficiently to guarantee healthy revenues from advertising.

The company has been active on the acquisitions front, taking over CompuServe in 1998 (adding 2.5 million subscribers), and in the same year it took its chance to acquire Netscape for $4.2 billion. The business world had not long recovered from the Netscape deal, when AOL made the shock announcement in early 2000, of a planned $166 billion merger with media giant Time Warner. Analysts weren't convinced that the Time Warner deal made sense and dumped stock, causing a 20 percent drop in its share price. Quite what the analysts saw that was so bad is difficult to understand. Despite the fears that Time Warner was carrying some fat in comparison with AOL, there is no question that it has significant assets. AOL gained an extensive voice network capability. Yet this may to turn out to be a sideshow. AOL already parted with the first network it built in return for CompuServe's subscribers. It's just as probable that AOL will sell off the networks acquired courtesy of Time Warner. The main prize is the content. AOL with Time Warner's movie and music business – with its publishing and television – all efficiently managed and running at Internet speed, would be a powerful combination. Such a combination perfectly fits Case's take on the future of AOL:

"What we're trying to be is a global leader in interactive service – the concept of interactive service is really a concept that embraces media and communication in a pretty central way – and commerce, too.

And the way I think is better to look at it is, we want a company that helps build and plays a central role in building this new interactive medium. If we're successful, we believe the AOL brand will stand for the way lots of people connect to this interesting new interactive world ... we really want to be their gateway into this exciting future.

But there's no question that ... advertising and commerce will grow and will be the main profit center."[2]

So far so good, for Case and AOL. Roughly 80 percent of the world's online users log on to AOL in some way. And while they are there, traipsing around the online shopping malls, they part with over $10 billion dollars a year. AOL itself saw revenues of over $4.5 billion in 1999 and $6.5 billion mid-2000. As of April 2000, too, AOL had 22 million subscribers, and was adding 12,000 a day. This rate of subscriber acquisition looks unsustainable, but is still impressive. The markets and the competition have been waiting for Case and AOL to stumble for a long time now. Case may have stubbed his toe once or twice, but they may have to wait for sometime before he slips up.

Notes

1. *Forbes Online*, April 2000.
2. *Washington Post*, 1997.

VINT CERF

In 1994 *People Magazine* listed Vinton Gray Cerf as one of the "25 Most Intriguing People." Intriguing he certainly is, but his true significance extends well beyond the merely curious. Cerf (born 1943) is routinely referred to as the father of the Internet – which in e-business terms places him somewhere near God's right hand. His curriculum vitae, including professional memberships, academic honors and publication credits, runs to 11 sides of A4 – in small type. If any man can lay claim to be the principal architect of the Internet then it is probably Vint Cerf.

Cerf was first introduced to the ideas underpinning the Internet at UCLA where he was a graduate student from 1967 to 1972. He had already obtained BS in Math and Computer Science from Stanford University and was following up with an MS in Computer Science (he wound up with both a Master of Science and PhD in computer science). At UCLA he worked in the laboratory of Professor Len Kleinrock, helping to develop the host level protocols (rules governing communication) of the ARPANET – the forerunner to the modern-day Internet. And it was during this period at UCLA that he first met Bob Kahn with whom he would eventually co-design the TCP/IP protocol and architecture of the Internet.

In late 1972, Cerf moved back to Stanford University as a faculty member for electrical engineering and computer sciences. Once again, Cerf came into contact with Bob Kahn who was by now working at ARPA. Kahn was trying to solve the problem of how to interconnect different networks and allow the computers on them to communicate with each other without them requiring any knowledge of the underlying networks. He asked Cerf to work with him and try to develop an open architecture that would facilitate this kind of communication.

The co-operation between Cerf and Kahn resulted in the submission of a preliminary paper, outlining the concepts underlying the Internet, to the International Network Working Group (INWG). The paper was subsequently revised and published in May 1974 in the IEEE (Institute of Electrical and Electronics Engineers) transactions on communications.

Following its publication, Cerf, still at Stanford, continued to develop the concepts outlined in the preliminary paper with the help of a group of graduate students. This led to the first full draft of the Transmission Control Protocol in December 1974. In 1976 Cerf became project manager at the US Department of Defense's Advanced Research Projects Agency (DARPA), with special responsibility for managing the internetting research programs.

Over the next few years, Cerf continued to drive development of the TCP and implement its use on the ARPANET. An important step along the way was the separation of the Internet Protocol (IP) from the Transmission Control Protocol, resulting in the TCP/IP protocol suite. In January 1983, ARPANET made the switch to TCP/IP and by the end of 1983 all hosts on the ARPA-sponsored network were running TCP/IP.

By then Cerf had moved on from ARPA to MCI, the Internet services and infrastructure company, where he headed up the engineering of MCI Mail – a commercial email service. Cerf's professional relationship with Kahn was not at an end, however; in 1986 Cerf and Kahn worked together again at the Corporation for National Research Initiatives (CNRI), a start-up non-profit research firm that Bob Kahn had founded. At CNRI, Kahn and Cerf worked on information infrastructure related areas, such as knowledge robots, and a digital library. It was a busy period for Cerf who also became a member – and later chairman – of the Internet Architecture Board. In 1992, he co-founded the Internet society, where he was the first president and then chairman. He remains on the board and is still chairman of the newly created Internet Societal Task Force – given the task of making the Internet accessible to everyone and monitoring and analyzing international, national and local policies surrounding the use of the Internet.

Cerf continues to pass on his wealth of knowledge about the internet and his insight into its future through his position as senior vice president for Internet Architecture and Technology (responsible for design and development of advanced Internet systems) at the MCI WorldCom corporation. Not that his interest in the Internet, stops at the doors of MCI WorldCom. A man of prodigious energy, in addition to his responsibilities at MCI WorldCom, Cerf is chairman of the IPv6 Forum, dedicated to raising awareness and speeding introduction of the new Internet protocol. And he is also on the boards of the domain names body ICANN, (the Internet Corporation for Assigned Names and Numbers), the Internet Policy Institute (IPI), the Endowment for Excellence in Education, the MCI WorldCom Foundation and the Hynomics Corporation.

Recognizing his expertise in the Internet, even the US government has sought his opinion on Internet related matters. Cerf has given testimony before Congress and is a member the US Presidential Information Technology Advisory Committee (PITAC). He is also a fellow of a number of prestigious organizations including the IEEE, the American Association for the Advancement of Science, the American Academy of Arts and Sciences, the International Engineering Consortium and the National Academy of Engineering.

Not surprisingly for a man who has made such a significant contribution to the development of the Internet, Cerf has picked up an award or ten, along the way. These include, among others, the Marconi Fellowship; the Alexander Graham Bell Award (presented by the Alexander Graham Bell Association for the Deaf); the NEC Computer and Communications Prize; the IEEE Alexander Graham Bell Medal; the IEEE Koji Kobayashi Award; the Computer and Communications Industries Association Industry Legend Award; the Yuri Rubinsky Web Award; the Kilby Award; and the Yankee Group/Interop/Network World Lifetime Achievement Award.

You might assume that Cerf's life revolved entirely around Internet technology. Not so. His personal interests are said to include "fine wine, gourmet cooking and science fiction." Certainly Cerf is a keen sci-fi fan, for nestling among his many achievements is a credit for an appearance on Gene Roddenberry's *Earth: Final conflict* – a top sci-fi TV show in the US for which Cerf served as technical advisor. Fittingly, he played Cy Vincent, the US President's Chief of Staff in Episode 21.

JOHN CHAMBERS

– *Cisco*

T he rumor is that the Internet is going to change the business world as we know it. But while investors get their portfolios in a twist over volatility in the share price of dot-com companies, spare a thought for the people who make the whole thing possible.

Cisco Systems is now the worldwide leader in networking solutions for the Internet. Surf the Internet for a couple of hours and chances are you will have accessed dozens of sites supported by Cisco products. The company supplies 80 percent of the Internet's routers – specialized computers that direct the packets of information speeding along the information superhighway making sure they take the quickest route to their destination. No routers – no Internet. And then there are Firewalls, Web Servers, Web Cache, Ethernets and a whole load of other essential network products.

Husband and wife team Sandra Lerner and Len Bosack, founded Cisco in San Jose, California, in 1984. Both worked at Stanford University, but on different computer systems. In trying to figure out a way to send and receive emails between their incompatible systems they came up with the idea of the router. It's a product that collects and sorts data and then distributes it. The beauty lies in its open architecture which enables it to provide data that can be passed across different networks and still be understood by each. Although that's how Cisco's business started, it quickly grew from a few gray boxes – the routers – into new areas such as switches, and other networking infrastructure.

Today, the company serves customers in three target markets:

- *enterprises*
  large organizations – corporations, government agencies, utilities etc., with complex networking needs often spanning different locations and computer types;
- *service providers*
  companies such as ISPs (Internet Service Providers) offering information services; and
- *small/medium business*
  companies that need data networks with connection to the Internet or each other.

Cisco's big selling point is that it delivers an end-to-end service. It provides the hardware, the software, and the expertise to install the systems and support them. The company describes itself as a "Global Networked Business." The Global Networked Business model, according to Cisco, uses the network to gain competitive advantage by "opening up the corporate information infrastructure to all key constituencies." Using this model Cisco itself makes operating cost savings of over $550 million a year.

Much of Cisco's success is down to the leadership and deal making ability of CEO, John Chambers (born 1949). When Chambers became CEO in 1995, Cisco had a market capitalization of $9 billion. At the time of writing, it was over 50 times that. Cisco owns 80 percent of the router market. It also has a voracious appetite, swallowing up more than 60 companies – an investment of $20.4 billion. Chambers has observed:

> "The companies who emerge as industry leaders will be those who understand how to partner and those who understand how to acquire. Customers today are not just looking for pinpoint products, but end-to-end solutions. A horizontal business model always beats a vertical business model. So you've got to be able to provide that horizontal capability in your product line, either through your own R&D, or through acquisitions."[1]

Chambers graduated from West Virginia University with both a business degree and a law degree. He then obtained an MBA from Indiana University. Before Cisco, he worked for two companies that shaped his managerial style. At IBM, where Chambers was part of the sales team, he saw the stifling effect that bureaucracy and uniformity could have on a company. In 1983, he moved to Wang, where he witnessed how betting on a proprietary technology could break a company. It was a tough lesson to learn as he found out when he was charged with "downsizing" the workforce to the tune of 4000 people. Chambers remembered the pain and vowed never to relive the experience:

> "The bleeding went on for 15 months. One person after another would sit across the desk from me and ask "What did I do wrong?" And the honest answer is they didn't do anything wrong – it was management acting more like Santa Claus than like business leaders. It was the most painful thing I have ever gone through. I never want to go through it again. I will do anything to avoid it."[2]

Having learnt what not to do, Chambers adopted his own strategy at Cisco. To date, it has been a winning one. Observers point to a number of reasons for his success. High on the list is Chambers' obsessive pursuit of the customer and customer satisfaction. It's an approach in keeping with the philosophy of the company's co-founder who assumed the role of "customer advocate" once the company was under way.

"John Chambers is the most customer-focused human being you will ever meet," notes venture capitalist John Doerr. Chambers is both competitive in acquiring customers, attentive to their needs and charming in his approach to making the deal. Known for his old-school manners it has been said that he is happy to take a handshake over a contract – a disarming approach from a law graduate.

Another factor in Cisco's stratospheric rise under Chambers is the culture he has instilled at the company. Chambers understands people. Maybe it's in the genes – his mother was a psychologist. Motivation is one of his strengths. Employees all have stock options for example. With the rise in the value of stock, this means several managers at the companies are sitting on stock worth $ millions.

Cisco is willing to embrace others into its culture, too. In absorbing a large number of acquired companies into the Cisco empire, Chambers has managed unlike almost any other CEO to retain the talented employees of the targeted companies. Acquisition often kills two birds with one takeover: it adds to the Cisco talent pool and saves on R&D costs. Not that Cisco doesn't do R&D – over 70 percent of products are grown in-house. Chambers judges the success of his acquisitions by two criteria: the percentage of people retained and the revenue generated two or three years down the line.

Finally, and crucially, Chambers 'gets' the Internet; he understands the benefits of scale and speed it offers corporations. The company's famous grasp of its metrics (performance measures) is partly due to the effort that has gone into enabling systems to deliver key statistics to

Insight

All-embracing company culture

One reason for Cisco's astonishing success is the Chambers' take on takeovers. The company isn't afraid to buy other companies, figuring it's a great way of acquiring talent and technology. And Chambers knows how to absorb the new employees into the all-embracing Cisco culture by giving them some short-term targets that are achievable and clearly mark out the direction the company is heading in.

A realistic approach to risk-taking

At the same time, Chambers believes in creating a risk-taking environment – not just paying lip service to the idea. He gives short shrift to the approach of some companies. "Anyone who takes risks and does not make mistakes is kidding themselves – you're not taking a risk. And companies who say, 'We're risk takers' and then you ask their key employees, well, what happens if you miss and they say 'I get shot,' they aren't risk takers either."

key individuals via the company intranet on a daily basis. The company doesn't just provide the means to transact business over the Internet, its own Website is one of the largest e-commerce sites in the world. Some 90 percent of Cisco's business is done online.

Links

www.cisco.com

Notes

1. *Business 2.0*, October 1999.
2. *Wired*, March 1997.

CHRISTOS COTSAKOS

– E*Trade

While the brokerage firm Charles Schwab & Co and others pursue the clicks-&-bricks road to sharetrading domination, E★Trade has opted for the Internet pure-play. Under the stewardship of its driven CEO Christos Cotsakos, the company based in Palo Alto, California, has emerged as an online trading phenomenon.

During the 1990's, widespread media coverage of the growth of the Internet led to a speculative feeding frenzy. Hardened stock traders and, in unprecedented numbers the general public, gorged themselves on technology stocks. Many a company with even the most tenuous connection to the world of e-commerce saw a severalfold increase in its stock price. A favorite pastime among the frequenters of investment chat rooms was predicting the next company to reinvent itself as an e-business and set fire to its stock price. And, as part of a virtuous circle, the resultant explosion in Internet stock prices created unprecedented online opportunities in the financial sector and in particular share trading over the Internet

E★Trade started life as an electronic trading network Trade Plus. The company was founded in 1982, by Bill Porter, to provide trading services to Fidelity, Charles Schwab and Quick & Reilly. Porter hadn't always intended to enter the world of business. At the age of 16, he left high school to join the US Navy. After a brief stint in the service he followed his father's advice and went to school, first at Adams State College in Colorado then Kansas State University where he studied for a Master's degree in physics. Work at the National Bureau of Standards, General Electric and the Textron Corporation followed – then in 1967 Porter decided to go to MIT, graduating with an MBA.

Shaking up the market

At the time Porter started Trade Plus, the stock trading market was still dominated by a few traditional stockbrokers. Because of the restricted access to the stock market for would-be purchasers, these traditional brokers were able to charge relatively high commissions. Porter saw an opportunity to use technology to bypass the brokers and instead plug individuals directly into the financial markets using their personal computers. The theory was great, but putting it into practice proved more difficult.

In reality it was an idea that was ahead of its time. The pre-Berners-Lee World Wide Web Internet was not a user-friendly place and it was difficult to attract large numbers of private traders onto the system. The 1987 stock market crash didn't make things any easier.

Reinvention beckoned. By 1992 the company was no longer Trade Plus but the E*Trade Group – and part of that group, E*Trade Securities was providing share dealing services via AOL and CompuServe. With the advent of the WWW and the GUI (graphical user interface) browsers, the Internet had come of age and the securities market was a perfect proving ground for the argument that the Internet would eradicate traditional distribution channels.

"The middle man gets squeezed," Porter has observed. "Why pay someone to do what you can do for yourself?"[1]

Using the Internet as a distribution channel meant E*Trade could cut costs associated with the provision of securities dealing services and offer a cut-price service to a mass market. E*Trade's service was comparatively low-frills compared with the likes of Charles Schwab or Merrill Lynch. The traditional brokers typically offer services with extras such as investment advice priced in. And, of course, the old guard had bricks-and-mortar premises with all the attendant costs. Economies of scale meant that in the period between 1991 and 1995 E*Trade was able to reduce its commission charge seven times.

The company quickly made inroads into competitors' market share. But things really took off when, in 1996, E*Trade.com was launched, followed swiftly by the hiring of Christos Cotsakos, a Vietnam veteran as CEO. Cotsakos (born 1948) had a clear vision of what would be needed to stay ahead of the competition as well as the personal drive, desire and managerial savvy to achieve it.

In order to survive, E*Trade needed to fight a battle on two fronts. On one side were ranged the deep-discount brokers that were springing up online. Numbering more than 100 they were, by then, undercutting

E*Trade on price. On the other side were traditional players like Charles Schwab & Co (the No. 1 online share-trading outfit), Merrill Lynch, PaineWebber, Prudential, and Morgan Stanley. They charged more, offered added value, pursued a clicks-&-bricks strategy and above all possessed strong brand image.

By 1998, Cotsakos decided it was time for drastic action. Even though the company had turned in a $7 million profit on $72 million sales, Cotsakos knew that it was on the back of a short-sighted strategy. He told the board that it was not enough for E*Trade to merely accept a position as a major player in the share-trading market. What was needed was a bigger vision, a transformation into the biggest and best. The company must provide an all-singing, all-dancing, financial portal covering insurance, financial news, banking and other financial sectors. In short, it had to become a one-stop destination for online financial information services and products.

To make the transition from security trader to financial portal would require a significant injection of cash. Billions of dollars were needed to pay for technology and marketing. This would be at the expense of profits for some time to come. However, the pot of gold at the end of the rainbow, Cotsakos predicted, would be worth the sacrifice. The breadth of services available at a reasonable price would attract customers from the deep-discount brokers, while the extra financial services at the one-stop destination would pull in customers from the likes of Merrill Lynch *et al*.

It was a bold strategic move. Seeing it through would require particular attributes, among them – resolve, toughness, and good managerial skills. As it turned out, Cotsakos was well qualified for the challenge. His earlier experiences had created an exceptional individual. He rose through the ranks of management the hard way. Born to a family of poor Greek immigrants, Cotsakos was the fourth of five children. His father was a store clerk, and Cotsakos grew up on the streets of Paterson, New Jersey.

As a boy, he was caught helping himself to communion wine at St Athanasios Greek orthodox church and received a timely lecture on the responsibility of leadership from the priest. The incident stayed with Cotsakos, who was impressed by the fact that the priest regarded him as leadership material. Whether he realized it or not at the time, the young Cotsakos had leadership qualities; he was the ringleader of his block and captain of the altar boys at St Athanasios.

It was the Vietnam War that would turn those qualities into something more productive. In March 1968, still aged only 19, Cotsakos earned a Purple Heart and Bronze Star when he single-handedly killed four Vietnamese soldiers who had his unit pinned down – he was later wounded in action. He returned home and attended Paterson State College in NJ, majoring in communications. After graduating, Cotsakos went to work for a rapidly growing FedEx, moving quickly through the ranks so that by 1988 he was running European operations. Staying in Europe, he switched to the market research company AC Nielsen, then a unit of Dun & Bradstreet Corporation. Once again he rose swiftly, but his style put a few noses out of joint along the way. "Christos didn't follow the rules," says Robert Weissman, D&B's former CEO. "He made people feel unsafe."[2]

In 1995, Cotsakos was promoted by Weissman to co-CEO and given responsibility for knocking the company into shape before it parted ways with D&B. Unfortunately things didn't go well for Cotsakos who struggled to find common-ground with his fellow co-CEO Robert J. Lievense. The result was that Cotsakos left for E★Trade.

Tour of duty

Cotsakos brought his own idiosyncratic management style with him to E★Trade – an approach that derives more from his experiences in the army than management textbooks. Unorthodox to say the least, Cotsakos employs unusual methods to instil his own special brand of company culture at E★Trade. Examples of Cotsakos' tactics include: subjecting new recruits to an initiation ordeal involving standing on a chair during a meeting and revealing something insightful about themselves; getting employees to carry around rubber chickens to lighten the mood; and taking executives off for some team-building at … cookery school.

Getting employees to give their best and pull together is Cotsakos' speciality. And if the employees don't fit, they are swiftly ejected like the new recruit who left after he didn't take kindly to being asked to stand on a chair. "It's all about getting people excited about how they can make a difference as a person and as a team," says Cotsakos.[3]

He expects every man and woman to do their duty: "My job is to make people do the impossible. I push people hard and I don't tolerate excuses. I'm very intolerant of people who makes the same mistakes over and over."[4]

Although Cotsakos might lead by example, he's a tough act to follow, cramming 48 hours into a day. In addition to his heavy workload at E★Trade, Cotsakos serves on the boards of a number of leading technology companies. These include: FOX Entertainment Group Inc.,

> ### Insight
>
> Cotsakos exemplifies what executive grit and pure force of personality can achieve. He has very clear views on what it means to be a manager in the new economy. Becoming a manager, he says, involves taking responsibility. A manager no longer has the right to say "I don't know" or "I can't do it." If that sort of accountability doesn't suit an individual's personality then as far Cotsakos is concerned he or she isn't cut out for the job.

Critical Path Inc., Webvan Group Inc., Digital Island Inc., PlanetRX.com Inc., and Tickets.com. He also finds time to study for a PhD in economics at the University of London.

How successful Cotsakos' reformation of E★Trade will ultimately turn out to be is uncertain. In the short term, the company has, as he predicted, bled money and posted mounting losses. At the same time in terms of share of average daily trades it has consolidated its position as No. 2 behind Schwab. It has also, however, seen a substantial rise in customers from fewer than 100,000 to more than 2 million, putting it firmly in third place behind Schwab and Fidelity Investments in terms of online accounts.

In the quarter ending March 31, 2000, E★Trade added 603,000 new accounts, up 83 percent on the previous quarter's 330,000. It also announced its intention to offer wireless access to its trading facilities through a partnership with Verizon Wireless, and rolled out the E★TRADE bank, the largest pure Internet bank in the US.

Along the way, the company has been aggressively predatory, acquiring among others a leading pure-play bank Telebanc Financial Corp for $1.8 billion – and thereby continuing to increase the customer base. Other plans underway include a personalised financial multimedia experience – "digital financial media." Cotsakos is also embracing the world of mobile computing, so E★Trade's services can be accessed through a wide range of multi-media devices – PDAs, mobile phones, PCs, cable, satellite or terrestrial television.

Cotsakos isn't coy about his plans for E★Trade. It's a war and he wants to be on the winning side. As he said in a recent interview: "It's all about loyalty and trust and who you have in the foxhole with you. At E★Trade, we're an attacker, we're predatory. We believe we have a God-given right to market share."[5]

If, or as Cotsakos would have it, when, E*Trade is firmly entrenched as the leading online financial services provider it will be largely due to the vision and sheer bloody-mindedness of Cotsakos.

Notes

1. Sloan-MIT Website – http://mitsloan.mit.edu/news
2. *Business Week online,* 2000
3. Ibid.
4. Ibid.
5. *Business Week,* 1999.

JIM CLARK

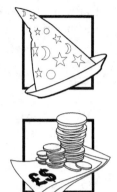

If there is one man who encapsulates the restless pioneering spirit of the new economy, then it has to be the hyperactive Jim Clark. He founded Silicon Graphics, Netscape and Healtheon – the first Internet healthcare information provider. The former Stanford University Professor also played a part in the creation of Sun Microsystems and a host of other Silicon Valley companies.

Clark (born 1944) has the Midas touch. The companies he started have created tens of billions of dollars of shareholder value and made him a billionaire. On hearing of Clark's involvement in a venture, investors form an orderly queue to hand over their money. Part of Clark's success can be attributed to an uncanny ability to foresee how technology will affect the future. No mere businessman, Clark is a card-carrying techie, who has made genuine contributions to the science of computing. In the 1970s, he benefited from a spell at Xerox PARC and a six-year stint at Stanford University as Associate Professor of Electrical Engineering. He was also involved with the DARPA (Defense Advance Research Projects Agency) project of the late seventies, that produced the business-oriented research teams from which Sun Microsystems, Silicon Graphics and MIPS Computer Systems all grew.

Jim Clark came from a poor family. He grew up in Plainview, Texas, dropping out of school in 1961 at the age of 16 to join the US Navy. Some reports have it that he was suspended for telling a teacher to "go to hell" when she admonished him for failing to read *The Rime of the Ancient Mariner*. It wasn't that Clark lacked academic ability, he had a natural aptitude for math and technology, it just wasn't the right time for him to study. He lacked the necessary motivation. His time in the Navy, however, persuaded Clark that education was worth pursuing. The Navy gave him a standard math test and his score was so high that the administrators assumed he must have cheated and made him take it again. When he repeated the feat, they moved him into technical work with computers. Clark's mind came alive.

He also revealed a shrewd business brain, running a loans business on the side, lending money to the other sailors until their payday – at 40 percent interest. In 1971 Clark graduated from Louisiana State University with an MS in Physics, which he followed in 1974, with a PhD in computer science at the University of Utah. At Utah, Clark met Ivan Sutherland, widely regarded as the man behind interactive computer graphics, an area where Jim Clark was to make a big impact.

The pattern of Clark's early working life is that of a bright, restless and easily bored individual seeking a challenge that would hold his attention. After his doctorate Clark was seduced by the romantic notion of academic life, and embarked on a teaching career at the University of Santa Cruz. The romance soon wore off though and Clark quit to take up consulting. Consulting he liked even less. A contract with Boeing persuaded him that life as a small cog in a large machine was not for him. Instead, he determined to return to teaching but only if he could combine it with developing his business interests.

In 1978, Clark took up a position at Stanford University. Although he had his teaching duties to attend to, he had funding from DARPA to lead a team of graduate students conducting research into computer graphics technology. Over a period of three years Clark and his team came up with several breakthroughs. Not least of these was a "geometry engine." The team managed to shift the processing of 3-D graphics from software to hardware, embedding the instruction set into a chip.

What Clark had achieved at Stanford was revolutionary, yet it seemed only Clark and others associated with the project had the vision to realize how important and potentially lucrative an invention it was. Clark did the rounds of traditional computer companies trying to sell his technology but with no luck:

> "I concluded after talking to DEC and IBM and all these companies that they didn't understand how to use what we had in the first place, so they would surely screw it up. Since they didn't feel the passion for getting these kinds of graphics into computers, what was I going to do? Try to convince them for three years while I died?"[1]

Instead, Clark decided to have a crack at developing the graphics technology himself. In 1982, he took six of the Stanford team, raised $500,000 and left Stanford to found Silicon Graphics (now SGI).

His mission was to push 3-D computer graphics as far as possible, outperforming all the existing products and ultimately bringing 3-D capability to personal computers. It was an ambitious vision, but Clark delivered.

By the time Clark resigned from SGI in 1994 the company had been growing at an impressive rate of 40 percent for about eight years and revenues were heading for the $2 billion mark; the company employed more than 5000 people; and its machines were the state of the art "best of breed" in high-end computer graphics.

As chief technical officer Clark had overseen the development of workstations, a graphics engine and a user interface that allowed real time creation and manipulation of 3-D objects. For the first time the SGI machines enabled designers to visualize objects by rendering them with a computer. They could then rotate them, morph them and manipulate them to give an accurate representation of how the object would appear in the real world. The company sold workstations to an "A" list of clients, including NASA, the US military and British Aerospace. In the early 1990s Hollywood, too, caught on to the potential of the SGI technology. The result has been a string of out-of-this-world special effects in films such as *Jurassic Park*, *Terminator II* and the computer-generated *Toy Story*.

When Clark left SGI it was out of frustration at the direction the company was taking. Clark had brought in Ed McCracken as CEO to concentrate on the management side. As befits a man of vision and restless genius, Clark looked into the future and saw that multimedia would become increasingly important. He was determined to bring SGI innovation and quality to the masses and not just those who could afford the very expensive high-spec SGI machines. Others at the company were not convinced. The entrepreneur in Clark wanted to move at speed, but SGI had itself morphed into a large and less agile company:

> "A lot of the things that I was trying to get done at SGI were going as rapidly as a company that size was going to be able to push them. I wasn't happy with the pace."[2]

So in February 1994 Clark went his own way. The company he had founded had made him a rich man. He would have been richer still had he not relinquished 400, 000 shares in an effort to convince possible investors in any new venture that he had made a clean break.

Clark wasn't out of the action for long – less than 24 hours in fact. When he resigned from SGI he already had an idea what he wanted to be involved with next. The same morning he resigned he sent an email

Insight

So what are the secrets of Clark's success? He puts it down to leadership qualities and building the right team. It's a combination that has served him well throughout his career from the research days at Stanford to his portfolio of start-ups. "It just comes down to leadership. It comes from a combination of being persuasive; believing in what you're doing; having integrity ... and knowing how to judge good people, because you can't afford to have anything but good people early on in a company."[3]

Clark likes to surround himself with people he respects and can get on with. "I look for intelligence and a certain measure of humility," he observes. "People who are boastful or too proud may be really good, but they're not my kind of people. A business is about teams, and teams mean getting along with people. There's just not enough room for a lot of super-egos in a company."[4]

Greed is not good

Despite his personal wealth, Clark is not a fan of avarice. Instead, he says, his success has come through sharing with others. Don't hoard the money, he advises: "Don't try to keep it all. A hallmark of this era is making the wealth distribution within an enterprise more democratic. Everyone gets to share in it."[5] Putting his money where his mouth is, Clark refuses to invest in companies that don't have employee stock options.

to a young programmer, Marc Andreessen. Andreessen had invented the NCSA Mosaic browser for the World Wide Web. Clark thought it was a product with a great future – in interactive television. For once, he was wrong. At the time the Web was in its infancy, everyone who hadn't been touched by the Web still thought interactive television was where it was at. Fortunately for Clark, Andreessen was as good an evangelist for the Internet as Clark was for 3-D graphics. Fortunately for Andreessen, Clark unlike the computer companies he had tried to sell his graphics technology to, was a good listener. As it turned out the Internet was everything interactive television could have been and more.

Netscape started life in 1994 as Mosaic Communications Corporation with $6 million of Clark's money and $6 million venture capital. The strategy was a radical one: give the product away, gain market share, become the "standard" for the Internet. It was an incisive strategy and it would have worked if it hadn't been for a certain company based in Redmond, Washington. As it was, it worked well for a time. Long enough at least to make the Netscape Navigator browser familiar to virtually every Internet user; and to build up a devoted customer base, some almost as fanatical as the famously devoted Apple Mac faithful. By 1996, Clark and Andreessen's company had captured over 80 percent of the market.

Netscape may have given the browser away to non-corporate users, but it charged for the server software and corporate versions of the browser. When the company had its IPO, it was valued at some $2 billion, making Clark the first Internet billionaire. All good things come to an end, however, and Netscape eventually succumbed. The company was sold to AOL. Clark left substantially richer than before.

Although Netscape eventually lost the browser war to Microsoft on a technical knockout – a points draw at best – Clark and Andreessen's achievements at Netscape should be measured in more than sales figures and revenues. Along with the work of Tim Berners-Lee, it is the Netscape browser that is primarily responsible for the explosive growth of the Internet.

Since then, Clark's enterprising spirit has seen him involved in several start-ups. Healtheon, for example, the online company that electronically hotwires the healthcare industry, is another of Clark's multi-billion dollar hits. Healtheon subsequently merged with WebMd. That puts his tally at three multi-billion dollar businesses.

These days Clark takes time out to concentrate on his other interests, flying his stunt plane, or crewing his $30 million 155-foot sailboat *Hyperion* for example. (Planes and boats are interests he shares with Oracle's Larry Ellison.) Even at play, however, his fecund and innovative mind is at work – he designed the complex control system on his boat.

Clark is a very wealthy man, even by Silicon Valley standards. But his appetite for start-ups appears undiminished. Since Healtheon he has set up myCFO – a financial service for the money-rich but time-poor; and Shutterfly.com an online family photo management service. Don't count on Clark packing up his whiteboard anytime soon.

Notes

1. *Wired*, January 1994.
2. *Wired*, October 1994.
3. MyPrimetime.com interview 2000.
4. *Ibid.*
5. *Ibid.*

MICHAEL DELL

– *Dell Corporation*

Michael Dell made history when he became the youngest CEO ever to run a Fortune 500 company. Today he heads one of the most profitable and innovative businesses in the world. Along the way, he has joined the ranks of the most revered entrepreneurs in America – as the man who took the direct-sales model and elevated it to an art form. (In 1999, Dell Computer came fourth in Fortune's ranking of America's Most Admired Companies, behind GE, Coca-Cola and Microsoft.)

The company Dell built is not the biggest in the world. Nor are its products the most innovative. Dell Corporation is that rarity: a corporate model, the benchmark for how companies can be organized and managed to reap the full potential of technology. Michael Dell (born 1965) is the Alfred P. Sloan of the high-tech age. But, while it took Sloan decades to meld General Motors into his organizational image, Michael Dell is still a young man.

Dell started young. By the age of 13, he had become a dab hand at taking apart the motherboard of his Apple II computer. But his interest in business pre-dated even that:

> "I first experienced the power – and rewards – of being direct when I was twelve years old. The father of my best friend in Houston was a pretty avid stamp collector, so naturally my friend and I wanted to get into stamp collecting, too … I started reading stamp journals just for fun, and soon began noticing that stamp prices were rising. Before long, my interest in stamps began to shift from the joy of collecting to the idea that there was something here that my mother, a stockbroker, would have termed a 'commercial opportunity.'"

Dinner-time conversations in the Dell household reinforced his interest. The talk was about what the Federal Reserve was doing and how it affected the American economy, the oil crisis, and which company stocks to buy and sell. By the age of 16, young Michael was putting what he'd learned into practice.

He got a summer job selling newspaper subscriptions of the *Houston Post* and quickly realized that the list of phone numbers the company handed out was an inefficient way to drum up new business. Dell speedily identified a pattern for new subscribers. Feedback from potential customers convinced him that the best groups to target were newly-weds and people who had just bought new houses or apartments.

From the local courthouse he and his friends obtained lists of those who had applied for marriage licenses. From another source he compiled a list of people who had recently applied for mortgages. He targeted the two groups with a personalized letter. Subscriptions poured in.

When the school term started, an assignment from his history and economics teacher asked students to complete a tax return. Dell calculated his income based on his successful newspaper subscriptions business at $18,000.

His teacher, assuming he had put the decimal point in the wrong place, corrected it. She was dismayed to learn that there was no mistake – her student had made more money than she had.

By then the fledgling entrepreneur had a new hobby – computers. While at the University of Texas, he rebuilt PCs and sold them. The Dell Corporation was kick-started with a $1000 investment. Dell is living proof that having too little capital is better than too much. It forced him to re-invent the computer industry. Dell has achieved a handsome return on the $1000; in early 2000 the value of his share in the company was estimated at over $12 billion.

Dell's inspiration was to realize that PCs could be built to order and sold directly to customers. This had two clear advantages. First, it meant that Dell was not hostage to retailers intent on increasing their mark-ups at its expense. Dell cut out the middlemen. By doing so, he reduced the company's selling costs from a typical 12 percent of revenue to a mere 4–6 percent of revenue.

Second, the company did not need to carry large stocks. It actually carries around 11 days of inventory. "The best indirect company has 38 days on inventory. The average channel has about 45 days of inventory. So if you put it together, you've got 80 days or so of inventory – a little less than eight times our inventory level," says Michael Dell.

In any language, high profit margins and low costs make business sense. In the fast-growing computer business they are nirvana. In its first eight years Dell grew at a steady rate of 80 percent. It then slowed down to a positively snail-like 55 percent. By the middle of 2000 its yearly revenues were up to $27 billion.

Inspired by such raw statistics, emulators have come thick and fast. In an effort to keep ahead, Compaq introduced programs which offer the ability to have PCs built-to-order. Crucially, they were still sold through intermediaries. The trouble for established companies like Compaq is that once the middlemen are in place it is very difficult to ease them out of the picture. Another Dell competitor, Gateway, opted for a half-way-house approach – it introduced "Country Stores" to provide potential customers with a physical site to learn about products in person – the equivalent of a car showroom and test drive.

Emulation is the purest form of desperation as well as flattery. Dell's insight was, after all, blissfully simple. "There is a popular idea now that if you reduce your inventory and build to order, you'll be just like Dell. Well, that's one part of the puzzle, but there are other parts, too," Dell has said. He explains the company's success as "a disciplined approach to understanding how we create value in the PC industry, selecting the right markets, staying focused on a clear business model and just executing."

While the notion of selling direct is appealing, companies which do so are only as good as their ability to deliver. Dell's model creates a direct line to the customer, which the company has proved highly adept at maximising. Direct knowledge of the end consumer builds a satisfied customer base – increasing Dell's brand strength, lowering customer acquisition costs, and boosting customer loyalty. The result is "mass customization" as opposed to the traditional method of broad market segmentation.

Dell, the interloper which cut out the money-grabbing middleman, has a strong rapport with its customers – in a way that Microsoft, for example, has manifestly failed to achieve "To all our nit-picky – over demanding – ask-awkward-questions customers. Thank you, and keep up the good work," read one Dell advertisement. "You actually get to have a relationship with the customer," explains Michael Dell. "And that creates valuable information, which in turn allows us to leverage our relationships with both suppliers and customers. Couple that information with technology and you have the infrastructure to revolutionize the fundamental business models of major global companies."

Dell has proved highly efficient in utilizing the full power of modern technology to create reliable logistics and distribution systems. It is among the pioneers of selling by the Internet. "The Internet for us is a dream come true," says Dell. "It's like zero-variable-cost transaction.

The only thing better would be mental telepathy." In 1997 Dell's online sales alone exceeded $3 million a day. During the year 2000 the online sales figure reached $50 million. Roughly 50 percent of the company's sales are Web-enabled.

A slight blip in performance early in 2000 prompted anxious murmurs from some sections of the industry analysts. Donald Selkin, chief investment strategist at Joseph Gunnar, the New York securities and banking firm, said of Dell, "I believe it's glory days are over; I hate to say it, but it's old technology."

It is a little early to be counting Dell out, though. Michael Dell has made his shareholders rich through an ability to predict market trends. And he has not lost his touch as investments in Cerent Corp and Rambus have shown. Dell has already begun to diversify. While the company is best known for its PCs, it also offers an impressive array of other products that provide better profit margins. These include Internet-related products such as servers and storage network devices. In the quarter ending April 31, 2000 for example, sales of these types of products accounted for 48 percent of the systems sales total. There was a 100 percent increase in sales of storage products and Dell accounted for 40 percent of the worldwide industry growth in the server market.

The beauty of the Dell model is that it can be applied to a range of industries where middlemen have traditionally creamed off profits. Its low overheads also mean that Michael Dell has no need to mortgage the business to expand. This year's model, may be around for some time. The same can be said of the man who built it.

Dell had been consistently ranked No. 2 in the world in liquidity, profitability and growth among all computer systems companies, No. 1 in the US. With that sort of performance, many a CEO would be pleased to take a bow and enjoy the applause. Michael Dell merely describes it as a "great start.":

> "I believe we have the right business model for the Internet age. We have a significant lead in dealing direct with customers and suppliers."

If that's a good start, what's he going to do for an encore? Still in his thirties, remember, he's still just a slip of a lad – a whole decade younger than Bill Gates

When people ask when the growth will slow down, he points out that his company happens to be part of what could soon be the largest industry in the world, and, just for good measure, adds that the company still has only a small percentage of total market share:

"If we had 50 percent market share – like Coca-Cola – I might be a little more concerned about our growth slowing. There's no such thing as a company that executes perfectly forever. But the real key to our success comes from within ... It comes from being willing to challenge conventional wisdom and having the courage to follow our convictions. It comes from an innate fascination with eliminating unnecessary steps."

Unnecessary steps! Beware – you have been warned.

Links

www.dell.com

MATT DRUDGE

– *The* Drudge Report

O n the night of January 17, 1998, the world changed for ever. Two things happened. One was a last-minute decision by editors at the American news magazine *Newsweek* to spike an article about the president of the United States and an obscure, young White House intern. The other, even more significant, was the decision by a 31-year-old renegade reporter to post the story about *Newsweek*'s decision on his Website. In doing so, he broke the Monica Lewinsky story to a gossip-hungry world. The reporter was Matt Drudge. The Website, the *Drudge Report*.

Drudge (born 1967) is the chronicler of the *Drudge Report*, an Internet site packed on a daily basis with gossip, tidbits, and news on everything from the latest political scandal in Washington DC to mysterious goings on in far-flung corners of the globe. Love him or loathe him – and many establishment journalists are in the latter camp – Matt Drudge is part of a revolution. It is a revolution that has turned the cosy traditional world of journalism on its pompous head. E-journalism is an earthquake that is sending tremors around the world.

"The king of new junk media," is how *Time* magazine described Drudge. Matt Drudge sees it differently: "All truths begin as hearsay, as far as I'm concerned. And some of the best news stories start in gossip," he says. He's right.

"I started it as a lark," Drudge has said of his eponymous online newsletter. If "hits" on his Website counted as readers Drudge's circulation would be up with the heavyweights he delights in scooping. With one press of the Enter button on that fateful night in January 1998, Drudge became an Internet phenomenon. From his LA apartment, he continues to be a thorn in the side of the US political and journalistic establishment. But while many in the media establishment vilify him they still cannot resist paying a visit to his Website.

As a teenager Drudge used to walk the streets of Washington DC gazing in awe at the pantheon of journalism, the *Washington Post* newsroom on 15th Street. With no publishing connections and lacking the benefit of an expensive education (he graduated 325th out of 350 in his class at Northwood High School and skipped college), Drudge figured his chances of winding up in the newsroom of one of the pillars of the US media establishment were zero. And he was right. Drudge's last job before leaving Washington was in a Seven-Eleven store. Hardly a breeding ground for would be Bernsteins or Woodwards.

After moving to Hollywood, California, Drudge settled into a mundane job at the CBS gift store. It was here that he learnt the value of gossip. Drudge discovered that people were sometimes careless with information and he would listen in to conversations and even rifle through the trash cans, for his own amusement. On a visit to his son, Drudge's father bought him a computer. When Drudge hooked up to the Internet he realized he had found the perfect medium to give vent to his journalistic ambitions.

He quickly progressed from posting up the tidbits he accumulated on newsgroups to starting his own Website. A few email addresses became a mailing list called the *Drudge Report*. Before he knew it Drudge was the cutting edge of renegade Internet journalism. Thousands, and then hundreds of thousands of people were reading his news reports. The *Drudge Report* Website was a natural progression.

The newsroom Drudge operates may lack the prestigious location of the *Washington Post*. It lacks the bustle as well. Drudge's newsroom is an apartment in one of the less affluent parts of Los Angeles. He gets his information from culling a stack of daily newspapers, wire services and thousands of daily email tips. "From a little corner in my Hollywood apartment, in the company of nothing more than a 486 computer and my six-toed cat, I have consistently been able to break big stories, thanks to this network of ordinary guys," he told the US National Press Club in 1998.

The Internet is the conduit for most of Drudge's information. Chat room buzz, news wires and most importantly emails – Drudge receives, he has said, some 10,000 a day – these are the raw material from which Drudge fashions his articles.

From his position outside the establishment press, Drudge, has scored several notable scoops. He has broken US political scandals –

the Paula Jones and Kathleen Willey stories; the CBS's firing of Connie Chung and Bob Dole's choice of Kemp as running mate.

But his biggest coup came when he scooped the Lewinsky story. *Newsweek* had the story but decided not to publish it. Drudge reported both the story, and *Newsweek*'s decision not to run it. The story spread on the Internet. After several days, it was finally picked up by the *Washington Post* and *Los Angeles Times*. Drudge recalls the moment he put the story out into the ether. "My life won't be the same after this," he thought. On this point, at least, he was 100 percent accurate.

Drudge was launched on a dizzy merry-go-round of media appearances. It was the start of an uncomfortable relationship between Drudge and the traditional journalistic establishment. While many in the media are happy to be seen criticizing Drudge and his methods, they also are the source for a lot of his stories, leaked from the newsrooms of press and television.

Cyber-muckraker

In *The New York Times*, Todd Purdum described Drudge as the "cyber-muckraker with the Dickensian name" dispensing "breathless tips on topics from Paramount Pictures to Paula Jones."

Muckraking journalism has a long tradition in America. At the turn of the century the legendary muckraking journalist Ida Tarbell railed against Standard Oil and its oil monopoly. Then there was William Randolph Hearst, the 23-year-old newspaper proprietor, using the *San Francisco Daily Examiner* and its writers like Ambrose Bierce to dish the dirt. By the 1950s the press barons' control of the media was sufficient to drive many reporters who sought to expose corruption outside of the traditional press.

George Seldes and I.F. Stone are famous examples of media critics who did their news reporting through the medium of the newsletter. At its peak, Stone's newsletter had a circulation of over 60,000. This is the tradition in which Drudge follows.

Drudge has been relentlessly criticized by the traditional media. His methods are suspect in the eyes of many trained journalists. "Like a channel catfish, he mucks through the hoaxes, conspiracies and half-truths posted online in pursuit of fodder for his Website," editorial luminary Doug Harbrecht observed at a talk Drudge gave to the National Press Club in 1998. It's not just a question of accuracy, sources and the like. Some of the stick has been plain condescending.

Take this example at the same 1998 address to the National Press Club. Mr Harbrecht again: "Here's a question that just came up. With all due respect, in the past half-hour you have been inaccurate 8 to 10 times – about history, government, the media. You said there were no suits approved by a president, no profits in early newspaper and radio. Do you think journalists should have any minimum educational requirements?"

Or the introductory remarks: "Matt, know this: You may be, as the *New York Times* recently dubbed you, the nation's reigning mischief-maker; you may get it first sometimes, you may even get it right some-times, your story of success is certainly compelling. But there aren't many in this hallowed room who consider you a journalist. Real journalists live and pride themselves on getting it first *and* right; they get to the bottom of the story, they bend over backwards to get the other side. Journalism means being painstakingly thorough, even-handed, and fair."

Some days Drudge must feel like a modern day Daniel walking into the lion's den. Yet a senior writer at *Time* said he had book-marked the *Drudge Report* on his computer and speculated that every other reporter in Washington would have done the same.

Online writers are not much kinder. "Matt Drudge is a new variety of vampire," said Lewis Koch, a special correspondent for "*Cyberwire Dispatch*, "a nasty little mammal who bites and laps the blood of its journalist victims. Drudge's Warholian fame, what there is of it, is due to living off the journalistic blood of other reporters."

Drudge counters

Drudge, however, is quite able to look after himself. He packs a powerful verbal punch, a sharp wit and a keen turn of phrase. He counters his critics by justly drawing attention to his scoops. Likening himself to the pamphleteers of old, he claims he is just speaking his mind, the difference is that the world is listening. Why shouldn't he report? – "You don't get a license to report. You get a license to style hair," he says. At the *Drudge Report* you can get the newswires from across the globe, raw and unfiltered news, refreshingly free of spin.

Poetically he puts his finger squarely on the issue that most terrifies the establishment:

"We have entered an era vibrating with the din of small voices. Every citizen can be a reporter, can take on the powers that be. The difference between the Internet, television and radio,

Insight

Matt Drudge was quick to realize that the Internet offers the biggest readership of all. This is something the traditional press was slow to pick up on.

On the Internet everyone can be a reporter. In the professional media a new style of journalism is taking shape. Faster, shorter. Distillation is of the essence. We're moving pell-mell towards real-time reporting. Why? Because no one has time to read everything. No one who is remotely in the game of getting things done can afford to invest so much time in reading about what others are doing. You can get a pithy distillation of *The Economist* by email – digested. Better yet, you can sign up for business this week or politics this week. You can scan what's in the full edition and choose which bits are worth reading. Ditto *Business Week* and the rest. It's not a new idea: the *Wall Street Journal* and other newspapers have done it for years. They crunch the news down to a single panel. Everything you need to know about the world in a few words.

As information becomes ever more widely available, private individuals exert a growing influence over the fortunes of entire companies. This process is compounded by the Internet. Until recently, large organizations maintained power through the management of information inside and outside their borders. Today, that is no longer possible.

Matt Drudge has shown that accuracy is often less important than audience. Over time, though, the quality of the journalistic filter determines the credibility of the information. Get it wrong too often and you're dead.

magazines, newspapers is the two-way communication. The Net gives as much voice to a 13-year-old computer geek or someone like me, as to a CEO or Speaker of the House. We all become equal. And you would be amazed what the ordinary guy knows."[1]

And this is the nub of it all. Drudge may not yet have worked out how to turn this new journalism into big bucks. He has made his money, not from the *Drudge Report*, but from selling his column to *Wired* magazine and AOL and, until he was axed, appearing on his own show on FOX

TV. He may be defending a lawsuit from White House recruit Sidney Blumenthal for $30 million, for a story which he hastily retracted and is fighting with the aid of libertarians. And yes, he might be a little sloppy at times – he has claimed in the past that his stories are 80 percent accurate. But he understands the power of the Internet to transform the news industry. He understands the power of the modem. And he understands that, in cyberspace, we are all reporters if we choose to be.

Links

www.drudgereport.com

Notes

1. Matt Drudge, "Anyone With a Modem Can Report on the World," Address before the National Press Club, June 2, 1998 (Moderator: Doug Harbrecht).

ESTHER DYSON

A mong the growing number of self-appointed e-gurus, Esther Dyson stands out. She is someone that the new business élite listen to. When Dyson speaks, even people like Michael Dell sit up and listen. In 1986, for example, Dell Corporation was storming the PC market with its direct sales business model. In fact the company's success created something of a problem. The phones were ringing with offers of capital and the question everyone wanted an answer to was: "When are you going to go public?" At the time, Michael Dell wasn't sure where the company was headed. So he called a brainstorming meeting and invited a select group of thought leaders from outside Dell to contribute. One of the first names on the list was Esther Dyson.

Dyson was born in Zurich on Bastille Day 1951 into an intellectual household. Her father was the famous science writer and astrophysicist Freeman Dyson, her mother the mathematician Verena Huber-Dyson. As a child young Esther grew up in Princeton New Jersey. Along with the usual childhood toys was a computer.

Precociously bright, Dyson attended Harvard aged 16. There she worked on the college newspaper *Crimson* before graduating with a degree in economics in 1972. After Harvard, Dyson took her skills to *Forbes* magazine, as a fact-checker and reporter (1974–77), and then to New Court Securities (1977–80) followed by Oppenheimer & Co. (1980–82) as a securities analyst specializing in the computer and software industry.

Eventually Dyson started her own company Edventure Holdings, and started to disseminate her views about how the Net would change the world. For Dyson 'Net' is an all-embracing term encompassing the network we call the Internet as well as the other formal and informal networks growing up between individuals, companies and cultures. The Net she believes has the power to change the role of the individual in society, the way we relate to organizations and institutions of power.

It is a view she elaborates on in her well-received book: *Release 2.0: A design for living in the digital age,* published in 1997. The Net matters says Dyson: "Because people use it as a place to communicate, conduct business and share ideas, not as a mystical entity in itself … It will suck power away from central governments, mass media and big business."[1]

Edventure.com is the home of Esther Dyson's online business. A small but diversified company, Edventure focuses on emerging technologies, emerging markets and emerging companies. Its interests include *Release 1.0* , a well-respected newsletter for the computer-industry. A monthly publication, *Release 1.0* comments on what is going to change the world and who will make it happen. The report's style is witty and informative and it is renowned for the accuracy of its crystal-ball-gazing. Dyson is editor and an occasional contributor to the magazine, which is managed by Kevin Werbach.

Dyson is also involved in the sponsorship of a number of influential conferences. The Hi-tech Forum is held in Europe and brings together over 200 individuals engaged in the tech industry – including analysts, investors, scientists, economists and entrepreneurs. In 1999, delegates from over 20 countries gathered on the banks of the Danube in Budapest to participate in the Hi-Tech Forum's tenth anniversary. In the US, the Edventure-sponsored PC Forum, which has been convening for over 20 years, attracts some of the most important people in the US tech industry through its doors.

Another important aspect of Dyson's work is her involvement in Eastern Europe: helping entrepreneurs and funding promising start-ups. Dyson has investments in Russia, (she speaks fluent Russian), Hungary, and the Czech Republic. The country, which seems to hold the most attraction for Dyson's investments, however, is Poland. She has been instrumental in helping Poles access the Internet by plowing money into the start-up of the Polish ISP Poland OnLine (Polska OnLine) and continues to fund its growth. The Central and Eastern European investments may not, in the short term, prove to be exceptionally profitable. Dyson, however, is familiar with the culture and politics of the region and is happy to take a long-term view.

Dyson also chairs the Internet domain name authority ICANN (the Internet Corporation for Assigned Names and Numbers). During her tenure she has at times been embroiled in controversy about the role of

---

Insight

Esther Dyson is the living embodiment of her own theories. Just goes to show what a brilliant woman with a modem and a frequent flyer pass can achieve in the wired world. Precociously bright and possessing boundless energy has enabled her to carve out a unique niche. If that's the key to business success, which it probably is, then Dyson has cracked it.

---

the organization. When ICANN proposed a tax levy of $1 per domain name registration, it and Dyson in particular came in for a lot of criticism prompting the Clinton administration to lobby for its repeal.

A multi-tasking woman, Dyson somehow finds times to help out at a large number of organizations. Those she is involved with include: the President's Export Council Subcommittee on Encryption; the Electronic Frontier Foundation; Poland Online Cygnus Solution; E-Pub Services; Trustworks (Amsterdam); IBS (Moscow); iCat; New World Publishing; Global Business Network; Perot Systems; the Internet Capital Group; the Santa Fe Institute; the Institute for East-West Studies; the Eurasia Foundation; the Russian Software Market Association; (US) Software Publishers Association; the Software Entrepreneurs Forum (Silicon Valley); the Russian Internet Technology Center; and the Soros Medical Internet Project. Whew! Busy lady.

At this point you may wonder how it's humanly possible to spread yourself across so many different interests and activities. At the very least, you may wonder whether it was possible to do justice to them all. In most cases this assumption would be bang on the money. But Dyson appears to be an exceptional individual. Her stamina is legendary enabling her to cope with a grueling global travel schedule that would guarantee most hardened business travelers a spell in a sanatorium.

Dyson, it seems, has settled into her own circadian rhythm, often rising at 4.30 a.m. to fit in everything she has taken on. She has racked up over six million air miles (enough, you'd think, to buy an aircraft of her own). She estimates that she averages a flight every other day. She spends sufficient time in Moscow to warrant being a member of a health club there and retaining a locker for her possessions.

For Dyson, wherever she lays her laptop that's her home. She is a phenomenon of the digital age – an information guru; Internet pioneer; venture capitalist; sage to governments and leaders. Dyson is a Renaissance woman. Her opinions are much sought after. She has advised among others, Bill Clinton and Bill Gates, as well as governments from around the world. Small wonder that *Fortune* magazine named her as one of the 50 most powerful women in US business. All the more reason to check out the Edventure Website.

Links

www.edventure.com

Notes

1. *Financial Times*, December 1997.

RICHARD EGAN

– EMC

We're living in the information age. The growth of the Internet has created an unprecedented avalanche of data that needs to be sifted, sorted and stored. The current king of storage is the EMC corporation. The relatively understated company, based at Hopkington, Massachusetts, has quietly transformed itself into the archivist of the Internet.

EMC corporation was founded in 1979 by Richard Egan and a college friend Roger Marino, (who lent their initials to the company name) and Egan's wife Maureen. The company was financed with their life savings. Egan had worked at Intel under Andy Grove as general manager of the systems division – an experience Egan claims taught him more than business school ever could. As the 1970s drew to a close, however, Egan was ready to set up his own company.

The original business proposition was that EMC would make money from the supply of add-on memory boards. But Egan quickly realized that add-on memory boards were likely to be superseded by new technology. In order to survive the company needed to come up with a different game plan.

So in 1989 the company refocused its attention on the growing need for specialized data-storage systems. It sank money into R&D and came up with a new take on information storage. The result was its flagship Symmetrix product line. The provision of intelligent storage systems, made up of arrays of smaller hard-disks, allowed companies to access data faster and more efficiently than ever before. This RAID technology (Redundant Array of Independent Disks) has become the accepted industry standard. With the introduction of this technology, corporations woke up to the fact that the ability to access information efficiently and reliably could convey a winning competitive advantage.

In 1994, Mike Reuttgers, EMC's CEO, took a bold step to secure the company's position as No. 1 in the market. For EMC's systems to become the obvious storage choice, Reuttgers realized, the company had to work with non-proprietary servers. The wider the range of servers that could access EMC storage units, the better for the company and its customers. The company invested a $1 billion or so developing software to enable mainframes, servers running NT and various flavors of UNIX to access EMC's integrated hardware/software storage systems. The fact that over half the world's biggest server manufacturers resell EMC units with their computers proves that it was the right move.

EMC, like many of the leaders of the new economy, has made several strategic acquisitions to bolster its services. Epic Systems for example was bought in 1993. A specialist in data-backup, it provided EMC with the best open-systems back-up technology available. By the end of the 1990s, EMC had distribution partners in over 50 countries and alliances with leading software and database companies such as Microsoft and Oracle, plus a list of prestigious resellers that included Silicon Graphics, Groupe Bull, Siemens and Unisys. After Dell, it was also the second best-performing stock in the S&P 500.

EMC's sparkling performance has however focused the attention of some potentially formidable competitors on the data-storage market. Computer manufacturing giants like Compaq, Sun Microsystems and IBM have all entered the data-storage fray. IBM once a partner of EMC has its own storage solution – the Enterprise Storage Server or Shark. Compaq has an agreement to resell Shark. Sun, which is the biggest player in the UNIX server market, is also targeting EMC market share as is Hewlett Packard, which was also once an EMC reseller, but is now hawking solutions from Hitachi Data Systems.

EMC claims that the new competition is healthy, as it prevents the company from becoming complacent. In reality, however, it would be quite happy to be left alone. As the No. 1 data storage company, EMC argues that with no vested interest in selling a branded server – it does not manufacture servers. This, it says, means the company is in a better position to deliver the intelligent storage systems its customers require. It offers systems that work with any server regardless of make.

The competition counters by pointing out that EMC's networked storage systems are in fact proprietary – a strategy that has felled many a tech company in the past. Analysts forecast tremendous growth in storage area networks or SANs. EMC's SANs do not interconnect with other manufacturers' SANs unless those SANs support EMC's proprietary fiber-channel connection. Fortunately for EMC, its standards are *the standards* in the industry at the moment. And there should be room for more than one player in a market predicted to grow to $35 billion by 2001.

There has been talk of EMC becoming the Cisco of the data storage business. The figures seem to support the view. EMC's first-quarter earnings for 2000 were ahead of market expectations at $332 million from sales of $1.82 billion – a 49 percent earnings increase on the same quarter in 1999. Sales growth was a solid 23 percent and revenue growth was predicted to rise strongly through 2000.

E-commerce pure plays may be more glamorous, but Egan's EMC has shown that there's plenty of money to be made in the picks and shovels of the new economy.

Links

www.emc.com

LARRY ELLISON

– *Oracle*

Although its origins date back to the 1970s, software company Oracle has reinvented itself as a new economy powerhouse. It is best known for its database software, used to store the wide variety of information companies need for their day-to-day operations. This includes: customer lists, employee lists, transaction details, product inventory – and so on. The company's success is due in no small part to one remarkable man, its founder and CEO Larry Ellison. He has grown the Oracle Corporation from humble origins to superstar status.

Ellison (born 1944) was raised on Chicago's South Side, a district that was described by *Look* magazine as the oldest and worst black ghetto in the US. He lived in a Jewish lower middle-class area surrounded by Puerto Rican, Latino and black ghettos. In today's world that might sound like a difficult place to grow up but in 1950s America things were different. Back then, drugs and guns were a lot less prevalent and Ellison says he was unaware that it was a "bad neighborhood" until he left.

As a child Ellison hoped to become an architect. He had a natural talent for mathematics and science and studied math at the University of Chicago. In his spare time, Ellison taught himself how to program a computer. Like other famous entrepreneurs including Bill Gates, he dropped out of university, deciding to head for California. There, based on his self-taught skills, he got a job as a computer programmer. One of Ellison's first jobs was at Amdahl, a company founded by Gene Amdahl. The company was 45 percent owned by Fujitsu, and soon Ellison was dispatched on a business trip to Japan. It was a trip that was to have a long-lasting influence on his life.

Japanese culture struck Ellison as fundamentally different to the American way of life. Japanese society, Ellison thought, contained some interesting contradictions. The Japanese were both aggressive and incredibly polite; they were arrogant and yet humble. The other quality that struck him was the emphasis on the group rather than the individual. It was an attitude that percolated through Japanese corporations, and seemed to him to be the antithesis of individualistic entrepreneurial America. These observations made a deep impression and, when Ellison eventually founded Oracle, he tried to instill in his organization those Japanese cultural values.

The origins of Oracle, lie in a seminal paper published by IBM Research called "the System R Project." IBM had also, at the time of the paper, developed a computer language for accessing databases – SQL (pronounced sequel). The paper, published in November 1976, was the culmination of ten years' work in the IBM research labs conducted principally by Ted Codd. When Ellison read the paper, it was an epiphany. He immediately recognized the commercial implications of the research. If, Ellison figured, he moved fast enough, he could beat IBM to the market. Popular opinion at the time said that database programs were not commercially viable, but Ellison thought differently, and backed his instincts. Bucking the received wisdom of the time gave him a useful head start.

To get his business off the ground Ellison needed money. And he needed it quickly. But raising venture capital back then wasn't as easy as it is today. For Ellison and his partners, the VC industry offered little encouragement:

> "They wouldn't even meet with you. They invested in hardware companies. But software at the time was this vague notion. There was nothing tangible; nothing you could touch. And, in fact, they would just leave you waiting in the waiting room for 45 minutes, until you finally got the idea they were not going to see you. And then the receptionist would search your briefcase to make sure you were not stealing copies of *Business Week* from the coffee table. We were *persona non grata* in the venture capital community."[1]

So, a frustrated Ellison, Bob Miner and Ed Oates, each put up $2000 of their own money to get the company started. The company was initially called System Development Laboratories, later changing its name to the Oracle Corporation. It took two years to produce the company's first product. The very first version of Oracle was sold to the Advanced Technology Division of the Wright Patterson Airbase, and installed by Ellison himself. Until then he and his colleagues had supported themselves by doing consultancy work in Silicon Valley.

Once the product was out, Ellison and Oracle never looked back. It was profitable from day one. In fact, Oracle has only ever lost money for one quarter, in 1990. To give an idea of the company's rate of growth, Oracle went public in March 1986 at which time revenues were $55 million dollars. It moved location to a campus style complex at Redwood Shores in 1989 – by which time revenues were $571 million.

The company's success has been largely due to the quality of product and the aggressive pursuit of market share. One of the lessons Ellison drew from the Japanese was their attitude towards competitors. Talking to a Japanese business executive while in Japan, the conversation had turned to competition in business. America, the executive maintained, had no appetite for competition. The attitude prevalent in the US was that competition could be tolerated provided the market was big enough. In Japan that attitude was unheard of. In Japan the executive said: "We believe our competitors are stealing the rice out of the mouths of our children. In Japan, we think anything less than 100 percent market share is not enough. In Japan, we believe it is not sufficient that I succeed; everyone else must fail. We must destroy our competition."[2]

Ellison may or may not have taken the lesson to heart. Certainly he has shown himself to be fiercely competitive. When he recounted the incident to a *New York Times* reporter he received a great deal of flak in the US. A story was printed with his picture and the words "It's not sufficient that I succeed; everyone else must fail." Whether the Japanese executive really taught him anything or whether Ellison's own competitive instincts were already well honed is a moot point. Oracle has ruthlessly capitalized on its market position, and has shown itself unwilling to peacefully co-exist with its rivals.

Another factor in Oracle's success is the team culture it has built. At the start Ellison vowed that he would "never hire anybody you wouldn't enjoy having lunch with three times a week." If the people at Oracle liked each other he figured then there would be less internal conflict. People would be pleased with their colleagues' achievements rather than envious.

He had seen how the Japanese overcame what seemed liked impossible tasks, using team spirit and with reliance on the group. The idea was to foster a competitive spirit between the people at Oracle and the competition outside, rather than promote competition within the organization itself. This strategy shows Ellison's understanding of what

Insight

Be your own man

Winston Spencer Churchill is one of Larry Ellison's heroes. Why? Because he had the courage of his own convictions; the courage to stand alone and ignore conventional wisdom. Larry Ellison has always believed in his own vision of the future. His opinions about databasing, the network computer and the Internet have at times been out of kilter with popular opinion, but Ellison has been happy to stand apart. Sometimes it takes intellectual integrity and courage to be a great business leader. Business fashion victims, take note!

motivates people and makes them tick. It is an instinctive understanding of how to get the best out of people that has served him well.

Ellison himself likes to live life to the full. A pilot who has flown his own fighter jet, Ellison is also a world-class yachtsman who was first across the line in one of the toughest ever Sydney–Hobart races in 1999. He is a man who appreciates the finer things in life; he hired craftsmen in Japan to build him a house by hand, then had it shipped to the US and assembled on his estate in Woodside, California.

His colorful lifestyle has sometimes made headlines, diverting attention from his business acumen. But under his leadership Oracle has always been an innovative company. Over the years, it has often introduced new technology that subsequently became mainstream. In 1996 Ellison decided to champion the cause of the network computer – a workstation without a hard-drive where applications were delivered from a third party on demand. While the idea never took off in quite the way Ellison envisaged, it anticipated the advent of Application Service Providers and Apple's Web-oriented PC range.

It was part of a strategic move by Ellison to steer Oracle away from the client-server model, a relationship where client computers and servers storing databases use "enterprise applications" software to communicate and manage database information.

In a bold move Ellison shifted from client-server products to applications that can run over the Internet via a browser. Ellison's embracing of the Internet and e-commerce was a strategic masterstroke coming at a time when one of Oracle's main competitors Microsoft was struggling to cover every commercial opportunity the Internet offered.

In 1998, under Ellison's dynamic leadership the company reinforced its strategic shift in direction. The flagship software product – the client-server version of Oracle Applications, was abandoned. Instead Oracle focused on the development of an Internet database. It was a risky strategy as Ellison realized: "If the Internet turns out not to be the future of computing, we're toast. But if it is, we're golden."[3]

In 1999 Oracle launched the world's first Internet database Oracle8i, a product that once again put Oracle ahead of the game. Today Ellison's change of direction has been vindicated. It has revitalized Oracle and boosted the company's value. Many of the leading e-commerce sites use Oracle's Internet products. The improvement in the company's fortunes is reflected in Ellison's own. His personal wealth is staggering; he describes it as "surreal." He now vies with Bill Gates for the title of richest man in the world.

Links

www.oracle.com

Notes

1. *Oral History*, Interview with Lawrence Ellison, President and CEO Oracle Corporation. October 24, 1995.
2. Ibid.
3. *Forbes.com*, April 2000.

SHAWN FANNING

– *Napster*

When a 19-year-old student came up with a neat software program in 1999, no one could have anticipated the outcry it would cause when it was unleashed on the Internet. Shawn Fanning was the student and the nifty software was Napster. Napster made it easy for individuals to trade music tracks over the Internet. It's a development that could shift the balance of power in not only the record industry but many other industries as well. Not surprisingly, the major record companies didn't like the idea and consulted their lawyers. Napster has become embroiled in what could be a landmark legal case, while the issues it raises for big business continue to reverberate around the World Wide Web.

Shawn Fanning was a computer science student at Northeastern University, in Boston, when he had his eureka moment. MP3 (MPEG3) had already taken off on the Net as a means of distributing audio files. The compression format meant that at last there was a way to keep music files to an acceptable size – and download times to a minimum. MP3 spawned a variety of consumer devices, such as portable MP3 players, as well as online companies hoping to cash in on business models built around MP3. Particularly popular among students who copied and traded MP3 audio files, the craze also provoked students to develop new software applications to make their new pastime more fun.

Fanning was one of those students. In his spare time at university he set about combining his interest in Internet Relay Chat (IRC) and MP3 to come up with a software application to enable individuals to share their collection of MP3 music over the Internet. Like Marc Andreessen, Linus Torvalds and other architects of the e-business revolution, Fanning designed his killer-app because of the inadequacies of an existing product or service. And, like Andreesen and Torvalds, Fanning didn't appreciate the commercial possibilities of his work immediately.

When the software program – dubbed Napster – was tipped as "Download of the week" by RealPlayer, download.com was overwhelmed with demand for it. Fanning realized the program had outgrown its "just for fun" status. He skipped his sophomore year and, with fellow student Sean Parker, founded Napster with backing from angel investors and the venture capital firm Hummer Winblad.

Napster in the house

The company provoked a furor in the record industry, and the lawyers' letters started flying. So why all the fuss? What Napster does is harness the power of the Internet to create a new distribution channel. Technically the process is called peer-to-peer file sharing. It works as follows. First you download the Napster software, or get a copy from somewhere. Then you type the chosen artist or song title into the search box. Now comes the clever part. When the software is downloaded users tell Napster where music files are kept on their hard drive. When the user searches they are connected to Napster's central user directory which then checks out all the other Napster users to see who has got the music requested and supplies the list to the user. The user then downloads it directly onto his or her hard-drive. It's a simple idea and harks back to the use of the Internet in the days before e-commerce. The problem is that it by-passes the record companies, which rely on making money from sales of the artists signed to them.

In less than ten months Napster acquired over ten million users. That's very fast growth even by Internet standards. To put it into perspective, it took AOL over ten years to accumulate ten million users. It was the kind of meteoric progress that made the people at Napster and its investors very happy. Not so happy, however, were the senior executives at the major record labels. For them it was a *déjà vu* moment. They were already staving off possible threats to their business from RealNetworks, MP3.com and others. Now a tiny software company was enabling millions of people to pirate their music.

If a sound track is capable of being 'ripped' to a digital file then it can be traded or swapped via Napster. That covers every CD and mini-disk out there, hence Napster being described by record industry executives with epithets like "the devil" for example, which are usually reserved for other members of the software community.

The music industry looks set for a long fight. Artists like Metallica and Dr.Dre have taken action over copyright issues as has the Recording Industry Association of America (RIAA). The war over the distribution of music on the Internet seems set to be a protracted one. Napster is entrenched but may suffer defeat, at least in the short term. Attrition however is likely, eventually, to wear the music industry down, forcing some sort of compromise. Quite what that will be is difficult to foresee.

Record majors, Sony, EMI etc. already offer songs for downloading on their Websites. The problem is it's not always the smoothest process, it costs money – several dollars – and there's a restricted amount of material available. One possible way for the record companies to protect their music would be to start their own file sharing. They might offer incentives for payment by, for example, allowing anyone who passes on a file to receive a small percentage of the fee thereby giving them an incentive to forgo pirating. But it's not a model that inspires confidence since people are too used to getting things free of charge over the Internet. Even Napster itself hasn't really figured out a way to turn its brilliant software into a profitable activity generating millions of dollars. The problem is that the pirating of sound tracks, while illegal, is almost impossible to prevent – all the more so since public attitudes fail to perceive it as a crime.

It's not just the record majors that Napster has annoyed. Napster users clog up the network, hogging bandwidth and irritating Internet Service Providers (ISPs), which didn't bargain on hard-drive based peer-to-peer activity on this kind of scale. Universities which rent expensive T1 lines for connection to the Internet also complain that students downloading MP3 files prevents the Internet from being used for academic purposes. Hundreds of universities have been forced to ban the use of Napster.

Napster has opened a Pandora's box. First out was Gnutella. If Napster was alarming for the record labels, Gnutella screams 'be afraid, be very afraid.' Gnutella is like an online fungus spreading its strands throughout the Internet. Taking a logical step on from Napster, Gnutella omits the central server from the equation enabling groups of like-minded individuals to link up directly and share the contents of their hard-drives. It's like a giant club and once a member you can communicate directly with all the other members. The implications are huge, because Gnutella isn't restricted to audio information. If it's digitally encoded then it can be downloaded. A thousand and one special interest groups are likely to start sharing information with each other.

Insight

Fanning didn't set out to create the monster that Napster has become. "Weird man, weird," is how he describes the whole affair. Instead he set out to fulfill a need, driven by his own personal interests. He's not the only Internet entrepreneur to start out this way. EBay and Yahoo! are two examples of the same phenomenon. For budding entrepreneurs maybe the best advice is don't spend hours racking your brains for the best business model ever. Instead find a better way of doing something you are already interested in. Then think long and hard about the legal implications.

Ironically, Gnutella was the brainchild of an AOL subsidiary Nullsoft. The irony is that AOL/Time Warner is one of the biggest music copyright owners in the world. Posted up on the Web, the Gnutella application was rapidly taken down again when the Napster litigation began in earnest. It was up for just one afternoon. Long enough for over 10,000 copies to be downloaded. Today there are many different versions of Gnutella available.

To date, what has really prevented peer-to-peer file sharing from entering the Internet mainstream is the security issues it raises. Allowing someone to access your hard-drive and rummage around your files is much the same as going to work leaving a big sign on your house saying "come on in and have a good nose about." In fact, in peer-to-peer file sharing you're effectively still in your house – you can hear the eerie sound of the hard-drive whirring as your guest rifles through the drawers of your computer. You just can't see them doing it. Until people are comfortable with the idea of strangers accessing their PCs; or are technically literate enough to set up there own firewalls and partitions; then peer-to-peer file sharing is likely to remain the province of the techies and the naïve.

Whether or not Napster ultimately will succeed is impossible to predict. There is no question however that it has put a match to the tinder of a new Internet revolution. As for Shawn Fanning, he must be hoping his next big idea is a little less controversial.

Links

www.napster.com

DAVID FILO & JERRY YANG

– *Yahoo!*

Yahoo! is one of the best-known pure-play Internet companies. It was founded in 1994 by Stanford University electrical engineering students David Filo and Jerry Yang. Yahoo! started as a hobby. Yang and Filo decided to find a better way of keeping track of their personal interests on the Internet, while they searched for a great business idea. The hobby became a search engine, and the search engine morphed into one of the most profitable portals on the Web.

Today, the project Filo and Yang started for fun in their spare time has turned into a business with revenues of over $2 billion a quarter. For the quarter ending March 31, 2000, Yahoo! posted revenues of $228,384,000. It is a project that has made both of them very wealthy indeed.

Yang was born in Taiwan in 1968, the eldest son of Chinese immigrants. His father died when he was two years old and his mother, a professor of English, took the family to the US to avoid Yang and his brother from being drafted into the Taiwanese army. When the family arrived in San Jose, California, Yang could understand just one word of English – the extremely useful "shoe."

Yang, despite this limited vocabulary, made swift progress in the US education system. He picked up English easily, played tennis for his high school and was elected student body president. He arrived at Stanford on a scholarship, completing both his BS in electrical engineering and a Master's degree within four years. It was at Stanford that he met David Filo. In 1992, Filo, who was from Louisiana, and Yang traveled to Japan on an academic exchange program. It was there that the two became good friends. When they returned from Japan, the Stanford University campus was buzzing with the news of Marc Andreessen's Web browser Mosaic. Mosaic made the World Wide Web both accessible and immediate. Filo and Yang were already familiar with the Internet through the use of email and Gopher. They understood how Mosaic would bring the Web to a wider audience. Like other students at the time they set to work experimenting with different applications for the Web including a program on basketball, and a Website on Sumo wrestling.

The problem with the Web in 1993 was that it wasn't easy to find interesting information out in cyberspace. And once found, it was hard to keep track of it. The amount of information was growing daily and no one was attempting to index it. Mosaic allowed users to store a list of Web addresses in a hotlist – but only so many. When Yang and Filo built a Mosaic hotlist of all the things that interested them on the Net, the list quickly grew to unmanageable proportions.

The duo set out to design their own way of classifying information on the Web. They developed some tools that allowed them to hierarchically categorize information. The result was a hierarchical index – or Yet Another Hierarchical Officious Oracle (YAHOO) – although Filo and Yang say that they chose the name because they considered themselves yahoos. Once they had produced their own version of the hotlist, they made it available to the Internet community over the Web and included a search facility to allow people to find specific entries. Surfers flocked to use it.

During its infancy, Yahoo! lived on the Stanford University system with the Yahoo! index on Yang's workstation and the search engine on Filo's PC. All this time Yang and Filo had been searching for a great Internet idea while working on Yahoo! as a hobby. Eventually it dawned on them that Yahoo! was the great Internet idea. Fortunately, for the sake of the efficiency of the Stanford University computer network, Marc Andreessen, then at Netscape, suggested they moved their files over to a Netscape machine. Even better, Netscape didn't charge them. Filo and Yang took a sabbatical from Stanford to work on Yahoo! When they left it was initially for a period of six months. They never returned to finish their studies.

From that point the business just took off. Yang and Filo struggled on by themselves for some time before taking on extra staff. Even when they were operating from Netscape premises and getting 2 million hits a day, there was still just the two of them doing everything. When the VCs began to knock at the door they finally came to terms with the fact that the business had outgrown their hobbyist approach.

Today, the company is headquartered in Santa Clara, California and has offices in Europe, Asia Pacific, Latin America, and Canada. The company receives 100 million hits a month and its 1999 revenues were $588.6 million with a profit – still a rarity among Internet stocks – of over $60 million.

Yang and Filo have rewritten the textbooks on management structure. Although they share the honors as self-styled Chief Yahoos, what this means in reality is that Filo takes responsibility for dealing with the tech strategy and Yang tries to meet the challenge of staying ahead of the competition and exploiting the opportunities the Internet, and its ever changing technology present. He has a roving role trying to build a company that will survive both himself and Filo.

John Hennessy, provost of Stanford University and faculty adviser to Yang in the mid 1990s, described him as "everything from a technical visionary to chief strategist to corporate spokesman, cheerleader and lobbyist. He's also the company's conscience."

Neither Yang nor Filo ever imagined themselves running the billion-dollar business Yahoo! has become. They were more than happy to employ Tim Koogle, employee # 6, another ex-Stanford student, albeit from another generation, to handle the day-to-day running of the business as CEO.

Some might say that Yahoo!'s profits are more a result of luck than design. The business model was never really nailed down. When Yahoo! started out it had no revenue at all – it was free to put a site link up. It still is. While Filo and Yang were still working on Yahoo! as a hobby they were devoting a lot of time on developing other business models for Internet business. It was never obvious how Yahoo! could make the kind of money it generates today. But the company now has a wide range of revenue streams including: online auctions; online payment services; and advertising fees. Its evolution has been one of sharp growth driven by demand for the directory element of the site, coupled with an instinct for what services Internet users are interested in. The result – a portal that is all things to all people.

Advertising forms a large proportion of Yahoo!'s revenue. The company has cleverly honed its targeting skills to enable it to deliver personalized advertising and keep its advertisers happy. Yahoo!'s eclectic nature however may still prove to be its downfall. There are several portals that offer the same or a similar range of features to Yahoo! There has also been a move towards niche sites and vertical portals. An Internet trend away from the general towards the specific may eventually draw surfers away from Yahoo!. For the moment, however, Yahoo! reigns supreme.

Insight

Go for it

When Yang and Filo first started Yahoo! they were both working on their PhD theses. As interest in their creation grew, the twosome were faced with a tough decision, business or study. It might seem derisible that there could be any question which to choose but that's hindsight talking. At the time Yang and Filo were both intent on completing their theses. In an interview they gave at the time Filo admitted to having taken leave from Stanford to concentrate on the Yahoo! project: "Officially, it's two quarters that we'll be off. It kind of depends on how things go."

Years later Yang incredibly was still troubled by his decision to leave the PhD program but eloquently voiced the motivation behind the decision he and Filo eventually made: "It still bothers me. It's a personal goal that I never finished. But on the other hand, had I finished my thesis, what impact would I have had? Maybe 100 people in the world would have read it. And understood it? Maybe 5 … Whereas the attraction to Yahoo! was that millions of people were going to read what we produced. And that, to me, is sort of like a drug."[1]

Links

www.yahoo.com

Notes

1   *Forbes ASAP*, 1998.

BILL GATES

– *Microsoft*

D espite one of the most bruising and public competition cases in corporate history, today Microsoft remains the most power-ful, and feared, software company on the planet. Period. The debate about Microsoft's apparent stranglehold on the software business will no doubt rumble on, whether the company is broken up or not. Whatever the eventual outcome, the fact is that the influence of Bill Gates on the recent and future direction of Internet business is simply too significant to exclude him from a list of new economy architects.

What can be said is that William Henry Gates III is a computer executive based in an office on the second floor of building number eight of his company's headquarters in Redmond, Washington. He hasn't strayed far. Gates was born in Seattle, on October 28, 1955. His parents nicknamed him Trey from the III in his name and members of the family never called him anything else.

As a boy, Gates was precociously brilliant. He read the family's encyclopedia from beginning to end at the age of eight or nine. (His company would later create the first CD-ROM encyclopedia in the world, *Encarta*). But his real gift was for mathematics, at which he excelled.

At Lakeside, the elitist Seattle private school which attracts some of the brightest students on America's West Coast, his love of mathematics became an obsession with computers. Even at Lakeside, Bill Gates stood out as a bright kid.

By his junior year, Gates was something of a computer guru to the younger Lakeside hackers. Gates and some of his computer friends formed the Lakeside Programmers Group, which was dedicated to finding money-making opportunities to use their new-found computer programming skills. Already, a pattern was emerging. As Gates observed later: "I was the mover. I was the guy who said 'Let's call the real world and try to sell something to it'." He was 13 years old.

It was at Lakeside that Gates met Paul Allen. Though Allen was two years Gates' senior, they developed a remarkable technical rapport. Allen's role in the Microsoft story, and that of a small coterie of Lakesiders recruited by the company is often understated. Gates, Allen, Kent Evans and Richard Weiland – two other members of the Lakeside Programmers Group – would often spend the whole night hooked up, first to a minicomputer owned by General Electric, and later to one at the Computer Centre Corporation, sometimes not getting home until the early hours.

Gates' high IQ and massive personal drive ensured him a place at Harvard University. He arrived at America's most respected seat of learning in Cambridge, Massachusetts in the fall of 1973, all brain with no real sense of direction. Later, he would say that he went to Harvard to learn from people smarter than he was ... and was disappointed. The comment probably says as much about Bill Gates' opinion of himself as it does about Harvard. Listing his academic major as pre-law, Gates might have been expected to follow in the footsteps of his lawyer father. In reality, however, he had little interest in a career in law, and his parents had little doubt that their headstrong son would steer his own course.

As it turned out, a degree from Harvard was not on the cards. In 1975, while still at the university he teamed up with Paul Allen once more to develop a version of BASIC, an early computer-language. Fired up with the new world at his finger tips, in 1977 Gates decided to drop out of Harvard to work full-time at a small computer software company he had founded with his friend. The company was called Microsoft.

Since the early days of Microsoft, Gates has pursued his vision of "a computer on every desk and in every home." (Interestingly, the original slogan was "a computer on every desk in every home, running Microsoft software," but the last part is often left off these days as it makes some people uncomfortable.)

The rise of Microsoft has been both rapid and relentless. Gates soon proved that he combined both a bone-deep technical understanding with superb commercial instincts. When ill health forced Allen to leave Microsoft, Gates' position as leader was confirmed. Microsoft's rapid growth soon made it the darling of Wall Street. From a share price of $2 in 1986, Microsoft stock soared to $105 by first half of 1996, making Gates a billionaire and many of his colleagues millionaires.

The rise in Microsoft's share price also signaled the end of the old world order. There were technology giants before Microsoft, but they were in hardware. IBM, Digital Equipment, Motorola, were all technology companies. In Detroit, General Motors, Ford and Chrysler were based on their technological leadership, as was General Electric. What all had in common was that they put their logos on technology that customers could see and touch – even if they didn't understand how it worked. Microsoft was different. It put its brand on something called an "operating system."

To some commentators a defining moment in the history of business occurred when the market valuation of Microsoft – which owned little more than a few buildings in Redmond, some software and the Microsoft brand – exceeded that of General Motors – with all its physical asset, factories, components and inventory. (On September 16, 1998, the market valuation of Microsoft even passed that of the mighty GE, with a market value of $262 billion. The intangible brainpower brand had overtaken the physical.)

The secrets which lie behind Microsoft's spiral of success have been dissected from every possible angle. What can be safely said is that the company hires very bright, creative people and retains them through a combination of excitement, constant challenge, and excellent working conditions. The odd stock option helps, too.

Microsoft's own encyclopedia *Encarta* says that "Much of Gates' success rests on his ability to translate technical visions into market strategy, and to blend creativity with technical acumen." What sets Bill Gates apart from any other business leader in history is probably the influence that he wields over our lives. Whereas the power of earlier tycoons was usually concentrated in one sector or industry, through the power of software, Microsoft extends its tentacles into every sphere of our lives.

Gates hasn't had things all his own way, however. With any success story come the detractors. Criticism has constantly been leveled at Microsoft alleging that the company abuses its dominant market position. When the Internet revolution took off in the early '90s Microsoft was momentarily caught off balance. Possibly for once the normally prescient Gates failed to see the true potential of the global network and the Web. A company called Netscape sprang up giving away a neat bit of software called a browser transforming the Web from a techie's playground to a mass-market phenomenon. Gates moved quickly to counter, however. Microsoft licensed the Mosaic browser technology from a company called Spyglass – ironically it was Marc Andreessen, co-founder of Netscape who had invented the original Mosaic. The technology was tweaked and packaged as the Microsoft browser Internet

Insight

Tough love

To some in Microsoft, Bill Gates is a mystical almost religious figure, while to others in the industry he is the anti-Christ. Both views are outrageous, but underline just how great his influence is. (With all the hullabaloo about alleged abuse of monopoly power, it is easy to forget that back in the 1970s, IBM, too, was the target of anti-trust investigations. Yet, memory fades. Today, we have come to regard Big Blue as almost saintly compared with Microsoft. Such is the nature of power – we fear most what we understand least.)

For all its enormous success, customers have a curious love-hate relationship with Microsoft. Many use the software but don't have a good word to say about the company. Many of those in the IT industry are vociferous critics. Microsoft dominates the software market, but is the target of as much distrust as peace of mind. Microsoft and its high-profile leader are, it seems, victims of their own success.

Explorer, paving the way for the browser wars. Microsoft, covering all the bases, also bought WebTV, eShops, Hotmail and Vermeer the original developers of the Front Page HTML editing software. Catch-up is a game Microsoft excels at.

It was this kind of behavior by Microsoft that angered its critics so much. With millions of dollars of talent holed up at Microsoft's Redmond HQ why, asked the critics, did Microsoft just snaffle up key technologies using financial muscle rather than invent it in the first place? Microsoft countered, with some justification, that it has developed a number of important technologies and is still doing so. At one time or another it seemed most of the major players in the software market – Sun, RealNetworks, Netscape – were complaining about Microsoft's behavior. Matters eventually came to a head when the US Justice Department became involved in examining whether or not Microsoft was in breach of antitrust law. After a lengthy trial and a mountain of depositions, in June 2000 US District Judge Thomas Penfield Jackson ordered Microsoft to be split into two companies, holding that it had violated the nation's anti-trust laws by using monopoly power to push aside potential competitors to the detriment of consumers.

Microsoft immediately appealed and, barring an agreed settlement, at the time of writing the case looks set to continue for some time. Ultimately however it may not be the anti-trust ruling that poses the greatest threat to Microsoft's bottom line. Microsoft may still have a 90 percent share of desktop computer systems but the world no longer revolves around the desktop PC. Microsoft risks being sidelined by the sheer pace of technological progress. Handhelds and mobile phones may be the PCs of the future and those are markets dominated not by Microsoft but by the likes of Palm Computing and Symbian. Microsoft's own CE operating system has failed to emulate the success of the Windows OS. On its home territory of PC operating systems open source software such as Linux is gaining momentum threatening to eat into Microsoft's market share.

Meanwhile, for now at least, the revenues keep pouring in. Fourth quarter 2000 revenues were some $5.8 billion with net income up a touch year on year at $2.41 billion. With cash in the bank and tech talent on the Redmond campus, only a fool would write off Microsoft. Gates has masterfully orchestrated one of the greatest corporate success stories in history. Microsoft may be a little bruised but there's plenty of fight left in it yet.

GEORGE GILDER

George Gilder has established himself as one of the world's most respected new economy commentators. His path to the top of the mountain has been a long and winding one. Since leaving Harvard University, he has written speeches for the late former president, Richard Nixon; pioneered supply side economics; been President Reagan's most frequently quoted living author; and written influential books on the causes of property, wealth and entrepreneurialism.

Arguably, however, Gilder is most famous for his prescient and detailed examination of the semiconductor industry in his 1989 best selling book *Microcosm*, his contributions to *Forbes ASAP*, and his frequently controversial predictions for the future of technology and its implications for business.

Gilder was born in New York in 1939. He studied at Harvard, where Henry Kissinger was one of his tutors. At Harvard, he founded a journal of political thought, *Advance*, which he continued to publish in Washington DC after graduating. (Gilder's association with Harvard was later reaffirmed when he became a fellow at the Kennedy Institute of Politics.) In the 1960s Gilder found himself writing speeches for political heavyweights Nelson Rockerfeller and Richard Nixon. The ability to recognize a good sound-bite when he wrote it would prove useful to Gilder in his later career as technology guru.

In 1970 Gilder began to research the causes of poverty. His studies resulted in a string of books on the subject including: *Men and Marriage* (1972); *Visible Man* (1978); and the best-selling *Wealth and Poverty* (1981), which reached fourth on the *New York Times* best sellers list. With the publication of these books it became clear that, regardless of whether readers agreed or disagreed with Gilder's views, a libertarian right-wing perspective on these social issues, his work always provoked a reaction.

Wealth & Poverty was received by the right as "the bible of the Reagan revolution." Ayn Rand however, who was seen as a key figure in the libertarian movement, spent the last public speech she ever gave, at the Ford Hall Forum, denouncing Gilder and severely damaging his libertarian credentials. Not that it bothered Reagan. An analysis of Reagan's speeches has revealed Gilder as the most frequently quoted living author. And in 1986, President Reagan gave George Gilder the White House Award for Entrepreneurial Excellence

Others took exception at Gilder's book *Men and Marriage*. In 1974, he was named "Male Chauvinist of the Year."

After his investigations into poverty, Gilder turned his attentions to technology. He read *The Soul of a New Machine* by Tracy Kidder and became curious to discover more. A friend in the semiconductor industry informed him that micro engineering allowed transistors to be placed on an area smaller than a pinhead. This revelation fired Gilder's imagination. He wrote an article for *Forbes* on a semiconductor company, Micron, and wrote about the semiconductor industry for *The Rosen Electronics Letter*. To get up to speed he took tech lessons at Cal Tech from Carver Mead, the father of large-scale integrated circuits and the inventor of the gallium arsenide MESFET transistor. Gilder's thinking was profoundly influenced by Carver. One of the most important lessons Gilder learnt, he later explained, was "how crucial it is to listen to the technology and find out what it's telling you."

Somehow Gilder had stumbled into a new career. The role of technology guru was cemented with his book *Microcosm*, published in 1989. *Microcosm* is an in-depth look at the history of the semi-conductor industry. Gilder originally wanted to major on Bob Noyce at Intel for part of the book. However the journalist and novelist Tom Wolfe, whose writing Gilder greatly admired, had covered Noyce in a piece for *Esquire*. So instead, Gilder featured employee No. 4 at Intel – Andy Grove. Out of luck or judgment Gilder had hit upon one of the principal protagonists in the new business revolution.

Gilder's next book was *Life After Television*, a look at the future of telecommunications. Throughout, Gilder continued to voice his theories about the future of technology in his *Forbes ASAP* column.

In answer to those who call him a futurist Gilder claims in fact to be behind the times – just less so than most other people:

> "I don't predict the future. I project the implications of existing technologies. The existing situation is complicated, challenging

---

Insight

Gilder believes that predicting the future is more about clearly identifying existing trends – trends that have been building for several years – rather than crystal ball gazing. In a world where most of us know that by the time a technology affects our lives it is likely to already have become obsolete by a new breakthrough in an R&D bunker or garage somewhere, Gilder provides a fascinating window on the next big thing. As he says, he is not a futurist but an expert extrapolator. Most of us are staring at the light from distant stars. By the time we are aware of it the image is already out of date. Gilder offers early warning – and an informed take on what the impact on business might be. He is living proof that staying two steps ahead of the pack makes you look like you're leading the parade.

---

and baffling – and extraordinarily hard just to understand. Clearly describing trends that were already strong two years ago has led to my being called a futurist. But I'm really behind. If I can stay within two years, people will think I'm a futurist."[1]

And regardless of whether you concur with him, reading his opinions, which often appear outlandish at first sight, is sure to crystallize your own views. Gilder's most recent vision is how the "telecosm" model, as he calls it, will dominate industry. In his own words, in the telecosm model there is a communications systems infrastructure that will have "dumb fiber in the middle and wireless on the edges" and "all the intelligence will migrate to the edge." According to Gilder it's a model of the Internet as, "a knowledge-generating system." What that means exactly is unclear.

Gilder does go on to make more sense when he talks about "more high-level exchange and less-logistical friction" meaning presumably that there will an exponential growth in communication that will open up possibilities to transact business that wouldn't have happened before. There are echoes here of Mcluhan's "global village."

Other pronouncements include hedging his bets on the value of tech stocks: "the high value of these stocks is reasonable. At the same time it's impossible for any human being to predict just which ones are going to succeed." And, more interestingly, talking about how the Internet will create a first-choice society, as distinguished from a society where the media pitches at the lowest common denominator. This will be the ultimate consumer-driven society where consumers choose exactly what they want rather than settling for the best of what is available.

It might all seem a bit trite were it not for the fact that Gilder has been spookily accurate in his detailed predictions. And he is not usually one for sitting on the fence. Over the years he has taken a strong line on the potential of many emerging technologies. Those that he has been less than keen on include HDTV interactive television and 3DO game machines. And the ones he liked? The Java programming language and optical networks. Not bad going in an industry that's notoriously difficult to predict from one month to the next, let alone years ahead.

For those who want to learn more about Gilder's predictions, sign up for *the Gilder Technology Report* at his Website, gildertech.com. Or take an online trip to the Discovery Institute. But if it's a little light reading you're after, other Websites might be more suitable.

"Those who manage knowledge govern the economy and add value to it," Gilder has observed. "Eliminating noise on the communications channels leaves knowledge as the residual source of entropy in the system."[2]

Quite.

Links

www.gildertech.com

Notes

1. Interview with George Gilder, *Knowledge Management*, November 1999.
2. *Ibid.*

ROB GLASER

– *RealNetworks*

Seattle-based RealNetworks is the recognized leader in the delivery of streaming media over the Internet. Founded in 1994 by Rob Glaser, a Yale computer sciences graduate and ex-Microsoft manager, the company started life as Progressive Networks.

Glaser showed an interest in delivering media from an early age both as a performer and a technician. Aged 12 he was broadcasting over the radio as well as finding the time to install a private network at his high school. After completing a Bachelor's and Master's degree in Economics, Glaser then studied for a BS in Computer Science. At Yale, Glaser moved from the airwaves to print journalism taking on the responsibility of editorial-page editor of the Yale student newspaper the *Yale Daily News*. He also found time to run a video game company.

After Yale, Glaser found his way to Microsoft where he managed Microsoft Word. This was followed by a stint in the company's networking group, before moving to multimedia and consumer systems. Eventually Glaser found he was unable to pursue his ambitions within the Microsoft empire. There were reports, too, of internal political struggles between Glaser and other Microsoft managers. Glaser left Microsoft.

Linking up with an old Yale friend David Halperin, Glaser started a company called Progressive Networks. (Halperin subsequently became a speechwriter for President Clinton.) The idea was to combine TV technology and the Internet to serve various good causes. To this end the company was developing a new technology – streaming media. Streaming media was a different way of delivering audio, initially from server to browser. Instead of downloading the audio file to the user's hard-drive, the audio was delivered, real-time and on-demand, in a constant flow and in a way that meant it could still be experienced at slower modem speeds (video followed later). The opinion of friends and his own instincts persuaded Glaser to focus on the streaming technology. The business model was to give away the client software and sell the server software. Progressive Networks, or RealNetworks as it became in 1997, was to be a software company in the business of delivering multimedia technology to a mass-market.

Funding came from a group of Glaser's friends, among them Mitch Kapor the founder of Lotus, and the venture capital firm Accel Partners. Glaser sensibly held back 40 percent of the stock for himself. But though he had the technology, finance and a head start on his rivals, most notably Microsoft, success was far from certain. In particular, the company's original business model made it vulnerable to attack. As it turned out, events required adjustments to the business model. (Glaser has said that he views business models not as fixed static things but as evolving and changing.) As RealNetwork's business expands, other businesses start up, using Real Media products as an integral part of their own business models. This in turn allows RealNetworks to develop specific products for those companies. It's what Len Jordan, vice president for media systems, calls the *ecosystem*.

The ecosystem that RealNetworks operates in is a complex and fragile one. It consists of large content providers, including the major record labels, and tiny companies that deliver niche content. Then there are the end users, the millions of consumers who "experience" the streaming media. To remain as king predator, at the summit of the food chain, requires a special combination of qualities: diplomacy, speed, flexibility, aggression, vision, and guile. Under Glaser's guidance, RealNetworks has demonstrated all these qualities. At one moment the company reassuringly holds the hands of the big content providers while almost simultaneously launching a technological offensive against its rivals.

Glazier's vision has been nothing short of total domination of the market. He set out to ensure that the standards RealNetworks created became the streaming multimedia standards adopted by Internet users. The strategy required control of the means of delivery. If RealNetworks could own the standard means of delivering audio/video over the Net, then eventually it could cut out the middle men between the creators of the content and the end-users, thereby controlling the entire market.

Initially Glaser realized that success would be largely determined by the amount and quality of content available in Real format. If the content available via Real was appealing enough then the company would achieve significant market penetration. Deals were struck with content providers that didn't threaten the relationship between, for example, the record label and the artist. Record companies were understandably terrified of the potential of the Internet to deliver downloadable audio to users for free. Piracy on this scale would substantially eat into the record companies' bottom line. Streaming audio, RealNetworks style, allowed the content providers to retain control of the relationship both with the artist and the end user.

Glaser, surprisingly at first sight, embraced his competitors. He figured, correctly, that Microsoft was eventually going to join the streaming media party. After all, Microsoft could get its product to the user in large numbers by using the ubiquity of the Windows OS and the Internet Explorer browser, and Glaser was fully aware of the gargantuan struggle for browser supremacy between Netscape's Navigator and Microsoft's iExplorer. Glaser agreed to license the Real technology to Microsoft to use in any multimedia viewer the Redmond company might offer. In a way it was playing Microsoft at its own game. It wasn't long before the deal broke down amid claim, counter claim and recrimination. But the ensuing confusion bought RealNetworks enough time to bring out its next generation RealPlayer 5.0 followed by the G2 player. By this time RealNetworks players were streaming both audio and video.

By the end of 1998, Real technology delivered over 80 percent of all streamed content on the Net. By 2000, RealPlayer was the world's most popular online audio and video player with over 115 million unique registered users. Over 350,000 hours of live RealAudio and RealVideo streamed across the Internet every week, and that's without counting pre-recorded content.

First quarter 2000 results showed net revenues up 120 percent to $53.5 million from $24.4 million over the same quarter in 1999. They also emphasized the global nature of the market for RealNetwork products – some 30 percent of RealJukebox users, 40 percent of Real-Player users, and 25 percent of net revenues came from outside North America.

Despite this sucess, however, RealNetworks position is still far from secure. The online audio/video market continues to evolve at a phenomenal rate. The MPEG 3 codec (compression/decompression) standard allows listeners to download audio files quickly enough for it to be worth doing. Napster and Gnutella are software programs that allow individuals to access audio files on other enthusiasts' personal machines, bypassing servers entirely. This type of technology, certain to be extended to video, threatens not only the existence of record labels and film distributors but also RealNetworks. Litigation between the providers of services such as Napster and the record companies is likely to be bitter and protracted. However in the long term it's hard to see

Insight

Own the standard, own the market

At Microsoft, Glaser learned the importance of industry standards. He understood that the application that is adopted by a critical mass of users becomes the standard, conferring competitive advantage on its originator. At Microsoft he had been on the team that developed the Optical PC in a joint venture with IBM. The original idea was to create an inexpensive desktop computer with sound, video, and a CD-ROM drive built in. But what was meant to be a $1,500 machine turned into a $6,000 machine that was a year late. By then it was a total irrelevancy. Faced with abandoning the project and, with it, Microsoft's hopes for multimedia, Glaser's team switched track. They released CD-ROM software, including the Encarta encyclopedia, which they hoped would make consumers clamor for inexpensive multimedia computers, as well as the software standards to support them. "We got enough people drinking the Kool-Aid at the same time to create a virtual standard," Glaser notes. "That's why computers today have sound cards, video cards, and CD-ROM drives as standard equipment."

When he started RealNetworks he applied what he'd learned from the Microsoft project. Despite opposition from within the firm, he insisted that users downloading the free player software provided their names, addresses, and email addresses. This prompted concerns inside the company. Some engineers, in particular, considered it a violation of netiquette. Glaser went ahead anyway. "I was influenced by Esther Dyson's argument that in a networked economy, you don't sell; you build a relationship. I believed that if people were inviting us to take up a megabyte on their hard drives, they were inviting us into a relationship."

The strategy proved sound. In 1996, against the advice of his senior management team, Glaser offered users an enhanced RealPlayer – basically the same product, but with a few extra features It was priced at $29.95 and sold over a million copies.

how individuals can be prevented from downloading audio files from other individuals. That genie is out of the bottle and half way across the globe by now.

RealNetworks anticipated this threat with its Real Jukebox product. It allows the downloading and playing of a wide variety of audio formats. And the company is in a strong position to benefit from the broadband revolution, confidently predicted by Internet pundits to be close at hand. In a keynote address to the Kagan Streaming Media Summit, CEO Glaser predicted broadband users would grow from 6 million today to 27 million by 2003, and that 15 years from now a third of all viewing time would be on broadband-delivered programming. Glaser observed:

> "Over time, the impact of everything that we [Webcasters] are doing will have the same impact on traditional broadcast and cable that cable had on traditional broadcasting."

To survive, however, Real will have to demonstrate it still possesses all the qualities that have kept it at the forefront of the market so far. It will need to redefine the boundaries of its relationships with other companies. It may, for example, have to sacrifice its relationships with some content providers in order to acquire attractive content it can then restrict to the Real format.

Web music distributor Internet Underground Music Archive, for example, projects revenue figures for online digital distribution as high as $600 million by 2003 rising to $3.7 billion five years later. It's a cake RealNetworks won't want to pass up.

Links

www.realnetworks.com

SETH GODIN

– *Permission Marketing*

Y ou click on a banner ad for a bookstore. It triggers a pop-up box that asks you to fill in personal details. No way you think, sick of constant online requests to part with your consumer habits. But look again, what the text actually says is if you give us your details we will give you a free product. It's an enticing proposition. It's an offer we are all likely to see a lot more of. The person to thank, or blame, is Seth Godin, marketing guru and father of permission marketing.

Godin's idea was to persuade people to accept product pitches from companies by offering them an incentive. A permission marketing campaign might for example involve an airline offering free flights or a chance to win a trip of a lifetime. In return, the customer grants permission to the company to email offers of other products that the customer might be interested in. This model has become one of the most popular ways of marketing online.

Godin studied computer science and philosophy at Tufts University, graduating in 1982. He subsequently rounded out his education by completing an MBA with a marketing bias at Stanford Business School. After Stanford, Godin went to work at Spinnaker Software as a brand manager for some of the first wave of multimedia products. He moved on from Spinnaker to his first start up at Yoyodyne entertainment, the company named after the character in Thomas Pynchon's novel *The Crying of Lot 49*. At Yoyodyne he set about changing the world of online marketing.

As far as Godin could see, conventional advertising was both expensive and ineffective. TV viewers skip ads and don't pay attention to the ones they fail to skip. Direct mail is scarcely more effective, with recipients resenting the constant uncalled for intrusion into their lives. Godin notes:

> "The average consumer will see or hear 1 million marketing messages this year, that's almost 3,000 per day. So marketers end up trying to cut through the clutter with outlandish production, outlandish stunts, and a lot of noise. In a 30-second commercial, you're paying for 20 seconds of models and rock and roll, and you only get 10 seconds or less to talk about your product. So your product gets trivialized pretty quickly."[1]

This was no less true for advertising on the Internet than for the more traditional media. Advertisers shoehorned the conventional advertising model onto the net in the form of the banner ad. What was novel soon became mundane and click-through rates for banner ads swiftly subsided. Godin's idea was to improve on what he termed "interruption marketing." Initially the marketer needs to interrupt the viewer's activity in order to grab their attention. So, for example, on the Internet an interstitial will be a break in the flow of the viewer's experience. Wouldn't it be better, thought Godin, if at least after the first interruption the marketer obtained the "permission" of the consumer to market *with* them rather than *at* them (this eureka moment evidently came in the shower).

The premise is that consumers will willingly give up valuable personal information and grant permission for marketers to send them product information so long as they are given sufficient incentive. This then is the challenge for the permission marketer, finding the right incentive to persuade the consumer to grant permission.

Godin rolled out several variations of permission marketing campaign, during his stint at Yoyodyne. Email and Web promotions were built around competitions, gameshows and sweepstakes. In one case, the company ran a "Get Rich Quick" campaign with a prize of $100,000 put up by the sponsor. This was enough to tempt 250,000 players to the client's site. Following on from this initial contact, sponsors were able to build relationships with the customers through email messages that led to the next level of the game. This information was given in return for permission to pitch products. Companies like Geocities and ESPN SportsZone signed up to the concept and used permission marketing to build relationships with clients.

Godin offers four simple guidelines for permission marketers to remember:

- people are selfish – they care about themselves not the permission marketer;
- never rent or sell permission to a third party;
- permission can be revoked – it's not given for ever; and
- permission is not static – unlike buying an address.

Permission marketers have to be careful not to abuse their permission. Permission is effectively a state of mind. What if, for example, a customer enters into a permission-based relationship but then fails to maintain it? Does the permission once granted allow the marketer to continue sending offers to customer for ever? The common sense answer is obviously no. This means that a permission-based relationship is constantly redefined during its lifetime through a series of requests and hopefully, from the marketer's perspective, permissions.

The marketer must manage the relationship with the customer effectively. Regardless of what the marketer may think, if the customer believes permission has lapsed, then it has lapsed. They also have to manage the relationship if permission is revoked, or has lapsed. It's a fine line between emailing product information under permission, and spamming – bombarding people with junk email.

When Yahoo! bought Yoyodyne in 1998, Godin became Permission Marketing Yahoo! tasked with integrating direct marketing, permission marketing and Internet promotions into the company's Fusion Marketing Online program.

Although he remains a consultant to the company, in January 2000 Godin left Yahoo!, to pursue his next marketing brainwave – the ideavirus. Whether the ideavirus contains much that is new is difficult to say. On the *Fast Company* Website which helped publicize Godin's idea, a number of comments were posted by readers struck by the similarity of the ideavirus to Richard Dawkins work on "Memetics." There are also echoes of viral marketing, the equivalent of word of mouth, a concept that had been around for a while but found expression on the Internet with Hotmail. The theory of the ideavirus is expounded in Godin's book, *Unleash Your Ideavirus*. The book is available as a free download as well as in hardback. Visitors to the Website are encouraged to tell their friends and send the book to others. A view expressed in the book is that an idea spreads by "word of mouse" because it has merit – in which case one might assume no exhortation would be necessary.

An interesting part of Godin's argument is the message conveyed by two of his "six key steps for Internet companies looking to build an online virus":

Insight

Taking the medicine

As Godin astutely notes, for any ideavirus to be truly successful it is necessary to keep it in the public eye by nurturing, developing and revisiting it. He cites management writer, Tom Peters, and the successful sequence of books started with *In Search of Excellence* and the Tom Peters' branding as a good example of this. Assuming Godin takes his own medicine, expect to hear more from him soon.

- Fill the vacuum in the marketplace with your version of the idea so completely that competitors will first have to unteach your virus before they can unleash one of their own.
- Achieve "lock-in" by making it more and more costly to switch from your service to someone else's.

Critics say this seems rather too close for comfort to the tactics that Microsoft has been so heavily criticized for by its opponents. It might make sense for a company to try and own the standards of a particular industry and own the thinking on the subject as well, some say, but what happened to giving the customer what they want? Or offering the very best possible product or service? Regardless of the freshness or merits of the thinking, Godin gets his message across well and is certainly thought-provoking. His ideas have won a loyal following.

Notes

1. Seth Godin interview, *Ebusiness* Magazine, 1998.

JAMES GOSLING

– *Sun Microsystems & Java*

J ames Gosling's name will for ever be associated with the development of Java – the programming language that transformed the Web. But when he first came to Sun Microsystems it was to work on interfaces – windows systems and graphics. Fortunately for Sun and the wider Internet community, Gosling had a wide range of IT research interests and a knack for creating computing tools that was to lead him in a different direction and, eventually, to the development of Java, the "write once, write anywhere" programming language.

Gosling (born 1956), arrived at Sun in 1984 from IBM where he had been part of the research division. His great strength was the ability to build better task-oriented tools than those already available:

> "What tends to happen with me is that I get something in my head
> that I want to do and the tools don't work so I end up building
> tools and regressing backwards: 'well the tools aren't there so I
> better build tools for that.' So I end up spending most of my time
> building tools and not what I originally set out to do."[1]

Early work at Sun included the NewS windowing system – technically impressive but not a great commercial success; and development of an EMACS text editor, a popular programmers' program.

In December 1990, Sun set up an in-house research project to look at the future of computing. It was called the Green project. The original members of the team were Patrick Naughton, Mike Sheridan and Jim Gosling. (Later on, the work it spawned attracted the personal interest of Sun co-founder Bill Joy, the man *Fortune* magazine described as "the Edison of the Internet," and who championed the Java project). Coming from product groups within Sun, as they did, the original trio were interested in conducting more than purely theoretical research into technologies. They were interested in consumers and how they would use the technology. The Green project members were focused on the end product. It was this involvement in delivering products that were of interest to consumers, and developing the business models through which the products would be delivered that was to shape their research.

The group predicted that one strand of the future of computing lay in the convergence of consumer devices and computers. And because they were drawn from practical product-driven backgrounds they determined to produce a number of working prototypes – and a business plan. Gosling explains: "We subscribed to what Bill Joy called 'Hammer Technology' – taking a bunch of existing stuff and hammering it together. Learning by doing. We built things you can hold and use."

In April 1991, the Green project moved offsite to premises at 2180 Sand Hill Road, Silicon Valley, and recruited additional members (Chris Warth, Ed Frank, and Craig Forrest). The group worked prolifically producing a raft of different prototype multimedia products. Patrick Naughton, a project programmer and one of the original team recalls:

> "In 18 months, we did the equivalent of what 75-people orga-
> nizations at Sun took three years to do – an operating system,
> a language, a toolkit, an interface, a new hardware platform,
> three custom chips ... using new risky technology at every
> turn. We pulled out all our teeth and put them in each others'
> mouths."[2]

What came out of this product maelstrom was a host of gadgets (see box below). They also developed "a new small, safe, secure, distributed, robust, interpreted, garbage collected, multi-threaded, architecture neutral, high performance, dynamic programming language" which they called Oak. (The name came to Gosling as he gazed out of the window whilst constructing a directory for the new language). It was subsequently renamed Java when Oak failed the trademark search test. The language was used to allow various prototypes to communicate with each other. Among them, the Star 7, a PDA device that Gosling called a handheld remote control.

The Star 7 was completed and demonstrated around Sun impressing important people like Sun CEO Scott McNealy – and, crucially, Bill Joy. Sun, Gosling and Java next headed off down a siding with an abortive foray into the set-top box/video on demand market. This hit the buffers when Sun and the Green project now (incorporated as FirstPerson Inc) lost out to SGI (Silicon Graphics Inc) on a major contract.

Insight

The Java development process is now held up as a shining example of how big companies should do R&D. In common with other successful technology breakthroughs, the members of the Green Project were allowed to detach themselves from the corporate mindset. They holed up in their own offsite bunker in Sand Hill Road, and later worked with Bill Joy in Aspen, Colorado, away from the close-knit world of Silicon Valley. Their remit allowed them to wander widely, generating a host of new ideas. The focus on prototyping also meant they were driven to hammer together practical working models rather than spend too long on purely theoretical notions. The fact that Bill Joy recognized the potential in the Oak language also meant that it gained a senior management champion at a crucial time. Sun's current success is largely the result of this one magnificent endeavor.

The Green project

To give an idea of how prolific the Green project team was, here is Gosling's recollection of the products prototypes produced:

- a new SPARC based, handheld wireless PDA (known as the Star 7 or *7), with a 5" color LCD with touchscreen input;
- a new 16 bit − 5:6:5 color hardware double buffered NTSC frame-buffer;
- 900MHz wireless networking;
- PCMCIA bus interfaces;
- multi-media audio codec;
- a new power supply/battery interface;
- radical industrial design and packaging/process technology;
- a version of Unix that runs in under a megabyte, including drivers for PCMCIA, radio networking, touchscreen, display, flash RAM file system, execute-in-place, split I/D cache, with cached framebuffer support, etc.;
- a new small, fast, true-color alpha channel compositing, sprite graphics library;
- a set of classes that implement a spatial user interface metaphor;
- a user interface methodology which uses animation, audio, spatial cues, gestures, agency, color, and fun;

- a set of applications which show all of the features of the ★7 hardware and software combination, including a TV guide;
- a fully functioning television remote control;
- a ShowMe style distributed whiteboard which allows active objects to be transmitted over a wireless network; and
- an on-screen agent which makes the whole experience fun and engaging.

FirstPerson was dissolved, and about half of its staff moved to Sun Interactive to develop digital video data servers. But a few people still pursued applying Java's technology to network-based desktop systems. As it turned out all was not lost – Java was the nugget of purest gold in amongst the gravel. When Marc Andreessen developed the Mosaic browser for the World Wide Web, Gosling and the team at Sun could see that Java was perfect for writing Web-based applications. Valley lore has it that after witnessing his first Java demo, McNealy released an email that started: "Charge! Kill Hewlett-Packard, IBM, Microsoft, and Apple all at once."

By the summer of 1994, the first prototype was running and in Spring 1995 the program was released to the world after the *San Jose Mercury News* leaked its location on the Net. Sun gave Java away for free, thinking that this way Java stood a better chance of becoming an industry standard. The company also figured, rightly as it turned out, that Microsoft was likely to take an interest in Java and by releasing it into the public domain quickly and at no cost they could delay any Microsoft counter measures.

Java has now become one of the most important programming languages in computing – particularly in e-commerce, networks and Web development. And Sun has claimed Java territory as its own. Gosling and the Green project's invention have reenergized the Sun Corporation. As for Gosling he continues to work at Sun on various Java related and other projects; he is chief scientist of the Java software division. And although most people would settle for inventing one program as significant as Java, who's to say he won't come up with another invention that has the same impact?

In 1999, Gosling gave evidence at the Microsoft hearings. In response to a question about Microsoft's willingness to cooperate with Sun on issues relating to Java, he testified:

"Our view was that when Microsoft was holding out its hand, there was a knife in it, and Microsoft was asking us to grab the blade."[3]

When asked in the daily press conference what remedy he would suggest in the event of Microsoft losing the case, Gosling replied: "They should just issue cream pies to all the software developers, along with a plane ticket to Redmond."

Links

http://java.sun.com

Notes

1. meme 1.09 interview with James Gosling 1995.
2. www.sunworld.com/swol-07-1995/swol-07-java.html.
3. *Fortune*, November 1999.

BILL GROSS

– Idealab!

Now commonplace in the technological ferment of Silicon Valley, incubators – some prefer the term "business accelerators" – aim to speed up the time to market for start-up businesses and reduce the number of failures. Based in Pasadena, California, Idealab!, the company founded by Bill Gross, is widely regarded as the originator of the modern incubator concept. GoTo.com, eToys, CitySearch, NetZero, eWallet and Tickets.com are all companies incubated by Idealab!

Incubators are not in fact a new idea. Although sometimes regarded as purely an Internet phenomenon, in the US the establishment of organizations to nurture new ventures dates back to the 1950s, when non-profit agencies began setting up incubators to encourage commercial development. Local governments, for example, established incubators to stimulate regional business activity. Universities also set up incubators to capitalize on patentable technologies developed through academic research. Europe has followed a similar pattern, with industrial parks being established from the 1960s onwards, often in an attempt to foster economic regeneration in areas of high unemployment.

But Bill Gross (born 1959) hit on the idea to apply the formula to Internet start-ups. If you create an environment in which Internet start-ups could be hatched and nurtured, he reasoned, then eventually they would thrive and repay your kindness with hard cash – or at least some valuable stock. It seemed a sure-fire winner. And so it proved – initially at least. Idealab! has attracted prestigious backers, like the movie director Steven Spielberg and Compaq chairman Ben Rosen, who have pumped in several million dollars. And then there's Gross, the James Joyce of innovation – a constant stream of ideas flowing from his fertile imagination.

Gross, now CEO and chairman, has built a multi-million dollar company from the incubation model. Idealab! is a private company (at present) with offices in Silicon Valley, New York, Boston and London. Its mission is to develop great ideas into Internet success stories. The company identifies, creates and operates Internet businesses. For start-ups it offers a full range of resources to help them succeed. These include offices and network infrastructure, as well as consulting services relating to legal and financial matters, finance and marketing. Its services help start-ups acquire the momentum needed to survive and thrive in a dynamically changing marketplace.

Idealab! is not the first entrepreneurial venture that Gross has been involved with. He has always been full of ideas. First it was bulk buying candy bars at a discount in seventh grade and selling them on to his fellow students. Then a business called Solar Devices, selling solar energy conversion kits through the small ads in *Popular Science*. Tapping into the usual student interests, Gross sounded out the world of audio hi-fi at the California Institute of Technology. He designed loudspeakers and his company GNP Loudspeakers Inc. built them.

After graduating with a BS in Mechanical Engineering, Gross founded GNP Development Inc., with his brother Larry. The company made a Lotus 1-2-3 product (it was bought out by the Lotus Development Corporation in 1995). And in 1986, Gross joined Lotus as a software developer. By 1991, however, he was missing the entrepreneurial way of life and left to start another company, Knowledge Adventure. The company published educational software and was eventually sold to Cedant for $100 million.

Eventually in 1996 Gross had probably his best idea of all – Idealab! A perfect vehicle for a serial entrepreneur like Gross, Idealab!'s success depends on the generation and marketing of great ideas. At Idealab! Gross has created a life-support infrastructure for infant Internet ventures. Although Idealab! doesn't accommodate all the companies that it helps nurture, a large proportion start life in the 24,000-square-foot incubator space provided in Pasadena.

Start-ups get basic support services – phones, desks, network connections, Web servers and the like – plus advice on the range of issues: legal matters, marketing, branding, corporate structure and other similar services. Technical back-up is on-hand from a team of expert programmers hired by Gross to give substance to the countless ideas he throws off as well as provide critical technological know-how to the start-ups.

They also benefit from the assorted expertise of the start-ups on the premises, a resource that is often undervalued. As a company expands it moves to a different space on the start-up farm so as to accommodate the growing roster of employees. Finally, by the time the company is up to 60-plus people, it leaves the nest to soar in the sky – or crash down to earth. To help the start-up survive, Idealab! also injects some seed capital, anything up to $250,000. If further financing is necessary then Gross will help raise it from external sources. In return, the incubator receives an amount per person per month from its fledglings and retains sufficient equity to reward it for its efforts.

Idealab! has an eclectic approach to funding. It has invested in a broad portfolio of Internet-related companies from software developers to content providers. And Gross has a clear idea of what constitutes a viable Internet proposition. Underpinning this is the One Percent Rule, a mantra he fervently believes in: employees in a startup need at least one percent of equity to motivate them sufficiently. Not such a radical idea at first sight. But with only 100 percent to give away, if every employee is to get one percent, the maximum number of employees at any one company equals 100. Can this really be what Gross believes? It seems so:

> "It's like a chemical reaction! It unleashes new energy! I urge someone to do this in other industries. I think this is the new model for business in general, not just Idealab! Every 10,000-person company should be broken up into 100-person companies."[1]

If the incubator principle is a sound one, then Idealab! should continue to prosper. There have been some cracks in the edifice, however. Just how exposed to market sentiment incubators are was demonstrated in the period between late 1999 and mid-2000. A loss of $252 million on revenues of $134 million didn't make pleasant reading. With low stock value and lots of hungry start-ups to feed Gross was forced to go to the market for $300 million. And if too many of Idealab!'s companies turn out to be lemons, then the market will give Idealab!'s stock short shrift.

Neither are start-ups always keen to be hatched by an incubator. Some entrepreneurs may find the infrastructure benefits are outweighed by the degree of handholding and supervision. An Idealab! partner sits on every portfolio company board, Gross himself sits on many.

Insight

Incubators spawn new possibilities. Their product is not a physical thing but a company. In the past, the conglomerate was the benchmark, a large sprawling mass of disparate companies yoked together from HQ. Increasingly, the talk among incubators on both sides of the Atlantic is of symbiotic networks of companies, similar to the Japanese *keiretsu* synergistic corporate groupings. A number of US Internet incubators explicity see themselves as holding companies, with a stated aim of creating a symbiotic community of businesses to leverage internal synergies. The current fashion is for "economic networks," or "EcoNets" in the unfortunate parlance. The incubators that succeed will create powerful networks of companies in which they have a stake.

Prototyping

His experience of e-business start-ups also makes Bill Gross a source of insights for new economy entrepreneurs and intrapreneurs. To test an idea he prefers prototyping to traditional focus groups. The small initial costs make it possible to take an idea and set up a Website as if it were a business. To the consumer the fake Website looks bona fide. Gross will even stretch the prototyping to the extent of taking credit card orders for the imaginary product or service. The results of his prototyping experiments give Gross hard data about the consumers that focus groups simply cannot. Rather than asking what people think they might purchase, how much they would be willing to pay, how often they would make a transaction and the like, he knows how they will react. In the prototyping phase, customers actually think they re buying and make a commitment. The drawback is that customers who thought they were paying for something that doesn't yet exist might be less than pleased. But to keep them sweet, Gross sends them a freebie and refunds their card.

Diluting equity by up to 50 percent may not seem such an attractive proposition either.

Some commentators believe that the recent backlash against incubators has been overdone. Josh Lerner, professor of business administration at Harvard Business School, argues that the economies of scale might prove a critical competitive advantage. Incubators are also agile organizations. Most have portfolios with a wide span (although some experts argue that in future they will be more focused on specialist markets). If investment in one particular area proves unlucrative, then the generalist incubator can swiftly refocus future investment in other areas.

While Gross waits to see if his ideas are vindicated, he continues to expand Idealab! and forge new alliances. The company is now busily rolling out its business model to other parts of the world. The company opened an office in London early in 2000. It is headed by Larry Gross, Bill's brother. The company views its European base as an opportunity to create new Internet businesses, and to support the international expansion of US-based companies. In all, Idealab! currently has around 50 businesses in development, and specialises in generating ideas in-house for Internet start-ups, recruiting the management team to develop each business. It actively participates in the ongoing operation of its network of companies through board representation, information sharing, and facilitating collaboration. Idealab! offers a variety of levels of incubation, including a full range of operational support services.

To tap into the predicted explosion in broadband services Gross has recently forged a deal between Idealab! and Creative Artists Agency. It may turn out to be a shrewd move as Web-based programming takes off.

Links

www.idealab.com

Notes

1. *Wired* magazine, September 1999.

ANDY GROVE

– Intel

For more than three decades the Intel Corporation has doggedly remained at or near the leading edge of the technology revolution. In the "old" pre Internet world, the company rose to dominance on the back of the mass-market PC. Despite constant threat from competitors, it continues to lead the microprocessor market in the era of the Internet. That it has managed to successfully ride the waves of technological innovation, switching its strategic focus on several occasions, is largely due to one man – Andy Grove.

Intel was founded by Gordon Moore and Robert Noyce, who left Fairchild Computing to start the company in 1968. Although not technically a co-founder, Grove was at Intel from the beginning. He was the fourth recruit – "employee number four," as he came to be known.

Grove (born 1936) graduated from the City College of New York in 1960, with a Bachelor of Chemical Engineering degree and afterwards studied at the University of California, at Berkeley, where he received a PhD in 1963. His first job after graduating was at Fairchild Computing, the company formed by Moore and Noyce. When they set up Intel, they asked Grove to join them.

The original intention was to manufacture a new kind of memory; cheaper, more efficient, and more powerful than the standard magnetic core memory that was used at the time. To do this Intel planned to use semiconductor technology, then still in its infancy. In 1970 the first dynamic random access memory (DRAM) for commercial use rolled off the production lines at Intel. At the same time Intel had been approached by a Japanese calculator company, the Nippon Calculating Machine Corporation (NCM) to produce some logic chips. Intel, however, suggested an alternative, a smaller single-chip, general-purpose logic device. The Japanese agreed, but Ted Hoff who had been the principal motivator behind Intel's counter offer moved on to other projects and the work on the chip stagnated.

It was only when Frederico Faggin, a young Italian engineer, got to grips with the development, under pressure from the Japanese who wanted to see progress, that the product was completed. In the end it took Faggin an astonishing three months. The masterstroke was yet to come, however. When the Intel founders went back to the NCM they were met with a request for a price cut. The Intel team were reluctant but agreed on the proviso that instead of the ownership of the chip passing to NCM, Intel would retain the right to produce and sell the chip to others. It was this agreement that set Intel on the path to becoming the semiconductor giant it is today.

But what later cemented Intel's domination was the skillful repositioning of what had previously been no more than a commodity computer component into a household name brand. Through a series of TV commercials, it elevated its microchips to the status of an aspirational product. This enabled it to by-pass PC retailers to grab the attention of consumers. Consumers did the rest – insisting on an Intel inside. The Intel Pentium processor became as synonymous with the PC as the Microsoft Windows Operating System.

The vision of Andy Grove was instrumental in this. It was Grove who oversaw the growth of Intel from a fledging producer of memory chips to a giant of the microprocessor industry. He was the man who got things done. He organized the office space and manufacturing capacity, and later played a principal part in negotiations with IBM that saw Intel beat off competition from Motorola to supply the microprocessors for IBM's PCs. A strong hand on the Intel tiller, Grove was resolute enough to make some difficult decisions.

In 1985, for example, he made the tough strategic decision to refocus the company's efforts on microprocessors rather than memory chips. It was not an easy call, as it meant laying off thousands of employees. Time has shown, however, that it was the right call. In 1987, Grove became CEO of Intel. The tough calls kept coming. Grove dealt swiftly with a potential crisis when the company's flagship Pentium processor proved to have a slight flaw. Once it became clear that the technical problem could spiral into a public relations disaster he took decisive action to safeguard the carefully constructed Intel brand. Instead of using Intel's powerful position to pass the burden onto the PC suppliers and consumers, Grove offered to replace the processors at a potential cost of millions of dollars and in doing so preserved Intel's reputation. Despite the hiccup, profits went up.

During Grove's time as CEO the stock price went up a whopping 24 times making shareholders eternally grateful. In May 1998, Intel appointed Craig Barrett as CEO in a planned succession, with Grove remaining at the company but with more time to devote to Intel's Internet strategy.

Since his appointment Barrett has begun to diversify Intel's operations. In October 1999 the company announced its intention to purchase DSP Communications for $1.6 billion as well as investing approximately $5 million in Proxicom. The move to shift the focus of the company is partly a response to the imminent demise of Moore's Law. Moore's Law, named after its proponent and Intel's co-founder Gordon Moore, states that processor power will double every eighteen months. The law's validity so far has made Intel a very wealthy corporation. However, as the technology needed to build faster processors becomes more expensive and Internet access through devices other than the PC grows, Intel faces the prospect of seeing its revenues from chip manufacturing tumble.

Intel's diversification is also a sign that the company is embracing Andy Grove's belief that "all companies will be Internet companies." Developments such as the WebOutfitters site, a Website with content aimed at Pentium III users, demonstrates that Intel is keen to open a communication channel with its customers. Having established one of the most widely recognized computing brands, it intends to leverage it in a new way. That Intel is changing focus there is no doubt, the question is whether it can find a role for itself in the new business world that Grove so accurately foresaw.

Grove himself remains in demand. A respected public speaker, he continues to pass on his views and advice about how technology is shaping the future and what companies must do to survive. His vision and accomplishments at Intel have been widely recognized. He has been elected a Fellow of the IEEE, a member of the National Academy of Engineering and a Fellow of the Academy of Arts and Sciences. He has also been awarded an honorary Doctor of Science degree by the City College of New York, the 1987 Engineering Leadership Recognition Award from the IEEE, the 1993 AEA Medal of Achievement, and the Heinz Family Foundation Award for Technology and the Economy.

He has also authored a number of influential books – *Physics and Technology of Semiconductor Devices* (John Wiley and Sons, Inc., 1967), *High Output Management* (Random House, 1983), and his best seller *Only the Paranoid Survive* (Doubleday 1996).

Links

www.intel.com
www.intelweboutfitter.com

JEFF HAWKINS

– *Palm Computing & Handspring*

T he handheld-computer market is littered with over $1 billion worth of wreckage. Apple spent around half a billion dollars developing the Apple Newton only to eventually pull the plug. The GO Corporation funded by the VC firm Kleiner Perkins Caulfield & Byers spent a little less – $75 million or so – to achieve the same result. So how come Jeff Hawkins and Palm Computers, the company he founded, succeeded where so many others failed?

Jeff Hawkins (born 1957) comes from a family of engineers. His father was an inventor who experimented with forms of hovercraft. As a boy, Hawkins would help out in the workshop. At college Hawkins showed an aptitude and interest in biology, but when it came to choosing his degree major, he fell in with the family specialty. Graduating from Cornell University in 1979 with a BSEE (Bachelor of Science, Electronic Engineering) he went to work for Intel. Three years later, Hawkins was ready to move on. He wanted more responsibility; Intel wanted him to get some more experience under his belt.

His next job was with another Silicon Valley company. GriD Systems specialized in cutting-edge portable computing. Hawkins' job was to write computer code. While there, he developed an interest in neurobiology, cognitive science and the workings of the brain – an interest that has stayed with him. In fact he maintains that his work at Palm, 3Com and Handspring are really a means to find the platform and financial support to promote his ideas about intelligence and the mechanics of the brain.

Acting on advice from his wife, Hawkins channeled his curiosity about the human brain into a biophysics course at the University of California, Berkeley.

"I want to solve the major problems in the study of human intelligence," he has said. "I want to achieve a theoretical understanding of how the brain works. My research into human cognition is a lifelong pursuit. It began before Palm, and it will last beyond Palm. The research and the company go together. I intend to use the next decade of my life to make my work on cognition much more visible."[1]

Hawkins wanted to pursue his passion about the human mind through a PhD, but it wasn't to be. Instead he left Berkeley with a greater understanding of neural networks – and an algorithm for handwriting-recognition software. The name he gave it – "PalmPrint" was to become a recurring theme in his career.

Armed with PalmPrint, now patented, Hawkins returned to GriD, licensing the software to the company. As vice-president of research he came up with the world's first pen-based computer. By today's standards it was a cumbersome contraption. But at the time the industry raved about how it would change the world of computing. Suddenly, all the big names in computing – IBM, Samsung, Apple – were working on what John Sculley, CEO of Apple had named a "personal digital assistant" or PDA.

Hawkins decided that it was time to move on from GriD. He raised some finance, around $7 million, and in 1992 started Palm Computing. It was a software company selling Hawkins' handwriting-recognition software to makers of handheld computers. The problem was the handhelds weren't up to running the software. The first handheld using the Palm application software was the Casio Zoomer. Only it didn't zoom, it plummeted.

The Zoomer had been designed and built through partnering with other manufacturers. Tandy brought it to market; GeoWorks worked on the Operating System; Casio built the hardware. Design by committee, Hawkins discovered, just didn't work. Poor sales, and a clunky design only escaped the blistering criticism of the trade press by hiding behind the Apple Newton which was released first, and received a lot of flak that would otherwise have been destined for the Zoomer. Instead of complaining about the shortcomings of the early handhelds, the Palm board suggested Hawkins should build his own.

Never one to pass on a challenge, Hawkins disappeared into his garage with some mahogany and plywood only to re-emerge with a low-tech prototype of the PalmPilot. As part of the design process he carried the model with him, in his shirt pocket, taking it out from time to time and pretending to look up an address or phone number on it. That first prototype is now in the Palm museum.

Donna Dubinsky left high school without a diploma, but still managed to get into Yale. After a job in banking, she attended Harvard Business School and in 1981 got a job at Apple in sales. It was a time of strong growth for Apple and Dubinsky prospered. In 1987 she switched within Apple to the Apple-financed Claris and spent time in Australia and Paris before finally ending up at a new start-up – Palm Computing. There she struck up a long-lasting and highly successful working relationship with Hawkins. They turned out to be kindred spirits with complementary skills – and their partnership has endured through Palm, US Robotics, 3Com and Handspring. As Dubinsky told *Fast Company* magazine: "One of my great purposes in life has been to create an environment where Jeff Hawkins can thrive."

Within Palm, Dubinsky provided a counterbalance to Hawkins. She provided stability, strategy and leadership, allowing Hawkins to give full rein to his creativity. To go it alone, Dubinsky decided, developing all the elements that would comprise the new product, Palm needed greater resources and more financial clout. In 1996 Palm was sold to US Robotics for $44 million. It was the right deal for Palm because USR was happy to bankroll Palm and not interfere with the running of the business. This enabled Dubinsky and Hawkins to assemble a team of individuals and companies with the necessary skills to manufacture the hardware and engineer the software for the PalmPilot. The members of the team were paid in cash and, more importantly, stock options. It was an innovative approach to building a product.

Within 18 months of its launch the PalmPilot had sold over a million units, making it one of the most successful electronic consumer product launches ever. The Pilot shipped faster than mobile phones or color televisions even. One of the reasons for the rapid sales was the price – below $300. Another was the policy the company adopted – making it easy for third parties to produce programs for the Pilot.

In 1997, US Robotics was in turn bought by 3Com. This time instead of leaving Palm with a high degree of autonomy 3Com attempted to integrate Palm into its global organization. It wasn't a situation either Hawkins or Dubinsky were happy with. Dubinsky later observed:

"It was becoming clear that that wasn't where we wanted to be. We were entrepreneurs, and we wanted to be running and creating an independent, influential company leading the next generation of computing. In the end, we decided we couldn't do that in the 3Com structure."[2]

Insight

Behind every great engineer is a great business person. Only very occasionally are the two combined in one individual. Hawkins was always a smart guy. But his career really took off once he met Donna Dubinsky. Dubinsky thrives on creating the space for Hawkins to do what he does best – innovate. Without the complimentary skills that Dubinsky offers, Hawkins would be weighed down with decisions on strategy, finance, and other areas essential to the effective running of the business. As Hawkins commented when asked about why he was leaving 3Com: "I'm a product person. I like to focus in on projects and drive that. Donna, in a similar way, likes being her own boss and being the CEO; and this gives her a chance to do that again."[3]

Before leaving, they went to see 3Com's CEO Eric Benhamou to explore the possibilities of 3Com spinning Palm off as a separate entity. They came away under no illusions. It simply wasn't an option. Ironically, 3Com did subsequently hive Palm off, but by then it was too late for Hawkins who had already gone. As he told the *San Jose Mercury News*, "If they had spun us out, I'd still be there."

Hawkins and Dubinsky left 3Com in 1998 to start up their own company, Handspring. The company's first product was launched in September 1999. It was a handheld device named the Visor.

The Visor looks like a sophisticated Gameboy. It has been designed to take add-on modules which will turn it into anything from an MP3 player to a camera. It's also cheaper than the Palm III. Given Hawkins' track record for innovative design, the Visor's success was almost a foregone conclusion. Handspring was overwhelmed with orders and soon racked up a four-week backlog. This was reduced to less than a week by January 2000.

Whichever way you look at it, a Hawkins–Dubinsky product is likely to dominate the market for some time to come. Handspring's main competition is 3Com's Hawkins–Dubinsky produced Palm IIIx, Palm V and Palm VII, although it's unlikely that Hawkins and Dubinsky will be comforted by the thought. There are echoes here of Marc Andreessen at Netscape, who found that Mosaic the Web browser he had originally designed, became the chief competitor to the Netscape browser. Hawkins, too, is fighting his earlier brilliance. Expect to see some exciting products come from Handspring, unfettered by any corporate restraints.

No doubt 3Com will be keeping an eye on Hawkins' garage. According to the research company Dataquest, the number of handheld computers is expected to increase from 8.2 million units in 1998 to 32.5 million in 2003. The question is: whose products will triumph?

Notes

1. *Fast Company*, June 1998.
2. Interview with Donna Dubinsky and Jeff Hawkins, *Fortune*, November 1999.
3. Interview with Jeff Hawkins, *Pilot Page*, October 1998.

STEVE JOBS

– *Apple Computer*

S teve Jobs has a special place in the history of the computer. It can be described in one word – usability. The graphical interface Jobs developed with Apple comrade Steve Wozniak made computing accessible to ordinary people. It also paved the way for the development of the World Wide Web. Without Apple, computers might still just be tools for techies. The principle of usability is as important to the creation of a wired world as it was to the adoption of personal computers. Without Apple there might have been an Internet, but there might not have been a Web. Apple's fortunes have fluctuated somewhat since then, but Jobs has to be regarded as one of the architects who laid the foundations for the current business revolution.

When Apple launched the iMac, the stylish Internet-ready computer which it hoped would re-energize the company's fading fortunes, "Chic Not Geek" was blazed across advertising posters. Beneath it were the Apple logo and the slogan: "Think different." The campaign epitomized what the Apple and founder Steve Jobs stand for. After a 13-year exile, Jobs was back where he started. The iconoclast who founded the computer company with attitude had returned in its moment of direst need. The wheel had come full circle. The world has changed in the intervening period with the arrival of the Internet, but Apple and its famous founder remain well matched.

Strong sales of the iMac have greatly speeded Apple's financial and brand rehabilitation. The iMac has also been instrumental in bringing new online recruits to surf the Web, many of them people who would not otherwise have plugged in. In summer 2000, Apple unveiled its new offerings, which drew mixed reviews from industry commentators. The new Mac Cube, Apple's most powerful technology packed into a clear plastic case the size of a toaster. According Jobs, it's the most beautiful thing the company has ever done.

Other recent innovations include an improved version of its iMovie software. And the company has revamped its Website creation program that allows users to set up shop online. Apple fans, though, will have to wait for a new wireless handheld device that some believe would take Apple into serious cyber contention. Unperturbed by the wait for the next move in cool mobility, fans of Jobs say the revival in the company's fortunes since his return in 1997 simply confirms his place as the king of the technology entrepreneurs.

Back in 1997 the story was very different. With mounting losses and declining market share, the company was all but written off. Enter Jobs. After a long exile he resumed command of the company. Today Apple is back to making stylish products. Revenues were up 17 percent, to $1.8 billion, in the quarter reported July 2000. (Unfortunately that fell short of analysts' expectations, pushing the share price down.)

For a time, Apple was quite simply the hippest thing in computers and corporate America. Founded in a garage by two college dropouts – Steve Jobs and Steve Wozniak – the company changed the face of computing with the Apple 1 and Apple 2. In a market where design went little further than beige boxes, the Apple machines stood out from the crowd.

Ownership of an Apple machine was a statement of identity: it was jeans and sneakers versus the suit and ties of corporate America. Apple had attitude. The two friends eventually fell out, with Wozniak leaving the company to become a teacher, but Jobs went on to launch the Apple Macintosh, with which he hoped to conquer the computer world. The crown went instead to Bill Gates, whose Microsoft persuaded 80 percent of computer buyers to use its operating system MS-DOS rather than buy Apple.

Many industry commentators still believe that Apple could have been sitting where Microsoft is today. That battle is over, but whether Bill Gates won it or Steve Jobs blew it remains an open question. Observers agree that an important mistake Apple made was refusing to license its operating system to other computer manufacturers. This left the door open for Microsoft's MS-DOS alternative. Some claim, too, that the company with attitude developed a little too much of the wrong sort of attitude, becoming arrogant and complacent.

After its early triumphs (the revolutionary nature of which should not be underestimated), a series of false starts, missed opportunities and product flops saw Apple's market share dwindle, despite the enduring appeal of the Apple name and high brand loyalty. In recent years, Apple's very survival has been in question after a succession of comeback attempts went wrong. Jobs himself was kicked out of the company in 1985, only to return 13 years later – initially as "interim CEO" and now on a permanent basis. It remains to be seen whether the second coming of Jobs will resurrect the fortunes of his famous creation.

Like all the best computer companies, Apple began life in a garage. In 1977, Steve Jobs conceived the Apple 1, regarded by many as the first real personal computer. Jobs and his technically brilliant partner Steve Wozniak built the first machine in a garage. They founded the Apple company. The Apple 2 followed, and then the Apple Macintosh with which the company planned to conquer the world.

Instead of writing commands in computerese, Macintosh owners used a mouse to click on easily recognizable icons – a trash can and file folders, for example. Suddenly, you didn't need a degree in computer science to operate a personal computer. Other companies followed where Apple led – most significantly Microsoft. But while Apple became the darling of the creative world, Bill Gates and crew never achieved the same iconoclast status.

One newspaper described Jobs as a "corporate Huckleberry Finn" (begging the question who was the corporate Tom Sawyer?), and said his early business exploits had already made him part of American folk history. The fairytale story came to a sticky end in 1987 when former Pepsi chairman John Sculley, who had been brought in to add some corporate know-how to the wilting Apple, removed Jobs.

In between his spells at Apple, Jobs plowed $250 million of investors' money into another start-up – NeXT Computer. It disappointed, selling only 50,000 units.

He also invested $60 million of his own fortune in Pixar Animation Studios, which eventually paid out with the computer-animated blockbusters *Toy Story* and *A Bug's Life*.

Back at Apple, Sculley himself was booted out in 1993 after a disastrous period that saw Apple's market share plummet from 20 percent to just 8 percent. He was replaced by Michael Spindler, who lasted until 1996, by which time market share had fallen to just over 5 percent. Apple was staring oblivion in the face as its long-term devotees began to switch to the Microsoft-powered PCs.

Spindler was shown the door, and Gil Amelio stepped into the hot seat. After 500 days in the post, Apple's market share remained unmoved and Amelio invited Jobs to come in and help. With two being a crowd, Amelio soon made his exit.

Since Jobs has been back at the helm, Apple has looked more like its old self. The iMac, a vision in translucent blue, sold 278,000 units in the first six weeks, an achievement that had *Fortune* magazine describing it as "one of the hottest computer launches ever." Wall Street, too, recovered its confidence in Apple – the company's share price doubled in less than a year.

The Jobs fans say the once and future king of Apple came in and saved the day. His actions since becoming CEO include dumping the NeXT operating system that he sold to Apple, ditching loss-making licensing contracts, and comprehending the potential of the Internet.

The iMac was the embodiment of everything Jobs believes in: eye-catching design, and simple operation. The iMac is also the product of a different vision of the computer industry. It doesn't have a disk drive – because Jobs believes they have been superseded by external storage devices such as zip drives and the Internet. Nor does the Apple CEO subscribe to the common view that the PC and TV are moving together.

Apple owners have always been passionate, fierce even, in their belief that Jobs builds a better mouse trap. Brand loyalty has always been high. The best news of all for Apple was that some 40 percent of early iMac sales were to new customers. This suggests that the iconoclast Apple brand can seduce a new generation of computer buyers, taking them online.

Links

www.apple.com

GUY KAWASAKI

– *Garage.com*

D espite the apparent abundance of venture capital, one of the biggest problems facing would-be Internet entrepreneurs is finding early-stage finance. Having a killer idea is one thing, getting it from the back of the envelope to the Internet is another. Until very recently, most venture capitalists have been reluctant to provide seed funding, preferring to back companies that are already up and running and which have a well-formulated business model. Corporations and business angels (wealthy private investors) seeking to invest seed money are faced with an unstructured, fragmented and disorganized market. It is this gap in the VC market that garage.com, based in Palo Alto, sought to exploit.

Garage.com was founded by Guy Kawasaki, along with co-founders Craig Johnson and Rich Karlgaard. It was one of the first so-called venture catalysts. Prior to becoming CEO and chairman of garage.com, Kawasaki had famously worked as the Apple Computer evangelist, tasked with spreading the Apple gospel. The author of a number of books, including *Rules for Revolutionaries* (HarperBusiness, 1999), Kawasaki has an excellent grasp of the nature of the relationship between start-ups and investors.

As well as timing, the size of investment a company requires can be an issue. Companies that require modest cash injections may be below the VC radar. The traditional VC market has experienced such success that it often looks for companies that require $5 million upwards of investment. It also concentrates on other factors that increase the chances of a leveraged return. VC firms may consider only companies projecting revenues in the $billions and that can sprint to an IPO. By contrast, companies which may be no less viable but have more modest ambitions requiring $500,000 to $3 million, may struggle to raise early financing.

This meant that entrepreneurs with great ideas were going unfunded simply because of the mechanics of the VC market rather than any fundamental flaw in their business plan. Kawasaki saw that there was a space for a matchmaker who could add value to both sides of the investment equation.

"I wanted to democratize the process," he has said. "I saw it had become very difficult for people with good ideas who didn't have a pedigree or pre-existing relationships to get funding."[1]

Garage.com bridges the gap between what Kawasaki calls the three Fs – friends, fools and family – and the big venture capitalists. By using the Internet and Garage's network of contacts, the company acts as a matchmaker between start-up and investor. It provides entrepreneurs with a way to maximize their chances of receiving investment through a mixture of selection and exposure. And, for the investor, garage.com acts as a quality filter. In the same way that recruitment agencies protect companies from an avalanche of unsuitable candidates applying for a position, garage.com makes sure the investor is considering only ideas that have some promise.

The aim for garage.com is to secure enough financing for the start-up to enable it to take the business to a stage where it is ready for its first big round of venture capital. In practical terms this means enough money to allow the founders to devote all their time to the business and give up the day job. Often that means sufficient funding to build a working Website to demonstrate the potential of the business.

Despite Kawasaki's admission that most entrepreneurs have only a one in a hundred chance of obtaining funding, garage.com does all it can to shift the odds in the member-companies' favor. In one interview Kawasaki said:

> "They know that it's a long-shot thing to be an entrepreneur. But if we can help educate them, we can increase their chances of success."[2]

Garage first carefully scrutinizes applications. The garage team looks for business plans that:

- hit the right target markets – especially networking, software, computer hardware and peripherals, semiconductors and the Internet;
- are at the right stage – that is, with the idea, the strategy, a team of players and maybe some money already raised from friends and family;

- have an aggressive business plan – the company is looking to grow quickly, dominate its market and start producing good returns to investors within a reasonable time frame; and
- have a talented team – that understands the business model, and the technologies required to implement it.

Once past the screening process, garage.com provides a wealth of resources to support the start-up. These include advice from experts, research and reference materials and topical forums. Member companies also get their start-up details posted on the garage.com Website in a password-protected area named Heaven. Potential investors can then peruse the details and decide whether to make an investment.

Garage.com makes its money from charging the investors for membership. In addition, its broker/dealer affiliate receives a placement fee from the entrepreneurs when funding is agreed. On top of this, garage.com operates two investment funds that co-invest in start-up companies on the side.

Predictably, venture capitalists were initially skeptical of garage.com. One argument was that garage.com would only attract ideas that didn't deserve to get funded anyway. Another was that any perceived added-value services garage.com was offering had always been and still were available from the established VC market. Today, however, perceptions have shifted. Garage.com has proved its worth in the finance market and demonstrated that a gap did indeed exist. Garage.com has already helped direct $100 million to start-ups. The VCs for their part have joined the growing throng of 2000-plus investors, including the likes of Microsoft, waiting to snap up the promising companies garage.com has identified as suitable for investment.

Garage.com also operates another money-spinner off the back of its start-up advice service. The company has held a number of conferences for potential entrepreneurs. These bootcamps, as garage calls them, are sponsored by *Red Herring* magazine and can cost over $700 a place. From Apple evangelist to start-up evangelist, Kawasaki and garage.com have dispensed their entrepreneurial wisdom at venues across the US – though none of them in a garage.

The NASDAQ mini-crashes in late 1999–2000 as well as the failure of a number of high-profile dot-com companies have dampened the mood of the venture capital market in the US. Companies are more circumspect about the start-ups they invest in. It's no longer a question of backing the buzz but rather backing the business plan. With a rapid

Insight

Ice factories

When Guy Kawasaki is asked why big corporations should pay attention to the Internet, he likes to remind them about the ice factories. There used to be an ice harvesting industry in America during the 1800s. People harvested ice in the north, cutting blocks from the frozen lakes. Then came the ice factories which could create ice on demand by freezing water at any time of the year. The ice harvesters went out of business. The ice factories were in turn put out of business by the refrigerator companies. With a refrigerator in the home there was no longer any need to go to the ice factory, buy blocks of ice or have the ice man make a delivery.

The important point in all this, says Kawasaki, is the fact that no company ever made the transition from ice harvester to ice factory to refrigerator company. "Big companies that don't look at Internet startups are ice factories," he says. "They should jump to the next curve or they will melt."

Companies seem to be getting the message. So-called corporate venturing means many established companies are now actively investing in start-ups. They include the likes of Intel and Xerox, which have earmarked corporate money to back entrepreneurs. Thus far in the history of Internet business, most big companies have shown themselves to be poor at identifying early investment opportunities. This provides fertile soil for garage.com and other venture catalysts. Over time, however, as companies establish in-house capability and become more experienced in this area, they may have less need for external help. But even if this is the case, garage looks well placed to move into other areas. Its brand strength relies on its ability to select high-quality investment opportunities. Whether it backs them itself through its established funds or acts as a matchmaker for others, it has successfully positioned itself in one of the key markets for the future.

IPO less certain, the likelihood of turning in a profit before the next century has also moved up the backer's agenda.

There has also been some criticism leveled at so-called venture catalysts about the fees that they charge. Companies have been asking why they should give up a share of their business not only to the eventual investor but also to the matchmaker – especially if the middleman takes a monthly fee in addition to placement fees. Despite the rumblings of disaffection, however, start-ups will still flock to garage.com all the time they are unable to find seed money elsewhere. And garage.com continues to expand its own services into Europe and the hi-tech clusters of Israel and the Middle East.

Angel investors are starting to group together to become a more effective force in the financing market. They may yet prove a threat to operators like garage.com, but only if they become adequately organized. The rapid growth of Internet incubators, too – including many with VC connections – offers an alternative route to seed finance. But many incubators are currently struggling to realize their investments. Alternatively, if the whole market including later-stage financing slows down, or even if companies seeking later-stage money suddenly seem a less attractive proposition, then garage.com might get squeezed by the bigger VCs moving down the start-up food chain.

Meanwhile garage.com continues to offer its unique take on personal ads for start-ups; providing new meaning to the phrase "a match made in Heaven."

Links

www.garage.com

Notes

1. *Fortune,* July 2000.
2. *Red Herring* Online, 1999.

HARRY KNOWLES

– Ain't It Cool News

Internet revolutionaries come in many guises. Harry Knowles is a cyber guerilla on a one-man mission to give Hollywood's slick PR machine a run for its money. Since April 1996 he has been the star of his own show, the movie news Website, Ain't It Cool News. In the click of a mouse, Knowles has come from nowhere to become one of the most influential voices in the US entertainment industry. He exemplifies the new breed of e-journalists who are challenging the media establishment.

The Hollywood film industry, a powerful and market-led sector, now has to answer to Knowles, a film-buff who posts film reviews from his bedroom in Austin Texas. In its own inimitably crass words: "Ain't It Cool News is a Harry Knowles production bringing you the latest in movie, TV, comic and other coolness that's got Hollywood's panties in a bunch."

As Harry describes his own growing fame, so also the network of informal alliances begin to grow around him:

> "Wow, here ya are! Well my little site keeps on growing, much to my shock. As you will find, I attempt to cover all stages of development of the films that you and I look forward to, without the 'studio line' clouding our judgment.
>
> "This site works with the help of people like you. Now everyone has a chance to be a 'spy,' because inevitably at some point there will be a moment where Hollywood enters your life, before it enters ours. If you see something filming, a trailer, an advance screening or something I can't even imagine. If you read a script, hear something from behind the scenes ..."

As a child, Knowles had a bad accident, which forced him to rest for many months; he spent much of his time in bed watching films. His father dealt in movie memorabilia, so the young Harry was immersed in the movies from an early age. He studied journalism at college, but the Internet offered him the perfect medium to express his views. He started tinkering, writing comments on movies he had seen and posting them up on the Net. For a while he worked with another cyber journalist Matt Drudge, posting reviews for the *Drudge Report*.

But things were happening in his home town of Austin, Texas. It may not be Hollywood, but Austin has a thriving independent film scene. A group of film critics, fed up with the influence that the major studios had over critics, set up their own newspaper, the *Austin Chronicle*. The paper was a success and bred a spin-off independent film festival. The upshot is that Austin now has more than 20 screens that show only independent and foreign films. It was this kind of anti-Hollywood establishment atmosphere that inspired Knowles.

Mouse, modem, action

Remarkably Knowles still operates out of his bedroom in his small two-bedroom house. From there he covers films from pre-production to screening. He covers the entire process of filmmaking – the scripts, casting, filming, direction – and all the details are up on his Ain't It Cool News Website (the "ain't it cool" name is taken from a John Travolta line in the movie *Broken Arrow*).

Knowles describes his approach as akin to: "Two friends walking from a theatre, going to a bar and talking all night. The only difference is that you hear my voice, and not the other person's, which I allow you to write underneath my review and talk back."

Through the medium of the Internet, Knowles gives the comments of thousands of other movie fans an airing. It's a two-way exchange, quite unlike the autocratic voice of most film criticism.

What started as hobby for Knowles has grown into one of the Net's hottest entertainment news destinations. Knowles has an army of sources, over 700 he has said, in the movie industry.

When Knowles first started, he would follow the stories in *Variety* magazine and then investigate them further. After spending hours during the day chasing a story he would put a piece together, but rather than say that he had done all the investigative work himself he would invent fictitious reporters. Colonel Travis, for example, was one of the network of undercover agents Knowles would have his readers believe were passing back secrets from the studios.

Soon, however, fantasy became a reality. People started emailing Knowles offering their services. Over time he built up a real-life network of agents sending back dispatches from the movie front line.

"CNN likes to talk about having 2400 worldwide reporters," Knowles says. "Well I've got about two million readers a day, and they can all be my reporters."

Many of these spies work on film sets. Knowles protects these sources fiercely, knowing that many are low-ranking, movie-production people. If the studios caught them leaking material they would be fired. Regular sources of information Knowles refers to as "St Francis Desales," patron saint of journalists. If the information comes from an actor then it's "St Genusius," the patron saint of actors.

Media mogul

It's hard to believe but this low-brow approach has brought Knowles considerable power within the film industry. He is, he says, a friend of Robert Rodriguez, for example, the independent filmmaker and director of *The Faculty*. He is also in touch with a number of other filmmakers who allow him exclusive previews of their scripts. Such is the power of Harry Knowles' Website that when the film *Jackie Brown* was about to be released, he and his family were taken out on the town in Austin by Quentin Tarantino and his cohorts. Although Harry does not see it as such, it could be viewed as a slick piece of lobbying by Tarantino on behalf of his own film.

Knowles claims to have the power to make or break movies. He created a buzz for *Gods and Monsters*. After watching the movie at the Sundance Film festival he immediately wrote 3000 words on the movie titled "Attention Distributors: Don't Miss This Academy Award-Winning Movie, *Gods and Monsters*." Although Knowles' attempt to drub up a distribution deal for the movie didn't work initially, he plugged the movie on his site, whipping up interest. It eventually picked up a distribution deal, was nominated for several Academy awards and won an Oscar.

Ain't It Cool has an excellent track record of breaking movie stories. Knowles has posted inside information on the *Star Wars* prequel scripts, advanced news of the *Blair Witch Project* and more recently news from the set of the *Lord of the Rings*. To his credit he has even managed to persuade his audience to check out *The General*, by Buster Keaton, from local video stores.

The studios are less delighted about the rise and rise of Harry Knowles. He doesn't go out of his way to endear himself to them. When he met the head of Twentieth Century Fox at the premiere of *Alien: Resurrection*, Knowles told him the movie "sucked." In another possibly less-than-smart move Knowles has made unflattering comments about parts of the anatomy of Harvey and Bob Weinstein, two of the most powerful figures in the film business.

Because Knowles says what he thinks regardless of what the PR people would like him to say, studios have complained about his ability to build negative buzz and kill a film before release. On this, like most subjects, Harry Knowles has a frank opinion: "Bad films deserve to die, and if I can help dig their graves, then fine."

Learn to love the Web

Like Matt Drudge, another anti-establishment figure who understands the influence of the Internet, Knowles believes filmmakers must embrace rather than shun the new technology. He cites secrecy over the *X-Men* film project as an example of how not using the Internet can work against filmmakers. The studios decided to keep a tight lid on the project, whereas the fans wanted the inside story. Unable to get any news, fans became negative about the movie, creating a bad vibe, although the film went on to do well at the box office. At the other end of the scale is *Lord of the Rings*.

Peter Jackson, director of the *Lord of the Rings* (LOTR) trilogy, emailed Knowles offering to answer questions about the forthcoming movie. Over 36 hours, some 14,000 questions poured in from Middle-Earth fans with Jackson answering two lots of 20 of the best. From this interaction between Knowles and Jackson sprung a host of other LOTR Websites. Now there's a community of fans doing the PR for the movie, desperate for its release. The only way this movie is going to bomb is if it's a real stinker and Knowles, who has read the script, assures his viewers it's a winner.

Internet auteur

Another reason for the studios to take the new technology seriously is the hordes of kids, some as young as ten years of age, who are out there shooting digicam movies on their home kit and sending them to Knowles. They've got an iMac and some software and they can cut the whole movie together themselves, effects, sound, the lot. And then

Insight

Talking to the barber

Knowles makes bold predictions for the future of film criticism and, by extension, other forms of criticism. He sees gigantic databases chock-full of viewers' reviews instantly accessible via the Internet. And when you think about it, who would you rather be guided by? A straw poll of other ordinary film lovers, or the opinions of the professional critic?

Knowles recounts the story of Mel Gibson directing reshoots from the film *Payback*. For various reasons he didn't receive a director's credit. It went instead to his barber. As Knowles points out: "You don't go to the publicists and say can you confirm this? No, you go to the barber." And if Internet users care to know about such things in the future they too will be going to the man who shaves the fluff off Hollywood.

they distribute the clips over the Internet. When broadband becomes ubiquitous, what then? It's a whole new business model for the entertainment industry.

So far Knowles has resisted the temptation to cross over to the world of the mainstream critics. He realizes he has to play the game to a certain degree to get his views out to the masses. *Entertainment Weekly* may tout Knowles as one of the hundred most powerful people in the film industry, but Knowles is happy to snipe from the fringes. Not that he balks at taking a few perks that come his way – but not the kind of perks you might imagine. For a true film-buff like Knowles, heaven is the opportunity to play a bit part in a movie like *The Faculty*.

Links

www.aintitcool.com

MARTHA LANE FOX
& BRENT HOBERMAN

– Lastminute.com

astminute.com is one of the European Internet standard bearers. Founded in 1998 by Martha Lane Fox and Brent Hoberman, the company is based in London, England, and offers late deals on a range of time sensitive goods and services – "perishable inventory." The company has established itself as one of the UK's leading online brands. This is largely to the publicity the company and its founders received in the run-up to the company's IPO early in 2000.

When lastminute.com listed on the London stock exchange, it did so in a blaze of media attention. One of the first dot-com listings in the UK that members of the public could sign up for, lastminute.com triggered a share-buying frenzy. Much of the press coverage was down to the company's photogenic co-founder Martha Lane Fox.

Fox, or "Fast Lane Foxy" as she was apparently known at school, is the daughter of an Oxford don. After university she went to work for the management consultancy Spectrum Strategy Consultants. It was there that she met her eventual collaborator and co-founder of lastminute.com, Brent Hoberman. While at Spectrum, Fox was asked to carry out a study for the Department of Trade and Industry on the use of the Internet and the implications of the associated technology. It was through this work that she began to glimpse the possibilities that the Internet offered for business. After Spectrum, Fox moved to the media company Carlton Communications, before leaving to start up lastminute.com with Hoberman.

Unlike many people living in England at the time Hoberman was fully aware of the potential the Internet had to shake up business. He grew up in New York with his father and had already been exposed to the Internet revolution. As a management consultant, Hoberman worked on Internet strategies for companies like the telecoms giant Cable & Wireless. He then left Spectrum to work with several Internet-related companies, including BT LineOne, the Internet service provider where he was business development executive, and QXL, the online auction company. At QXL Hoberman was in from the beginning, gaining experience of working in the fast paced hothouse environment of an Internet start-up. It left him in no doubt that he wanted a piece of the dot-com action. He left QXL after only four months to start his own Internet company. Hoberman's idea was to start an online business specializing in offering goods and services – including flights, holidays, restaurant bookings and hotel rooms – at late notice through its Website. This became lastminute.com.

Hoberman recalls how:

"From day one I loved the idea of buying goods over the Internet. At that point I couldn't find anything on the Web that I wanted to buy, yet I could recognise a compelling business case for Internet transactions. In my eyes, once the Web as a medium had attracted a sufficient mass of people, it was the place to make money."[1]

Fox, however, was less convinced. At first, she admits, she thought the idea a terrible one. Initially she was reluctant to throw in her lot with Hoberman, but he eventually persuaded her that the lastminute concept was a winning idea. The two then pressed ahead at Internet speed. Between March 1998 and the company's launch in October of the same year, Fox and Hoberman wrote the business plan, raised £600,000 venture capital, planned, designed and built the Website and put up a beta site.

Fox's appearance – young, blonde, attractive – was an added asset in generating column inches and TV coverage to drum up interest in the company's listing on the London Stock Exchange (LSE). The company listed at the peak of the dot-com hype and the public stampeded to buy the shares. Unfortunately for lastminute.com and the private investors, it marked the high tide of the speculative wave. Individual shareholders were disgruntled with their paltry share allotment of 35 shares – a result of massive oversubscription. Hiking the offer price, fittingly at the last minute, also stuck in the craw. The NASDAQ caught a cold shortly after and with it the FTSE index on the LSE. In reality, many investors were saved from big losses by their collective greed, which had rationed lastminute.com shares. The company that had been so hyped by the media duly took a drubbing at its hands.

Insight

First mover advantage is fleeting

Lastminute.com had first-mover advantage but ultimately that may not count for much. The kind of marketing spend required to keep the company in the public eye may simply be too much for it to bear. Lastminute.com is rolling out its operation throughout Europe and in other more far-flung destinations such as South Africa and Australia.

Late bookings is a competitive market and, if the big carriers and holiday companies such as BA and Airtours get their online act together, they will make significant inroads into lastminute.com's market.

The spectacular collapse of Boo.com, the online sportswear company, and another European standard bearer, shortly afterwards didn't help. Lastminute.com has a tough task ahead of it to achieve its aim of becoming "the global marketplace for all lastminute services and transactions." At the time of the lastminute.com IPO, its target market – online sales of unsold perishable inventory – was relatively uncrowded. By mid-2000, however, the competition was mounting.

An American company with a distinctly familiar name LastMinuteTravel.com, founded in 1997, was already eyeing the UK and European market. With extensive links with over 500 travel companies and 25 airlines, LastMinuteTravel.com poses a serious threat to lastminute.com. The big bricks and mortar travel companies and the airlines are also beginning to formulate a credible response to the Internet upstart. First Resort, part of the Thomson Travel Group, for example, intends to offer over 80 percent of its package holidays on the Internet.

Another serious threat to lastminute.com's ambitious bid to become the leading global player in its market is the company's burn rate. Although the IPO stocked lastminute.com's coffers with cash, it is spending it quickly. By the end of the third quarter 2000 lastminute.com had an impressive two million subscribers, a 50 percent increase on the previous quarter's figures. But the gross profit and operating costs were less impressive. Lastminute.com spent some £11 million over the three months to June 2000 against gross profits of £950,000. Total transaction value over the same period was up to £9.5 million, but lastminute.com only makes a small percentage on those sales amounting to just over £1 million. These figures indicate that the company was bleeding roughly £10 million every three months. Even with £122 million in the bank, lastminute.com will have to smarten up over the next couple of years or risk serious cash difficulties. Its profits are vulnerable for several reasons: there is always the possibility of its supply of "perishable inventory" drying up; larger bricks and mortar companies may muscle their way into the market; or competition may squeeze lastminute.com's margins. If lastminute.com is to become the first best-of-breed UK online business, the company must use its agility and innovation to stay one step ahead of the competition – before it's too late.

Links

www.lastminute.com

Notes

1.   *.com Magazine*, February 2000.

SCOTT McNEALY

– *Sun Microsystems*

un Microsystems is the networking giant that introduced the cross-platform Java technology. The company is one of Silicon Valley's legendary success stories. Founded in 1982, it has grown from a company with four employees to one employing 35,000 people, and generating annual revenues of over $15 billion today. It is a company driven by a vision: "The network is the computer." The vision has more relevance in today's world of Internet e-commerce than ever.

"Sun's vision continues to be widely accepted and resonates with bricksters, clicksters, service providers and network equipment providers," Scott McNealy, Sun's CEO and co-founder proclaimed early in 2000.

McNealy (born 1954), like his adversary Bill Gates, attended a top private school. He excelled at sports, but still knuckled down enough to get a perfect 800 score in his SAT college tests and a place at Harvard. He arrived intending to be a doctor, but left as an economics graduate. While at Harvard he pursued his interests in sports demonstrating considerable prowess at golf – he captained the Harvard golf team. McNealy was actually at Harvard at the same time as Bill Gates, who famously dropped out, although McNealy does not recall crossing paths. Given McNealy's avowed interests in beer and sports, this is not surprising.

After Harvard, McNealy embarked on a career in manufacturing, working in Illinois at a tractor body-panel factory. But agricultural machinery was not for him. When Stanford University Business School finally accepted McNealy, at the third attempt, he headed off to the West Coast.

Despite being at the heart of the computer revolution, McNealy persisted in his interest in manufacturing. When the call came to join a tech start-up, it was from Stanford colleague Vinod Khosla, now a partner at VC firm Kleiner Perkins Caulfield & Byers. McNealy was working in Silicon Valley at Onyx, a hardware company, as manufacturing manager. Khosla and some friends at Stanford had set up a network system at Stanford – the Stanford University Network – SUN. Khosla was looking for a manufacturing guy – McNealy was the man for the job, and joined as VP for manufacturing and operations. The year was 1982. By 1984 SUN Microsystems had already made its mark, tying up a three-year $40 million deal to supply Sun-2 workstations to Computervision.

Within the company, however, there was friction about who could best lead the company through the next phase of expansion and consolidation. It seemed that Khosla, then CEO, while perfect for driving the company through the start-up, had difficulties dealing with the more mundane staff communication role, and that this might hinder the company's progress. McNealy was placed in a difficult position, he was Khosla's friend and had joined Sun only because Khosla had invited him. McNealy had divided loyalties. Eventually, however, the company's other two founders, Bill Joy and Andy Bechtolsheim, together with McNealy persuaded Khosla to leave. Khosla went on to pursue a very successful career as a venture capitalist.

McNealy was installed as CEO. His appointment was an inspired decision. McNealy possessed the qualities needed to drive the company through a period of rapid growth. The company went public in 1986, had annual sales of $1 billion by 1988 and over $3 billion by 1992.

Early on, McNealy realized that the main cloud on Sun's horizon was Microsoft. Gates was pushing the Wintel (Windows operating system & Intel chips) combination on all fronts and it seemed only a matter of time before the Windows NT product started to take big bites of market share from the SUN UNIX platform. To combat Microsoft, McNealy shrewdly embarked on a campaign of antagonism that attracted the attention of the media and created a buzz around Sun.

Setting out his stall with a vision that was diametrically opposed to the one espoused by Gates, McNealy coined the phrase "the network is the computer." It was a vision which proved prescient as Internet use grew. He named his dog Network and made it the company mascot. While the tactics were astute it is doubtful whether they would have been sufficient to fend off Microsoft had it not been for the winning lottery ticket that McNealy was handed by his programmers.

Insight

The email trail

Like many other corporations, Sun has a formal organizational chart. And, like many other companies, it's hierarchical, pyramidal in shape, with delineated reporting lines. That's not how it works in practice, though. The real indicator of the *de facto* organizational structure within Sun is the email trail. Follow the emails and it is possible to trace the concentrations of power within the company. It is just a question of finding out who is getting the critical emails.

This is exactly how Scott McNealy found out about Java. When he kept coming across emails along the lines of 'Java group meeting' he guessed something important was happening within Sun. Something that he ought to become more acquainted with. And he was right. The network may be the computer, but it is also the company.

In 1994, a group of Sun programmers headed up by John Gosling and marshaled by Eric Schmidt pitched their newly discovered computer language at McNealy. It was called Oak and uniquely it could be used across different platforms. Write it once, run it anywhere – so the thinking went. It was ideally suited for use with Internet applications. McNealy got it at once. Here was the big stick to beat Microsoft with. Sun majored in the new language, renamed Java.

The computer community loved it. Kleiner Perkins rounded up a $100 million fund just for Java start-ups. Netscape incorporated it into its Navigator browser and, best of all, Sun licensed it to Microsoft. In truth, there was no choice. For Java to become a ubiquitous product it had to gain share in the Wintel market. Inevitably Microsoft would come up with its own Java-like language but by that time, Sun hoped, Java would be the standard.

McNealy was right. Java, designed to run on any computer, has revolutionized the world of programming. With its strong branding and open standards it has become a universal language. Java came along just in time to realize McNealy's vision of computing as network. With application service providers and peer-to-peer file sharing becoming more common, the Internet is sweeping all before it.

As Sun has grown in stature, so McNealy has been able to bring his vision to a wider audience. He is a renowned speaker, rated by

Forbes ASAP as one of the top 10 speakers in the technology industry; *60 Minutes* dubbed him "one of the most influential businessmen in America." McNealy's enthusiasm for selling Sun systems extends to some high-profile networking. Famously, he challenged Jack Welch, General Electric's celebrated CEO, to a round of golf. McNealy lost, but so impressed Welch that he received a place on the GE board.

McNealy is known to be a strong advocate of competition, believing it to be an essential pre-condition of innovation. "Without choice, there is no competition," says McNealy. "Without competition, there is no innovation. And without innovation, you are left with very little."

With McNealy holding the reins, Sun has blazed a trail of innovation through the technology industry. Growing at an astonishing rate, Sun reached $1 billion in revenue by 1988, the fastest ever for a computer company with a direct sales force. It now competes in the server and storage markets, holding its own against rivals such as HP and EMC. The company's results for the quarter ending June 30, 2000 took Sun past the $5 billion revenue mark for the first time. The company now operates in over 150 countries, employs over 35,000 people and has annual revenues of over $15 billion.

Sun is not resting on its laurels. The company is continually seeking opportunities to leverage its proven expertise in networking. In March 1999, for example, Sun embarked on an interesting joint venture with AOL – iPlanet. The aim of iPlanet is to help companies develop strategies to compete in the Net Economy. In its first year iPlanet helped 1000 dot-com start-ups using Sun's own Internet platform.

Links

www.sun.com

NICHOLAS NEGROPONTE

– *MIT Media Lab*

Nicholas Negroponte started out with a Venn diagram and ended up with the funding for a research laboratory at the Massachusetts Institute of Technology. It was money well spent. The laboratory he founded invented multimedia as it is understood today, and has gone on to produce some of the world's most innovative tech research. As you read this, the future of computing and the Internet is being determined in the MIT Media Laboratory.

A professor, lecturer, author, and pioneering researcher, Negroponte has been elevated to the status of technology guru. Many of his ideas appear to come not from the world of real technology at all but straight from the science fiction genre. The son of a ship owner on New York's Upper East Side, he is a man who despite an élite education has remained in touch with the masses. The work of the MIT Lab has touched the lives of a large percentage of the world's population.

His two best subjects at school were math and art. It was natural to combine them, so Negroponte went to architecture school. He graduated with two degrees: the first in architecture; the second in computer-aided design (CAD). It was CAD and his thesis advisor Steve Coons that got Negroponte fired up about computers. Coons was the man behind the math that made computer graphics possible.

From CAD it was a natural progression for Negroponte to computer graphics and from there to the interface between humans and computers. Negroponte has been present at most of the major milestones of computing since the 1960s. His work was influential on the early development of both the Internet and multimedia. Working at MIT's Architecture Machine Group, which he founded in 1968 with funding from the Office of Naval Research and the Advanced Research Projects Agency, and latterly at the MIT Media Lab, Negroponte has spent a good part of his life working on what he calls "man–machine symbiosis."

A good example of the man–machine symbiosis concept is the "Things that Think" research consortium. The aim of the research is to imbue everyday objects – clothing for example – with intelligence incorporating computing devices. In time, these computing devices may not be microprocessors; Negroponte sees a point in the future where computing will be on a molecular basis. He uses the example of the intelligent doorknob – a doorknob that can think, is conscious and has volition. It's a useful object, more so than the non-intelligent doorknob, because, among other things, it can tell you who's at the door. If this technology comes to pass, (and much of the MIT MediaLabs work does eventually), then it has incredible implications for business. That's why over 150 major corporations like Nike and FedEx, sponsor the research.

Today Negroponte works out of a small room at the Media Lab. It's small because he is rarely there, traveling some 300,000 miles around the world each year. He has no office at the Lab to speak of, deeming it unnecessary. Where does he file his paper? He doesn't use paper if he can help it. Books? Not at the Lab but on the shelves in his house in Greece (he's dyslexic and doesn't read a great deal). Yet, despite his grueling schedule and air-warrior lifestyle, Negroponte is famously contactable via email.

In 1985, when he started to raise the $50 million funding he needed to build the Media Lab, Negroponte would demonstrate his concept with the aid of a Venn diagram. The diagram contained three interconnected rings portraying the overlapping areas of research interest: computers, broadcasting, and publishing. Negroponte labeled them the interactive world, the entertainment world, and the information world.

The idea was to blend broadcasting (the audiovisual world of entertainment) with publishing (the world of information and knowledge) using the interactivity of the computer. To obtain the necessary funding Negroponte was forced to look outside the obvious sources, companies such as IBM and AT&T, because of the possibility of conflict of interest with MIT and its endowments. Instead he turned to publishers, Time Inc., Warner communications and other media companies. It was the publishers that were the original sponsors of the Media Lab construction.

Later MIT had to bow to commercial pressures, and Negroponte turned to the likes of IBM and AT&T for research funding. He admits that the publishers bore the brunt of the original costs. The split between the media companies and the tech companies is more like 50:50 today.

As an architecture student Negroponte had clear ideas of how the Lab should look and function. He drew on Xerox PARC for inspiration, but also Bauhaus, the German Modernist school of art. The Media Lab doesn't just look different; it employs an unusually eclectic range of talents for a tech research lab. These include typographers, photographers and filmmakers as well as the computer whiz-kids, engineers and physicists.

It's this cocktail of competences that makes the Media Lab a unique place. Its first and foremost role is "invention." It invents things. The Lab isn't a social science organization, and doesn't look at the social implications of its research. It does what it does exceptionally well, inventing product technologies and trying them out in the real world through its network of corporate sponsors.

Negroponte talks about the hijacking of ideas. The Media Lab throws out the technology; it's up to the corporation and the external world to appropriate ideas for their particular needs:

> "We are in a business where people 'steal' ideas ... that's a sign of success, that's why I like the word 'hijacking.' The more they can steal and take, the better."

Like all laboratories at MIT, the Media Lab is financially independent. The sponsors pay for the running of the lab and the research. They also pay for the students at the Lab. Students get tuition costs and a full salary. Funding research from external sources, as it does, raises the prospect of losing some independence. Sponsors might be inclined to try to drive the research rather than the other way about. However, with the kind of value sponsors are getting, most are keen not to upset the applecart.

Judging the success of an organization like the Media Lab is problematic. One metric could be the number of patents, another the level of sponsorship finance. But Negroponte likes to point to a third – the satisfaction of the people working at the Lab. Passion, he says, is one of the measurements he prefers to use. Four companies might give four different responses to a particular piece of research the Lab is conducting. But if the level of passion inside the Lab is high, Negroponte is happy.

External criteria are not easy to apply to its work. A lot of the research "loses" its connection with the Lab when it is released into the

Insight

Separating ideas and commercial applications

MIT Media Lab exemplifies the divide between creating great technology and exploiting it commercially. Companies can and do combine the two activities successfully for a time. But eventually, commercial pressures mean that most become mired in their own internal machinations. Better to hand over funding to people whose interest lies in creating the future, and then appropriate the best ideas for commercial exploitation. Inventors are often poor businesspeople; and businesspeople are rarely great inventors.

public domain. It is often the manufacturers who sponsor the research that receive the plaudits. Take Apple's QuickTime movie technology, for example. The movies were developed at the MIT Media Lab in conjunction with Apple. John Scully, Apple's CEO at the time, then took the idea and ran with it at Apple. Ultimately, few people are aware of the Lab's contribution. This is the way Negroponte likes things to be. He believes that the chances of the technology getting into the consumer mainstream are much greater if the organization "owns" the project. He's right, of course.

Ultimately, history can be the only true arbiter of the Lab's success. It's only when the lineage of tomorrow's great ideas is traced back to the Lab that it gets the recognition it deserves. Watch out then for forthcoming MIT Media Lab's treats coming your way. They may not be emblazoned with its name but they won't be that difficult to spot. If it's a smart, neat idea, well executed with a technology and media angle, then it could well have originated there.

Take software agents, for example. Not everyone can afford, or would want a personal shopper. In the future, however, they will be cheap, ubiquitous and non-human. At the MIT Media Lab, Professor Patti Maes is conducting research on intelligent agents – software that provides personalized and active assistance for carrying out tasks. So in the mildly hazy near future, an Internet user will purchase goods, order services, and collect comparative information as an automated process using an intelligent agent. If you want some tickets for a show, off the agent will go, finding the best-priced tickets, paying for them, arranging for their delivery, booking the taxi and the hotel for the overnight stay –

and haggling to get a discount on all. It's not pie in the sky, it's coming to a computer near you soon, courtesy of Nicholas Negroponte and the MIT Lab. And then there's electronic paper ... but that's another story.

Links

www.media.mit.edu

JORMA OLLILA

– *Nokia*

I f Silicon Valley has a new economy blind spot, then it is in the mobile space. Despite the current dominance of US companies in just about every other area, the huge potential that connecting to the Internet via mobile phones offers has so far eluded them. This apparent failure offers Europe's best opportunity to seize the advantage. The high-profile auctions of 3G (third generation) licences in a number of European countries, and the scale of the investments being made by network providers indicate that this is set to become a major battlefield – perhaps the major battlefield – in the next few years.

If, as many predict, Internet users discard their cumbersome, desk- or lap-bound PCs for the convenience and portability of mobile phones, then the landscape of the new economy could shift dramatically. Which company sold the most mobile phones in 1999? Not the US giant Motorola, but Nokia, a Finnish company that used to sell rubber boots.

The rise and rise of Nokia is due in no small part to its CEO Jorma Ollila. Ollila (born 1950) was a member of the first intake at Atlantic College, situated in Wales, in the UK. This unique educational establishment was founded by Kurt Hahn, a German national, who had evolved a distinctive educational philosophy (he also created early Outward Bound courses). The rationale behind the college was to bring together individuals with leadership qualities who would go on to become political or commercial leaders throughout the world. Ollila, aged 17, was recommended for a scholarship by his school headmaster. Ollila followed up Atlantic College by taking an MBA at the London School of Economics and went to work at Citibank. At Citibank Ollila worked on the Nokia account and in 1985 he joined the Finnish company as vice president of international operations. A year later, aged 35, he became CFO.

The Nokia of today started life as three separate companies: the Finnish Cable Works; the Finnish Rubber Works; and the Nokia Forest Products Company. When the three merged in 1967, the new company took its name from the timber mill, which in turn took its name from the Nokia River in southern Finland. The Scandinavian countries gained a head start in wireless telephony when they joined forces to develop the technology researched in Bell Labs in the US. Although the Nordic countries weren't the first with their 1981 cellular system, its extensive coverage resulted in the Nordic technical standards being adopted in many countries. The companies that profited most from this were Ericsson in mobile networks, and Nokia in mobile-phone production.

Despite its head start, Nokia still almost managed to give the market away to Motorola in the 1970s. It was the beginning of a bleak period in the company's history. At the time, Nokia and the then CEO Kari Kairamo had hedged its bets. The company used money from its more traditional businesses to fund tech operations. Nokia bought a computer business from Ericsson, for example, and a German TV company, as well as making mobile phones. And Kairamo underestimated how big the mobile business was going to be. Struggling to cope with the demand, Nokia lost market share to Motorola, which was geared for mass production.

One problem after another beset Nokia. In 1988 Kairamo committed suicide. Then in 1991, the USSR disintegrated, taking one of Nokia's main markets with it. It was an event that affected the entire Finnish economy. Nokia turned to is investors for support – but received little. The company's biggest shareholder even tried to sell its stake in Nokia to rival Ericsson. Ericsson, however, wasn't interested.

It was into this difficult situation that Ollila stepped in 1990, when he was put in charge of the mobile-phone business. His first decision was to hang on to the business rather than sell it. He set about raising morale and reorganizing the mobile-phone unit. He found he had a gift for motivation: he talked directly to the workers on the factory floor telling them of his plans for the business.

By 1992 Ollila was CEO. He rationalized Nokia, ditching the non-core paper, rubber, cable, computers and TV businesses. Needing to raise finance to pursue a telecom-oriented strategy, he looked to America. Nokia was already listed on European stock exchanges, but to raise the company profile, a listing in the US was a must. Ollila's deft handling of the company was enough to persuade some US institutions to participate

---

Insight

Go with the flow

Instead of pursuing its traditional core business to extinction, Ollila has given the Nokia rudder a heave and caught the winds of the new business revolution. In 1992 he came out of a brainstorming meeting with Nokia's new mantra buzzing in his head: "Telecom-oriented, global, focus, value-added." Ollila has spent eight-plus years driving these words down through the once unwieldy, old-fashioned conglomerate, to create today's shiny new corporate star. If the company can persuade Internet users that its vision is the right one, then the future could belong to the flying Finns.

---

in a private placement in 1993, and in 1994 Nokia was listed on the New York Stock Exchange.

Between 1994 and 1999 Nokia's stock price rose by over 2000 percent. Ollila had successfully dragged Nokia back from the precipice. He worked on the brand image. Abandoning a confusing array of mobile-phone brands, he concentrated the product line under the Nokia name.

In 1998, he emerged from a brainstorming meeting with a compelling vision of the future: "Telecom-oriented, global, focus, value-added." While competitors focused on bringing the size of the mobile phone down, Ollila went further. He brought in designers to make the look of the Nokia distinctive and fashionable, and technicians to create revolutionary scrolling text displays to make the phones as user friendly as possible. At the same time Nokia covered its bets by backing the range of technical standards from the European GSM to the Japanese PDS. Nokia's first digital offering in 1993 was meant to sell at least 400,000 units – in fact it sold over 20 million. Nokia's operating profit soared from nil in 1991 to $4 billion in 1999.

Internally Ollila has introduced a flat organizational structure. Things get done in the company through networks of individuals. It's an entrepreneurial, innovative environment within a large corporation. Then there is the Nokia Way. The Nokia Way is a means of tapping into root feeling at the company. Brainstorming at a series of meetings throughout the company is synthesized into a vision statement by the top managers, and this is disseminated back through the organization via a series of presentations. In many companies this might be a purely cosmetic and meaningless exercise. In Nokia it's critical because if an employee notices a project they are working on is missing from the presentation, then it may well be time to find a new project to work on. The Nokia Way keeps the employees plugged in to the company.

Nokia's future prospects look bright. It passed Motorola as the world's No. 1 mobile-phone manufacturer in 1998. The company is exploiting both WAP (wireless application protocol) and Bluetooth technologies. Most commentators agree that WAP is merely the prelude to the real m-commerce revolution. The future is Internet-enabled mobile phones and the servers to deliver the Internet to them – Nokia has developed both.

Under the leadership of Ollila, Nokia is in good shape to see off potential threats from other mobile manufacturers. If the mobile phone becomes a more desirable and ubiquitous object than the PC, Nokia may well be the new IBM, Dell or Microsoft. It is unclear how total revenues will be split between the mobile manufacturers, which are also developers of software, and the large pure-play network operators such as the UK company Vodafone and Japan's NTT DoCoMo. Coming up on the blind side, too, is China Mobile, which is already No. 2 by number of subscribers, (approaching 60 million) and closing in on Vodafone's lead.

For now, Nokia appears to be the right company in the right place at the right time. The threat is more likely to come from a dilution of culture through acquisition. The challenge for Ollila and his future successors will be to hold onto the innovative organizational environment that has made Nokia the world-beater it is.

PIERRE OMIDYAR

– *eBay*

 Website that sells valuable first-edition books, jewelry, beanie babes and grand-master oil paintings – it sounds like the online equivalent of Aladdin's cave, a collector's paradise; and that's exactly what eBay is.

eBay is the dominant player in the online auctions business. It has over 15 million registered users bidding on more than 4 million items. It is that most unusual of beasts, a dot-com business that makes profits. In fact eBay, started by Pierre Omidyar in September 1995, has made money almost from the word go.

Omidyar (born 1967), moved to the US from his native France, at the tender age of six, when his father took up a residency at the Johns Hopkins University Medical Center in Maryland. Like many of his generation of entrepreneurs, Omidyar was interested in computing from an early age – he cut classes to mess around with computers. Still at high school he was hired, at six bucks an hour, to write computer code that would allow the school library to print out catalogue cards.

After high school, Omidyar studied for a Bachelor's degree in Computer Science at Tufts University, Massachusetts. It was at Tufts that he met his future wife, Pamela, who had come from Hawaii to study for a degree in biology. Tufts has since benefited from the success of one of its star pupils to the tune of $40 million.

Spells at Claris as a software developer and General Magic Inc. on the engineering side were followed by Omidyar's first attempt at starting his own business. He founded Ink Development Corp. with three friends, writing programs to allow computers to interpret instructions received by pen rather than keyboard. Later renamed eShop, the Internet shopping element of the start-up was bought by Microsoft in 1996, making Omidyar a very wealthy young man.

A sweet idea

It was at General Magic that Omidyar had a conversation with his then fiancée Pam, now his wife, that led to the founding of eBay. She was an avid collector of Pez dispensers, (those candy brick dispensers with a cartoon character's head that tilts back). Omidyar's idea was to create a Website where collectors could come together to buy, sell and communicate with their fellow enthusiasts. It would be a consumer-to-consumer auction. "What I wanted to do was create a marketplace where everyone had access to the same information," says Omidyar.

eBay started life as a humble homepage hosted by Omidyar's local ISP (internet service provider). The name eBay stands for "electronic Bay Area" – an indication that Omidyar was thinking along local lines when he first set up the Website. Global ambitions came later. But what began as a hobby soon flourished, and by 1996 Omidyar had given up his day job to concentrate efforts on eBay.

"I didn't set out to create a huge business with eBay," said Omidyar in an interview with the *New York Times*, "When it happened, I took advantage of it."

It quickly became evident that the commercial potential for an online auction was tremendous. The Internet was the perfect medium for this type of business model. And, although Omidyar may not have set out to create the commercial giant eBay has become, his motives were certainly tied up with a philosophical desire to use the Internet to create a more efficient market:

> "I'd really given a lot of thought to the way efficient markets are supposed to work and how the financial markets work. What I realized is that individuals – ordinary people like you or me – usually can't participate in the most efficient markets because we don't get access to all the information the professionals do. The stock market is a great example of that. I wanted to create a place on the Web where – since everyone has access to the same medium – I could in theory create an efficient market."[1]

Online auctions offer the best of all worlds. Demand meets supply in cyberspace. After more than a century of fixed-price commerce, online auctions mark a return to more traditional – dynamic – pricing. They mean that market forces can do their thing. Friction is virtually eliminated. The great economist Adam Smith would have been ecstatic.

Further investment followed, notably $6.7 million from a then up-and-coming VC firm called Benchmark Capital for a 22 percent share of the company. (By April 1999 when Benchmark distributed part of its stake to the investors who put up the money, the value had risen to a staggering $5.1 billion – nearly one thousandfold. Its investment in eBay alone made Benchmark one of the most successful VC firms ever.) With hindsight, it was a no-brainer. eBay was profitable as early on as February 1996. From that point it was just a question of marking the milestones as eBay marched inexorably towards an IPO. Three million items sold by the end of 1997; ranked no. 1 e-commerce site on time spent by users in May 1998; completed its 10 millionth auction in May 1998; over one million registered users by August 1998.

The inevitable IPO took place in September 1998. On that day the company's share price rocketed from $18 a share to $53.50 at its highest, $63 million poured into the company's coffers and Pierre Omidyar's hobby made him a paper millionaire ($274.1 million). Back at the office ecstatic eBay staff formed conga lines.

To smooth the transition from a fledgling homepage to publicly quoted company, Omidyar astutely brought in the right people at the right time. His first move was to bring in a partner – Jeff Skoll, a friend and Stanford MBA. Then, in 1997, he recruited a CEO – former Disney marketing executive Meg Whitman was lured away from Hasbro (where she presided over the Mr Potato Head toy line among others) to handle the company's IPO.

Today, eBay is one of the Net's top brands, along with Amazon.com and Yahoo! It ended 1999 with a market value of around $20 billion. The company has expanded to handle some four million auctions a day. Customers can select from over 4000 categories, with 450,000 items going up for sale daily. eBay makes its money from a seller's fee and a commission on the realized price – often these commissions may only total a few dollars but we're talking about a lot of trades here. In the second quarter of 2000, for example, 62.5 million auctions were hosted.

It's not all been plain selling, however. In the run-up to IPO the company was plagued by technical glitches which closed down the Website on a number of occasions. And other online auctioneers are now banging their virtual gavels in competition. The nature of the business proposition means that the barriers to entry are more about

Insight

New business models are by definition new. Omidyar advises would-be entrepreneurs not to carry pre-Internet business baggage with them when thinking up business models. "Things are moving to business models that could not have existed without the Internet. eBay is the first example of that and there are many others. So I would encourage entrepreneurs to focus on this medium, which is almost pervasive, global and instant, and think of something new you could do with that."

He suggests focusing on something he calls "individual empowerment" – collective buying, for example, or using the public's input in the way eOpinions does for example.

user numbers, brand and momentum than technology or complexity of business model. "It's very hard for a new market to draw people away from an existing market," Omidyar has said. "So what we've seen with all our competitors is it's been very difficult for them to get lift off and get started."[2]

It is also a business susceptible to price competition. Yahoo!, Amazon and other major online companies have all jumped on the auction bandwagon but do not have to rely on revenue streams from that particular activity to turn a profit (assuming they do turn a profit).

So far eBay has remained ahead of the competition. It has bought into traditional bricks-and-mortar auctioneers to add to brand value and increase its user base. It has also expanded into Europe, and has a big enough war chest to acquire significant stakes in, or buy outright, online auction operators in Europe where its strongest competitor is QXL. Plus, eBay is also shifting upwards and capturing a share of some of the premium auction action – old-master oil paintings for example. And Omidyar thinks that the single-minded approach to eBay's business gives it a cutting edge in Europe:

"We're solely focused on person-to-person trading. All our competitors have mixed models. It's not clear. Are they really committed to the person-to-person trading community or are they doing retail or selling banner ads? Our singular focus has brought success in the States. I think it will bring us success here too."[3]

Despite commitments to the person-to-person model, however, eBay is exploring other revenue streams. It is venturing into B2B trading, hoping to benefit from the predicted explosion in business e-commerce. Increasing revenue in this area will potentially defray any downturn in the level of consumer-to-consumer auction activity. The eBay Business Exchange service was launched in March 2000. In mid-2000 the company acquired half.com, adding a fixed-price element to its trading platform.

Regardless of the ultimate success or failure of eBay, Omidyar's achievement is significant. By accident or design he was one of the first to demonstrate how the Internet has the power to change the nature of markets, allowing the equivalent of the village market – where producers and consumers deal directly with each other – to exist on a global scale.

Links

www.eBay.com

Notes

1. Interview with *California Computer News*, 1999.
2. *The Guardian Online*, December 1999.
3. *Ibid.*

KEVIN O'CONNOR

– *DoubleClick*

I n 1999, advertisers spent an estimated $4.6 billion on Internet advertising – up from $1.92 billion in 1998.[1] Managing the Internet advertising needs of the world's corporations is a complicated business – but one that DoubleClick, one of the top Internet advertising specialists, appears to have mastered.

When Kevin O'Connor decided he wanted to start an Internet company he already had the experience of four technology start-ups behind him. Rather than rush into it, he spent eight months cooped up in his house with friend Dwight Merriman, racking his brains for the killer idea. Eventually he hit upon a winner. On the Internet it is possible to track and monitor the surfing behavior of users. Why not apply it to a business? The business he chose turned out to be advertising.

Founded in 1996, DoubleClick has grown rapidly from its Silicon Alley, New York, HQ. It now employs more than 1800 employees and delivers services to over 7000 customers worldwide. It is the biggest player in the Web advertising infrastructure business. It's a market niche that could be worth as much as $11.5 billion in annual sales by 2003, according to Jupiter Communications, a research firm based in New York City.

DoubleClick does not conform to the conventional notion of an advertising agency. But then advertising on the Internet is a specialized market. DoubleClick does not create advertising in the traditional sense; instead the revenue comes from two main streams – selling advertising and serving advertising. The first is self-explanatory; the second is more complicated.

The majority of DoubleClick's revenue comes from ad-sales. The company has a network of sites on which it offers space to advertisers. Although individually many of the sites have less pulling power than the well-known Internet portals, banded together they offer any advertiser massive exposure. This collective approach is the secret behind DoubleClick's success in selling Internet advertising. It gives the smaller guys much more clout than they would have on their own.

Then there's ad serving, which provides a second and growing stream of revenues for DoubleClick. In fact, the future of its business appears to lie with ad-serving techniques. When an Internet page is generated in the browser of the user, it will almost definitely not have originated – or have been served – from a single source. The bulk of the page may be provided by one Web server, but the advertising component at least will come from another. And not just any old advertising.

This is where it gets a bit complicated. At the time the page is generated, a decision is made based on various items of information from the user's computer, cookies (hidden messages stored in a text file on the users hard disk), about which ad to serve. In the world of Internet advertising, the Holy Grail is the personalized or targeted ad. Two people view the same Web page at the same time, but are served different advertising fare according to their personal profiles. Disposable income, Website viewing preferences, location, interests; all these and many other factors will influence the advertising that the user sees in their browser. Using its clever proprietary DART (dynamic advertising, reporting, and targeting) technology, DoubleClick or advertisers themselves can use sophisticated profiling criteria to position adverts in front of the most receptive audience. Take a simple example: if a car manufacturer wanted to advertise on the Net, the model of car flashed in front of the target user might be different depending on their disposable income and family circumstances. So an affluent single man might see a sporty little number, while a family man with a similar income might view a more practical people carrier.

Tempting though the prospect of personalized advertising is, it does raise some difficult issues. Not least of these is privacy. It is at this point that the word 'cookies' rears its ugly head.

When a user requests a Web page, he or she may at the same time be sent a message, a cookie, that is stored in a text file on the users hard disk, cookie.txt. The transaction is a hidden one, with the recipient often unaware that the cookie has been delivered. Every time thereafter that the user requests a Web page from the same server the message will pass back to the server. The purpose was originally to make the connection between the server and the client (the user) more efficient. Cookies have, however, been hijacked by the online marketing and advertising world. Companies like DoubleClick realized there was potential to subvert the purpose of the cookie, using it to help deliver personalized advertising.

If a user fills out a form, or gives information about themselves on a Website, the data can be sent to them as a cookie and stored on their own hard drive. Then, when the user visits a Website, that information is retrieved and passed on to the ad server, along with a unique ID number. The ad server matches up the cookie information with the user profile it has, and serves an appropriate ad. So a motorcycle enthusiast and a butterfly collector see different ads even if they visit a site at the same time.

This use of cookies for building user profiles and targeting advertising has already come in for close examination. Privacy is a growing area of concern on the Internet and the Federal Trade Commission in the US has carried out investigations into the use of personal information for commercial purposes.

When DoubleClick announced its plans to merge with Abacus Direct, a mail order company, there was an outcry. Why? Because O'Connor planned to merge DoubleClick's database of user habits acquired via cookies with the catalogue-buying habits of the 80 million consumers who used Abacus mail order. This concern about the stripping away of the user's anonymity is unlikely to go away.

The nine members of the Network Advertising Initiative (NAI), which include DoubleClick, have struck a deal with the FTC, however. It's a deal that suits DoubleClick's business model. Under the terms of the agreement DoubleClick is free to continue monitoring the habits of users, subject to certain conditions. The conditions include: not using personally identifiable information about sexual orientation, social security numbers, and medical or financial data for marketing purposes; allowing consumers to opt out of data collection and have reasonable access to information collected about them; and notifying consumers when cookies are placed on their hard-drives.

The decision is good news for O'Connor, who stood down as CEO in the middle of 2000 to concentrate on the company's strategy in his role as Chairman, particularly as he had previously been forced to back down on the issue of personal profiling. In a company statement a repentant Kevin O'Connor had said: "It is clear from these discussions I made a mistake by planning to merge names with anonymous user activity across Web sites."

In the quarter ending March 31, 2000, DoubleClick, through its worldwide DART platform, delivered an astonishing 125 billion ads – a

Insight

DoubleClick, in common with a number of successful online business models, is a classic example of an Internet solution looking for a business question. The answer has proved a lucrative one, and one that looks set to remain so. Kevin O'Connor's approach illustrates an important lesson: ask not what the business community can do for your Internet application; ask what your Internet application can do for business.

substantial increase on the 77 billion ads in the previous quarter. It also posted increased gross profits of $57.6 million.

If the privacy debate continues to go DoubleClick's way, then the outlook is rosy for the advertising infrastructure company. Broadband and mobile computing pose no threat to the company, because Double-Click is equally capable of serving rich-media ads, WAP-enabled ads (or whatever comes after WAP). Providing the FTC is not forced to legislate over privacy, the only problem for DoubleClick will be when one of its potential competitors, like CMGI, really gets its act together.

Links

www.doubleclick.net

Notes

1. PricewaterhouseCoopers

TONY PERKINS
& CHRIS ALDEN

– Red Herring *Magazine*

Today, many regard *Red Herring* (the *Herring* as it is affectionately known) as the bible for the new economy investor. The "who's investing in what" magazine began life in a garage and is now an essential read for anyone interested in the power brokers driving the business revolution. When the magazine started chasing stories in Silicon Valley, the secretaries of the great and the good would answer the phone with "Red what?" Word spread of a new seafood restaurant in town. The jokes soon stopped, however, and the magazine began to fly out the door. Now staff at the *Herring* don't ring the money men – the money men ring them.

Tony Perkins, *Red Herring*'s co-founder and driving force, grew up in Silicon Valley. While working at the start-up Silicon Valley Bank in the late 1980s he realized there was a gap in the market for a magazine covering all the small private companies that were springing up in the Valley. So in 1989 Perkins founded *Upside* magazine. It was a magazine with a slightly irreverent tone that examined the tech industry from a people angle. It was a unique approach at the time. Advertisers were more easily persuaded to run advertising in magazines that were product-driven. Perkins set about converting them, explaining that the readership was a prime target audience for them.

His ambitions grew. There was an opportunity for another type of magazine, he thought. This magazine would eavesdrop on the financiers in the Valley, following the money trail to find out who was investing in which tech companies and why. It would be an inside view of the investment and finance industry. To start the new title, Perkins needed help. He was put in touch with Chris Alden, a young history graduate and son of a Silicon Valley entrepreneur. Alden had no journalistic experience at all but lots of enthusiasm and not a little talent. The two hit it off immediately. Alden also recommended a friend of his – Zack Herlick – and said he knew where they could set up office. He also volunteered his computer for service. They had a magazine.

Red Herring takes its name from Wall Street parlance. In the 1920s, American investment bankers called preliminary investment prospectuses – red herrings. This was to warn investors that the documents were not finalized. The prospectuses were bound in red covers. The name fitted the new magazine's ambitious intent. Today, *Red Herring* covers the hi-finance of hi-tech but its origins were avowedly low finance and low tech. Conceptually, the *Herring* was always intended to be a bigger and grander magazine than *Upside*. But Perkins wanted to produce it on a shoestring budget. Most magazines require a large initial investment. Launch money often runs into millions of dollars. They also generally require experienced staff, editors, writers, a sales team, and a survival fund to keep the magazine going until it can build a readership and the advertising revenue comes in. Not the *Herring* though. As Chris Alden wrote in the June 1998 edition of the magazine:

> "We raised zero in financing and made zero investment in our product – that is to say, we did not go into debt. In the *Herring's* first three years, we didn't have a single employee with any prior experience in publishing. During our first three years, we didn't send out a single piece of direct mail or build a structured sales department or hire a single copy editor. And we left the design of the magazine in the hands of someone (me, in fact) who had neither experience nor talent for the job (but did have the biggest computer)."

Jonathan Burke, the magazine's editor from 1993 to 1997, explains that there were no attempts to impress new hires:

> "Even with my expectations low, my introductory visit to the *Red Herring* was inauspicious. The interview took place in a converted garage equipped with a single Mac, a telephone, and a filing cabinet. One of the three founders was on a cruise; another was working out of a café. There were no graphic artists or writers on staff; most of the articles were contributed by bankers and sales managers."[1]

In spite of, or perhaps because of, this attitude and atmosphere, *Red Herring* thrived. Perkins had discovered an untapped well. The magazine had no competition at all. Once it had built up a network of contacts and a loyal readership, the *Herring* became almost unassailable. The first issue slithered off the presses in June 1993. It's target readership was obvious from the start. VC Whispers was billed as "the inside scoop" on what VC firms were funding multimedia and why. Heard in the Valley looked at what niche markets investment banks were interested in. And the *Herring* offered its own Top 20 list of "the hottest multimedia companies in America."

The approach may have been somewhat grandiose, but it was well received. The new magazine was a godsend for technology investors. Acting on the information in the *Herring* some became very rich. Perkins' appreciation of the Valley's *de facto* hierarchy of power also put him and his new venture in a powerful position. "As a banker," said Perkins, "I am less interested in coverage of personalities; what I like is keeping up with what the venture capitalists and private companies are doing. That kind of information – who knows what first, and what to know first – is the most powerful currency in Silicon Valley."[2]

Like his logic, Perkins' timing was impeccable. The success of the *Herring* was mirrored by the explosive growth of the Internet. Through a combination of luck and instinct Perkins had started the magazine just in time to ride the Internet wave through the 1990s. And with its network of contacts it was able to flag up the stars of the business revolution before anyone else. Soon the world was waiting expectantly, to see who or what *Red Herring* was tipping as the next billion-dollar e-business or rocketing market sector. At this point Perkins knew it was time to scale up the *Herring* operation and get in some professional management. A manager was hired for each of the departments. The content improved and the circulation went up. But some were nostalgic for the old days, as Jonathan Burke recalls:

> "We had no receptionist, so we took calls from our first sub-
> scribers between telephone interviews with CEOs. There were
> no public-relations cold calls. We could misspell people's
> names, print inside jokes, and run sarcastic replies to readers
> who wrote in with stupid questions. It was clear why so many
> people in America take huge risks to work at startups."[3]

As the Internet continued to expand, so did the *Herring*. In 1996 its Website was launched, as was an events business that offered venues where start-ups could deliver lightning pitches to woo VCs. The magazine also broadened its horizons beyond technology to cover a wider spectrum of cutting-edge companies. In 1997, Chris Alden was appointed president and chief operating officer and Perkins finally raised some

Insight

Breaking the rules

It's common knowledge in the publishing industry that over 60 percent of new magazines fail. Received wisdom also says that starting a magazine requires financial backing, experience, talent, and a lot of luck. Fortunately for the *Herring*, Perkins ignored conventional wisdom. What he had that many publishers lack was a clear understanding of his target readers, their interests and issues, and the fact that no one was meeting them. The magazine started up on a couple of home-owned computers, in someone's house, with meager wages and employees who had little or no journalistic experience, other than Perkins' brief stint on *Upside* magazine. Talent and luck they had in abundance. The magazine is a great success but it might never have been if Perkins hadn't been prepared to break the rules.

money – from Ziff-Davis, the publishing giant. To have reached $10 million in revenues without major financial backing, without going into the red and without failing to pay the staff, is an incredible achievement. But, once again, Perkins realized the need to move on. The magazine had to raise finance to leverage the brand and to stave off potential threats. If there were to be a lasting backlash to the new, get-rich-quick IPO mentality of many start-ups or a loss of investor confidence, *Red Herring* must be able to weather a downturn in revenues.

Perkins stood down as CEO in 1999 and appointed Alden in his place. The magazine continues to thrive. In 1999, the *Herring* contained 1450 ad pages compared with 3091 for the weekly *Industry Standard* and 1267 for the monthly *Business 2.0*. The magazine was also reaching an international audience. In the UK, *Red Herring* outsold *Forbes* and *Fortune*. Between 1997 and 1999 print revenues grew by 270 percent and online by 1700 percent – the Website receives over a million different visitors a month. Throw in 100 percent growth on the events side and it's a very healthy picture. And there are no plans to plateau, Perkins is looking at $80 million for 2000 and the *Herring* is already ahead of target. The aim is world domination. In the words of Perkins:

"Chris and I are committed to making *Red Herring* the ultimate global media brand in the business world, and it's hands-on work. People say, 'Wow, you're doing so well' but I always look up at the mountain we're trying to climb. As long as we're moving and not standing still, we're doing a good job."[4]

Notes

1. *Red Herring*, June 1998.
2. *Independent Online*, June 2000.
3. *Red Herring*, June 1998.
4. *Independent Online*, June 2000.

TOM PERKINS

– *Kleiner Perkins Caulfield & Byers*

I n the pantheon of venture capitalists, the name of Kleiner Perkins Caulfield & Byers has a special place. Based in Menlo Park, California, the VC firm is the equivalent of a top Hollywood film producer. KPCB finances the very best ideas Silicon Valley has to offer, assembling a top-class cast, and basking in the glory of the resulting box-office hits. The firm's ability to pick winners is legendary. The list of companies that have benefited from its investment reads like a *Who's Who* of West Coast tech companies. It includes AOL, Netscape, Sun Microsystems, Compaq, Intuit, and Excite@Home.

By the time Tom Perkins co-founded Kleiner Perkins in 1972, he already had a track record of working in successful high-tech companies. He worked at Hewlett-Packard, at one point as Bill Hewlett's assistant. While still at HP, and with its permission, he used $10,000 of his own money to start a company based on a low-cost laser he had invented. He later merged the company into Spectra-Physics, making a couple of million dollars in the process.

Perkins wisely decided to change career direction and become a venture capitalist. In Silicon Valley at that time, VCs were thin on the ground. There were probably less than ten major VCs in total in the US – some of the biggest names at the time being Tommy Davis and Arthur Rock on the West Coast and Fred Adler in New York. Venture capital had until then been the domain of wealthy individuals. It was time to institutionalize VC.

Together with Eugene Kleiner, who Perkins met through a mutual contact, Perkins co-founded Kleiner Perkins. Its first fund in 1973 was just $8 million – peanuts by today's standards when funds can total in excess of $1 billion. The firm scored two hits from that first fund

– Genentech and Tandem. By 1983 the partnership had added Frank Caulfield and Brook Byers. It never looked back.

So what exactly does KPCB do? John Doerr, a partner at KPCB, explains:

> "We help assemble and then invest in a team of entrepreneurs or scientists. Usually the ventures are startups. Sometimes they're already going – I call those "speedups" (like Intuit, Shiva, or Amazon.com). Occasionally, we'll see a huge opportunity, like two-way paging, or cable modems, and pull together "co-ventures" of entrepreneurs and corporate partners. MTEL/ Destineer and @Home are examples. In the end, we're recruiters who pay you for the right to help build your team. You reward us with shares of stock. We both work like crazy to make the stock valuable."[1]

KPCB doesn't just take a company's equity and run. The firm likes to get involved. This means taking a seat on the board of the companies it invests in and imparting advice – one of the reasons why the firm likes to invest in companies on its doorstep. As William Hearst III, KPCB partner and grandson of the newspaper tycoon William Randolph Hearst said in one interview: "Our focus is still on companies we can reach within half an hour from here. It's rare that we look at companies in New York. Outside the country, hardly ever."

It might seem a narrow view, but when the partners sit on the boards of over ten different companies, it makes sense. KPCB's role is about team building and creating the right environment to grow a great company. It's something partner Vinod Khosla calls "venture-assistance." The partners seem to gain a vicarious entrepreneurial satisfaction from helping their charges. It also ensures their investments are well looked after. The practical focus suits the background of the partners, which is predominately hands-on technical and entrepreneurial rather than purely financial. John Doerr worked at Intel and his own start-up, which he sold for over $100 million. Vinod Khosla was CEO of Sun Microsystems. The partners are entrepreneurs at heart. In fact, in an interview with *Red Herring*, Tom Perkins, the firm's co-founder, said that if he were 30 again, he would be an entrepreneur and not a VC (though not necessarily in the US).

A major part of Kleiner Perkins' success can be attributed to its *keiretsu* approach to investment. *Keiretsu*, a Japanese form of corporate organization with a grouping or "family" of affiliated companies, was adopted by John Doerr to describe the way KPCB has built up a synergistic network of investments.

From building alliances between portfolio companies to moving executives from one company to another, KPCB fosters relationships between the companies it invests in to promote their interests. So, for example, Netscape might sign up to receive services from other KPCB companies – such as search engine capabilities from Excite.

In some ways it looks similar to the old movie-studio system where the movie studio signed up its own exclusive list of stars. Everyone else at the studio profited by association with the stars. Some might argue that this approach could lead to difficulties. What if a company wants to look outside the KPCB portfolio for partnerships and solutions? Might they not feel undue pressure to enter into a deal with another company from the KPCB stable rather than go to an outside company? Also, in a situation where there is a great deal of interdependence, the failure of one company may severely damage other companies in the network. KPCB argues, however, that commercial sense will always prevail over family loyalty.

Whatever its potential pitfalls, the *keiretsu* system is an approach that seems to have worked both for KPCB and the companies it invests in. Investors aren't complaining either. The profits from any particular fund are divided up between the firm's own partners and the limited partners. The limited partners are institutional investors, that put up the bulk of the capital for the fund. When companies in the fund go to IPO or are bought, the resulting share of stock accruing to the participants in the fund is distributed. The partners can then sell the shares if they wish, provided they are not locked in. The VC's cut can be as much as 30 percent – and is it all profit, as the expenses of administering the fund are met by the limited partners who pay an annual management fee.

When the fund finally closes after a pre-determined period, the capital is returned. The investment funds are invariably profitable, even if the companies in the funds suffer reversals post IPO. This is because the fund buys into the company at pre-IPO prices. It is this discount to the eventual launch price that makes such investment funds so attractive.

For the people who would like to participate but are not partners in the firm or limited partners there is the side-fund. The side-fund reflects the main fund's investments. So if the main fund is a big hit, the side-fund will be, too. The average individual's chances of participating in one of the famous KPCB investment side-funds are slim, however. The list of participants reflects the new economy's affluent. It includes

Insight

Ideas are easy; teams are hard

A large part of KPCB's success is down to assembling great teams.
John Doerr is on record as saying the money is the easy part. He uses
Netscape as an example. Jim Clark had enough money from Silicon
Graphics, the company he had founded, to go on to start Netscape
without KPCB's assistance. He came to the firm not for the money so
much as the expertise in team building. John Doerr helped Clark hire
a brilliant team and set Netscape on the road to success. Says Doerr:
"Ideas are easy. Teams win."

the likes of Steve Case (AOL), Jim Barksdale (Netscape), Scott McNealy
(Sun Microsystems) and Andy Grove (Intel). These are rich people
getting richer.

The side-fund is also a way of rewarding people for supporting the
keiretsu of KPCB companies, and making sure that KPCB is high on the
list when successful entrepreneurs move on to their next deal. This is one
reason why KPCB gets to see so many promising start-ups.

Believe it or not, such success also has its drawbacks. KPCB may
be a temple of investment competence and probity, but the wider VC
industry is coming in for criticism. For example, there is increasing
discussion about whether it is possible for VCs to offer the same kind
of service to start-ups they once did. Some say it's a question of greed.
Keen to cash in while the going is good, some VCs, they say, have taken
stakes in far too many companies. How is it possible to give a start-up
the benefit of the VCs experience when the VC sits on the board of 15
different companies? Indeed in the rarified world of Sand Hill Road and
Silicon Valley, the term "drive-by VC" was coined to describe a VC who
stayed at the board meeting just long enough to have a quick cup of
coffee before disappearing without making any valid contribution.

Even stalwarts of the industry like Arthur Rock see significant
differences between the service offered by VCs today and that once
offered. "Just figure it out," says Rock. "If you sit on 17 or 18 boards
and you're looking for new deals, and you're looking for new employees,
how much time do you have for any one company?"

Some VCs look to get out of a company with almost indecent haste.
As Rock says: "These people today get in and out of deals very quickly.

If they stay with a company three or four years, it's considered an awfully long time. I was on the Teledyne board for 33 years. I was on the Intel board for 32 years. That's an awfully different atmosphere."

The fact remains however that start-ups need cash and, despite the VC detractors, firms like KPCB can make the difference between success and failure. They can also provide significant added value for their equity stake. KPCB remains the doyen of the venture capital industry and, as long as it continues to cultivate its incredible network of companies and contacts, it will remain so. The dot-com bubble may burst and a lot of Internet companies may be massively overvalued, but with KPCB able to pick the cream of the start-up crop it's not something that is likely to give the partners too many sleepless nights.

JON POSTEL

f the Net does have a God, he is probably Jon Postel," *The Economist* observed. That's quite an accolade. Yet many people have probably never heard of Postel. For users of the Internet, his achievement is akin to divine intervention. Postel switched Internet navigation from strings of numbers to the natty domain names we all know today.

Imagine a world where instead of a written address the only way to identify a location was a string of numbers. It's a postman's nightmare and a recipe for chaos. But it's still the way the Internet operates behind the scenes. Fortunately for businesses and Internet users, individuals such as Jon Postel took it upon themselves to ensure that the Internet is a user-friendly place by matching those unwieldy numerical Website addresses to the now familiar dot-com addresses.

When Jon Postel died in October 1998 in Los Angeles, at the age of 55, the Internet community mourned the passing of one of its most respected figures. Although Postel's work was widely acknowledged within the Internet industry, by such luminaries as Vint Cerf for example, a friend and colleague of Postel, it was only late in life that the true extent of his influence became known to a wider audience. This was partly due to Postel's desire to remain in the shadows.

"Jon was a very private person," said Cerf, "and didn't seek the limelight at all. He preferred to exercise his stewardship role in a very quiet but competent way." David Farber, who advised Postel on his thesis, agreed: "Being famous never drove Jon. He had tremendous influence, people respected his intellect."

It was his role in the founding of IANA, the Internet naming authority, and his involvement in a long-running debate about how the domain-name industry should be structured that brought Postel

Insight

Power and authority

Jon Postel was a prime example of how title and authority do not necessarily go hand in hand. Despite Postel's lack of title or position within the computer industry, he commanded immense power where the Internet was concerned. His authority came from the enormous trust and respect of his peers and the IT community.

As David Farber said in an interview with news.bbc.co.uk: "He really was the most powerful person on the Net. He came by that power legitimately, as the only person who could command the respect and loyalty of the whole community."

Those who would use the Net for commercial gain should be aware of and respect both Postel's legacy, and the history and ethos of the medium.

somewhat unwillingly to the attention of the world at large. He started his long association with the Internet at UCLA. It was there that he received his BS and MS in engineering followed by a PhD in computer science. It was also while at UCLA that Postel developed an interest in what was eventually to become the Internet. In 1969, at the age of 25, Postel was working on ARPANET – the forerunner of the Internet – and involved in the development of the Network Measurement Center.

Postel's interests encompassed a range of technical fields, all of which impacted on the development of the Internet. These included multimedia conferencing, electronic mail, very large networks and, in particular, computer communication protocols. He had fingers in a lot of pies. He helped establish the Internet Assigned Numbers Authority; edited the Requests for Comment – the Internet's technical standards; and ran the Los Nettos regional network for Los Angeles.

Despite the immense power he wielded within the industry, Postel never sought to profit from his position. Had he wished to, he could have been a very wealthy man. "Jon could have been a millionaire," says Farber. "It just wasn't his bag."

There was something of the sixties about Postel. He wore a flowing gray beard and had a famously casual style – when helping the US Air Force with its computers in the '70s, for example, he had to be asked to don a pair of shoes before boarding a USAF plane. But his attitude to money went deeper. Postel strongly believed in the public good and strove to avoid the Internet falling into commercial hands.

One example of the strength of his beliefs was an incident which saw him seize control, if only temporarily, of the registration of dot-com domain names. The authority to register dot-com domains resided solely with an American company Network Solutions. Network Solutions charge a fee to resellers and the general public for registering domain names. Postel strongly objected to this monopoly, arguing that it was against the public interest. Instead he suggested his own solution to the issuing of domain names and by 1997 had stimulated considerable debate. So much so that the US government became involved. Then in a demonstration of his power within the Internet community, Postel temporarily transferred control from Network Solutions to his own servers, redirecting half of the Internet's directory-information computers.

Decisions on domain naming, he asserted at the time: "... have to be made fairly and with the long-term benefit of the Internet community in mind. I'm not on any power trip." While he may not have sought power it was clear from this incident that he held it. When a researcher at the University of Maryland – which controlled one of the directory-information computers – was questioned by the *Washington Post* he commented: "If Jon asks us to point somewhere else, we'll do it. He's the authority here."

Postel's methods may have been unorthodox but they paid off. Although Network Solutions still registers domain names, it no longer has a monopoly. A number of other companies around the world now have authority to register the prestigious dot-com domain.

Until his premature death, Postel remained a director of IANA (as well as director of the Computer Networks division at the Information Sciences institute (ISI) of the University of Southern California). This is the Internet's main co-ordination, allocation and registration body for addresses and names, and has been since its early days. Throughout his tenure there, Postel continued to expand the organization, developing IANA's role and shielding staff from controversial debate about the management of the Internet to allow them to get on with their work – work which is critical to the Net's stability.

MICHAEL ROBERTSON

– MP3.com

MP3 technology allows music to be downloaded direct from the Internet onto a PC hard-drive. The company MP3.com has moved to take advantage of the possibilities presented, paving the way for the online audio revolution.

CEO Michael Robertson set up MP3.com in November 1997 and the site has quickly become one of the leading music destinations on the Web with an average of over 500,000 unique daily visitors. "MP3" even toppled "sex" as the most searched-for word on the Net – if only temporarily.

MP3.com wasn't Robertson's first start-up. Before founding MP3.com in November 1997, he had started the Z Company. Focusing on the convergence of search technologies and e-commerce, the Z Company developed a number of key products under Robertson's guidance. These included: Filez – the Net's largest and speediest file search engine; and Websitez – the domain name search engine. But the creation of the MPEG compression standards provoked Robertson to start MP3.com.

For the uninitiated, MP3 stands for MPEG audio layer 3. It's an audio compression format that takes sound signals and uses perceptual audio coding and psycho-acoustic compression to strip inaudible and unnecessary information. At around 12 megabytes for a minute of music, a CD or WAV file is a large file, making uploading and downloading over the Net with a standard modem a lengthy process. MP3 by contrast packs a minute of sound into about 1 megabyte, at near CD quality. Suddenly delivering music directly over the Internet becomes a viable prospect, as does copying music – hence all the fuss.

MP3.com is the centerpiece for the exploding MP3 music movement and works with more than 40,000 artists and hundreds of inde-

Insight

Creating a noise

Through a clever marketing campaign, MP3.com created a buzz about the MP3 technology. For online audio to take off, the irritating waits due to long downloading times needed to be overcome. From a quality point of view MP3 may not have deserved the attention it has received – it actually falls some way short of CD quality. However, it was enough to break the barrier of consumer resistance. And, critically, it spurred other programmers to build applications for the technology.

pendent labels to promote and sell their music. Robertson's DAM (Digital Automatic Music) CD program allows artists to market and distribute their music via the Internet while receiving a 50 percent royalty. With the My.MP3.com flagship service users can add, organize and listen to their MP3 music collection via the Web no matter where they are. No more lugging boxes of CDs around. The site contains over 387,000 songs and audio files from more than 62,000 artists. The site pays featured artists a royalty.

MP3.com has its detractors, however. The MP3 file format and its proliferation over the Net has raised concerns among music publishers and the writs have been flying. The Recording Industry Association of America, for example, has sued MP3 over copyright issues. The lawsuits may prove irrelevant. With hindsight MP3.com's greatest impact on online audio may prove to be exposing the possibilities of the MPEG compression format to a mass market. As a result of the interest, a software application called Napster was developed (see "Shawn Fanning and Napster"). The implications of the Napster technology could carry the Internet to a new paradigm. The frenzy whipped up over MP3 helped MP3.com's revenues in the short term. In the long term it could put the company out of business.

In the first quarter of 2000, MP3.com had net revenues of $17.5 million compared with a mere $666,000 for the first quarter of 1999. Despite the revenue growth the company still posted a loss of over $18 million. Revenues may be growing but to survive MP3 requires a business model that doesn't rely too heavily on revenues from music downloads. If peer-to-peer sharing is the future of online audio distribution, and many believe it is, then this presents MP3.com with some problems. With individuals openly copying audio files, the long-term success of MP3.com may well be bound up with the results of the various court actions over music copyright infringement on the Net.

Links

www.mp3.com

ARTHUR ROCK

T here would be no Internet, e-business, information revolution or new economy, as we understand them today were it not for the venture capital industry. And there might be no venture capital industry were it not for Arthur Rock.

Along with Tom Perkins and Eugene Kleiner, Rock was one of the first major VCs on the west coast of America. It was Kleiner who persuaded him to make his first significant investment. At the time, Kleiner was a young researcher working with William Shockley the Nobel-Prize-winning scientist. Kleiner wanted to develop silicon transistors, and Rock invested in Kleiner's idea, which became the pioneering company, Fairchild Semiconductor.

The son of a candy store owner, and a Harvard Business School alumnus, the astute Rock went on to provide early-stage finance for two of the companies that paved the way for the digital revolution: Apple Computer and Intel Corporation. In 1961, when Rock founded the venture capital firm Davis & Rock, the VC market was in its infancy. The only other comparable investors were American Research & Development. In fact VC didn't exist in the professional sense – and it wasn't known as venture capital either, a term widely considered to have been coined by Arthur Rock.

Rock's lucky break came while working at Hayden Stone, an investment banking firm on Wall Street. It was here that he met Kleiner, who happened to be the son of a client of the firm. Kleiner was looking for corporate sponsorship to keep the research team at Shockley's labs together; even if it meant leaving Shockley, with whom the team were finding it increasingly difficult to work.

After discussing Kleiner's letter with a partner at Hayden Stone, Rock and the partner flew out to the West Coast to meet Kleiner and his associates. Kleiner wanted to investigate the possibilities of manufacturing transistors from silicon – if the process worked it would revolutionize the computer industry. Rock and his partner liked what they heard and agreed to raise $1.5 million to finance the development.

They contacted a long list of potential investors, explaining the proposal and soliciting investment, but managed to raise nothing more than a few eyebrows. Eventually, however, Rock contacted Sherman Fairchild, an entrepreneur and inventor. Fairchild thought the idea was a good one and agreed to invest money through one of his companies, Fairchild Camera and Instrument.

The result was the new company Fairchild Semiconductor, the technological gene pool from which much of the new economy evolved.

The Fairchild investment focused both Rock and Hayden Stone's attention on the possibilities of investing in other West Coast companies. Rock found himself travelling to the West Coast investigating other opportunities. Eventually he met up with Tommy Davis, who was working for Kern County Land Company. The company was investing surplus cash in companies, but Davis wanted a free hand. So in 1961 he joined with Rock to form the investment partnership of Rock & Davis. It was a move neither was to regret.

There was little enthusiasm among institutional investors for the first Rock & Davis partnership fund. Instead the money was raised from private individuals. The first fund returned over $70 million to its limited partners – from an investment of roughly $3 million of the fund's capital. Needless to say the investors were a lot keener to participate next time Rock came knocking on the door.

From the beginning Rock & Davis' approach was about more than just investing money. As well as the injection of finance, Rock spent time working closely with the companies funded to enhance their prospects of success. Teledyne, one of the fund's first investments, was a good example. Rock was on the Teledyne board for 33 years.

There was no second fund, however, for Rock & Davis, and in 1970 Rock formed a new partnership, Arthur Rock & Associates. Rock had maintained his friendship with the founders of Fairchild and when Gordon Moore and Bob Noyce, two of the original eight, contacted Rock and said they were interested in raising finance for a new venture, Rock agreed to meet them. Moore and Noyce were disenchanted with life at Fairchild. Rock liked their vision of a semiconductor memory business and raised $2.5 million to invest in the new company, which was eventually to become Intel. Once again it was private individuals who put up the money, including Rock himself who invested $300,000.

Insight

It's the people, stupid

Arthur Rock has been asked what makes a good VC many times during his glittering career. Is it luck – or a good understanding of technology? Neither, he says. For Rock, being a good VC is about the ability to listen, having a diverse range of interests (not just technology) and above all the ability to read and understand people. And it doesn't come overnight. It even takes him a while sometimes to separate the fake entrepreneurs from the genuine ones.

Interestingly the company that became the world's largest producer of microprocessors started with a modest $5.5 million of private funding raised on the strength of a business plan written on one and a half pages. In keeping with his views about the role of investors and the value of his advice, Rock remains on the board of Intel 32 years after the company was founded.

Apart from Fairchild and Intel, Rock is most famous for his association with Apple Computer. When Mike Markkula, ex-VP of Intel, tipped him off about a fledgling computer company called Apple, Rock was not immediately convinced. Whereas Gordon Moore and Bob Noyce came with a reputation in the industry, Steve Jobs and Steve Wozniak, although they already had a growing band of devotees, were unknown quantities. It took a trip to the San Jose Homebrew Computer show to persuade him that Markkula might be onto something. Rock could not get near the Apple stand at the fair because of a crowd desperate to see the mock-up computer Jobs and Wozniak were demonstrating. Even then Rock invested only $57,000. Once again, he assumed his customary position on the board – a position that he had to relinquish years later when Intel and Apple came into direct competition.

In his time as a venture capitalist, Rock has seen big changes in the way VCs do business. He has also seen the astonishing growth of both the industry he helped put on a professional footing and the new business world he helped create. The young engineer Eugene Kleiner, whose letter first set him on the path to becoming a VC, went on to found his own venture capital firm – Kleiner Perkins Caulfield & Byers.

Today VCs move at a pace different from the days when Rock was financing Fairchild, or Intel even. Where Rock would have sat on the boards of four or five companies at the most at any one time, today's VCs sit on the boards of ten to fifteen different companies at a time. Rock used to hold onto his stock for long periods before selling. Many VCs now look to dump stock as soon as they can. Due diligence might once have taken over a month. Now it might take just two days. As Rock observes:

> "It's just a different world. It's an order of magnitude different. The pace of venture capital has changed. You don't get much time to look at the company. Sometimes you have to make up your mind that day."[2]

Notes

1. Interview with *Forbes ASAP*, May 2000.
2. *Ibid.*

LOUIS ROSSETTO

– Wired *Magazine*

L ouis Rossetto founded *Wired* magazine. He made the tech generation fashionable. He brought nerd culture to the attention of the US public and the wider world. Rossetto didn't just tap into the digital *zeitgeist*; he created it. As Michael Wolff observed in the *New York Times*: "There would be no cyberbusiness, no cyberculture without *Wired*."

In the late eighties Rossetto was working in Amsterdam, Holland, running *Electric Word*, a magazine he had founded with his partner Jane Metcalfe. The magazine concentrated on advance technologies that dealt with word-based information – from voice-recognition to word-processing. Rossetto realized that, despite focusing on a particular industry, in order to appeal to as wide an audience as possible it was necessary to find a *lingua franca* that crossed the boundaries of specialism. Couch the content in too technological a way, and a segment of the readership would be lost. This insight inspired Rossetto to focus on people, companies and ideas.

He was still in Amsterdam when these ideas crystallized into a business plan for another magazine. He put together a series of spreadsheets and a publishing model for a magazine with a unique take on technology – *Wired*. So far as Rossetto was concerned, technology was the new rock and roll. In publishing terms, *Wired* was going to be the Beatles, Jimi Hendrix and the Rolling Stones all wrapped up in one.

Rossetto and Metcalfe knew Europe was no place to launch the magazine. They wanted to be where the action was, and that was several thousand miles away, in Silicon Valley. So, in March 1991, the two uprooted themselves and set off for San Francisco. What they took with them was the idea for a publication that would showcase digital culture. Rosetto recalls:

> "The idea was based on the premise that we were entering a new era. And this new era was being created by the convergence of computing, telecommunications and media, and it was something that had been predicted for a good 10–15 years, foreshadowed in the work of Nicholas Negroponte."[1]

The initial response from potential investors, however, was unenthusiastic. They didn't get Rossetto's vision. Today, there are few people on the planet who aren't aware of the *Wired* culture, but back in the early 1990s technology was for techies – and the *Wired* culture didn't exist because Rossetto had yet to invent it. Rossetto remembered someone he'd interviewed while at *Electric Word*; someone enlightened enough to understand what he was trying to do. That person was the MIT guru Nicholas Negroponte. Here, thought Rossetto, was one of the few people sufficiently urbane and up to speed on the technology, to appreciate the idea – someone Rossetto pinpointed as playing a pivotal role in the *Wired* world.

Negroponte had founded the MIT Media Lab. He was also a polymath – his work at the MIT Media Lab granted him an insight into the massive impact that the technologies of the near future would have on society. Negroponte had himself been through the arduous task of raising the funds to build the MIT Media Lab and finance the research there. He was cognizant of the difficulties involved so he may have felt some sympathy towards the plight of Rossetto. Negroponte invested $75,000 of his own money. He later recalled:

> "I asked them, 'How much money do you need?' They gave me a number, and I said, 'Fine.' It was a handshake. I said early in the negotiation that I wanted to protect my investment, so to speak, by helping. If the magazine turned out to be a failure, I'd have only myself in part, to blame."[2]

It was a wise investment. Rossetto was driven by a desire to draw attention to the profound transformation the world was undergoing. Negroponte had been preaching the same gospel for years. Rossetto was about to make getting his message across a whole lot easier. Rossetto explains his goal:

> "Almost every aspect of the way we live today is being changed, and *Wired* was an attempt, or is an attempt to focus on this change and try to make it visible and talk about the effects on us as individuals and on our society."[3]

The first issue of the new magazine was published in San Francisco on January 6, 1993. In it Rossetto spelled out why people should read *Wired*:

> "Because the Digital Revolution is whipping through our lives like a Bengali typhoon – while the mainstream media is still groping for the snooze button. There are a lot of magazines about technology. *Wired* is none of them. *Wired* is about the most powerful people on the planet today – the Digital Generation."[4]

He also quoted at length from a wired icon, Marshall McLuhan (1911–81):

> "The medium, or process, of our time – electric technology – is reshaping and restructuring patterns of social interdependence and every aspect of our personal life. It is forcing us to reconsider and re-evaluate practically every thought, every action, and every institution formerly taken for granted. Everything is changing – you, your family, your neighborhood, your education, your job, your government, your relation to 'the others.' And they're changing dramatically."[5]

When Rossetto was searching for the voice of the magazine, he was influenced by a mix of technologists, futurists and literary writers. Bruce Sterling, Michael Crichton, George Lucas, Howard Rheingold, have all contributed to *Wired*, giving an idea of the magazine's range. Nicholas Negroponte was a regular contributor for many years, writing the often controversial endnote, "Being Digital."

The magazine was a runaway success. Its fast-paced style and trendy graphics encapsulated the essence of the digital revolution within its pages. The first issue, 1.1, was followed by bi-monthly issues until November 1993 when it became monthly. Influenced as he was by McLuhan, Negroponte and the futurist Alvin Toffler, it was always Rossetto's intention to cover the social aspects of technology. And the magazine gained "geek-cred" early on by assuming the role of free-speech advocate when a campaign was mounted against the Clinton–Gore administration's proposals for the Clipper encryption chip.

It wasn't long before Rossetto was planning an online offering. Word of mouth outed the proposal for a Web version of the magazine in 1994. When *HotWired* arrived on the Net in October 1994 it was more of a complementary product – an Internet agitprop for the digital unwashed. *HotWired* was a commercial Website that immersed visitors

Insight

Creating the digital culture

For the world to embrace the Internet, it had to find a place in the social consciousness. Popular culture and the Internet had to converge. Regardless of any debate about Rosseto's management skills there is no question of the contribution that Rossetto and his unruly creation has made to the digital and business revolution.

in the culture of the digital revolution. It wasn't so much a commentator on the revolution as one of its front-line fighters. It can justifiably claim to have invented Web media, as it was the first Website with original content and *Fortune* 500 advertising. In fact it was one of the first Websites to build a business around online advertising and sponsorship revenues, and among the first to recognize the value of community building through chat rooms and forums.

By April 1996, Rossetto's grand design had expanded. As a publicly quoted company, he wanted to push the brand to previously unimagined heights. Whether it was a case of being caught up in the hype, or truly believing the *Wired* brand was strong enough to justify a valuation close to half a billion dollars is not clear. With hindsight it now seems faintly absurd even by the standards of dot-com stock. But it must have been difficult for Rossetto, so passionate about the digital revolution, to maintain perspective seated as he was at the eye of the storm. The price of meteoric success is often a savage backlash. As clouds gathered over *Wired* the critics became more vociferous. "*Wired* may indeed be an interesting read," wrote Christopher Byron in *Upside*, "but as a business proposition, the company is a mess: a money-losing enterprise with a confused business plan and little likelihood of turning profitable for many years, if ever."[6]

Fortune magazine prophetically questioned the value of the business in a July 1996 piece:

"At a proposed offering price of $12 a share, Wired Ventures will have a market capitalization of $495 million, including options. That's real money ... In *Wired*'s case, forget operating cash flow: There is none. *Wired*'s valuation is nearly 20 times its $25 million in revenues ... For all the hype, isn't this still just a magazine company?"

Wired became a victim of its own success. It was almost as ubiquitous as the Internet itself. Book publishing, online publishing, a TV show, a move into Europe, and more. It all added up to soaring costs. By the end of 1996, the company was burning $3 million a month and employed over 350 people – a millstone around its neck. When the UK launch was aborted and the TV show ditched after 4 episodes, *Wired* began to lose some of its luster. Twice an IPO was planned only to be pulled.

Rossetto and Metcalfe conducted a deep cost-cutting exercise reducing staffing to about 150 and trimming the stable of *Wired* brands back from 11 to 4. It was the right move, just a little too late for Rossetto. The denouement came in December 1997 when he stepped down as editor of the magazine he had created, announcing that a search for a new CEO had started.

In 1998, *Wired* magazine, was sold to Conde Nast for around $90 million and the rest of *Wired* empire was plundered by Lycos for some $80 million; a total of roughly $170 million, a far cry from the $495 million valuation touted at the time of the first IPO attempt. In the new Lycos regime there was no role for Rossetto who left, as did Metcalfe. Kevin Kelly, who had been with Rossetto from almost the very beginning, stayed as editor. The *Wired* print magazine continues to preach its message. For Rossetto it was an unfortunate end to a great adventure.

His contribution to the digital revolution should not be underestimated, however. At a time when technology had the status of a minority sport, Rossetto dragged digital culture from obscurity, by the scruff of its neck, and thrust it upon an unsuspecting public. He had the vision to see that the social implications of technology affect all of us – and the desire to want to tell us how.

Notes

1. "The Story of *Wired*," a talk given by Louis Rossetto, Doorsofperception.com.
2. *Wired*, November 1995.
3. "The Story of *Wired*," a talk given by Louis Rossetto, Doorsofperception.com.
4. *Wired*, 1.1, January 1993.
5. Marshal McLuhan, *The Medium is the Message*, 1967.
6. *Upside*, February 1997.

JOHN SEELY-BROWN

– *Xerox PARC*

J ohn Seely-Brown (JSB to those in the know) is the chief scientist of Xerox Corporation and director of its famous Palo Alto Research Center (PARC). Regarded as a seer, and technology guru, his recent work has majored on the transfer of knowledge and ideas within organizations, and is at the heart of his latest book, *The Social Life of Information.*

Despite his reputation as a prophet of the digital future, at PARC Seely-Brown is haunted by the past. The story of how Xerox blew it in the 1970s is part of the mythology of Silicon Valley. The Palo Alto Research Center was set up in 1970 by Xerox Corporation and charged with the task of creating "the architecture of information." Under Bob Taylor, who had come from ARPA, the team at Xerox thrived in the hothouse atmosphere, producing a string of inventions that would change the nature of computing. "The father of the Mac is Xerox; the father of Windows is Xerox," Bill Gates has observed. Sadly for Xerox, the company did not ultimately profit from this research, failing to exploit the commercial possibilities of the work at PARC.

A pick of the PARC innovations include:

- the Alto, the first ever personal computer;
- the first What You See Is What You Get (WYSIWYG) editor;
- the first Graphical User Interface (GUI);
- the first commercial mouse;
- laser printing; and
- the ethernet – the global standard for connecting computers on a local area network.

With this kind of intellectual property Xerox should, by rights, be as big or bigger than Microsoft, Oracle, Sun, Apple and the other computer giants. Instead the people at Xerox fumbled the ball, allowing these companies to grow fat off the PARC produce. Xerox did successfully exploit the laser-printing technology – but its impact was insignificant compared with the PC or the GUI.

Despite the technology gems that emerged from Xerox PARC in the 1970s, its parent the Xerox Corporation passed up on the chance to spearhead the PC revolution. Seely-Brown has worked hard to prevent history repeating itself. The research conducted at PARC under his leadership could make as significant an impact on the e-business world as that under his predecessor Bob Taylor had on the world of personal and network computing.

The world has moved on since the men at the PARC rashly demonstrated their wonderful new GUI to a young man touring the center in 1979. His name was Steve Jobs and he immediately saw what would make Apple Computer famous. Since then, the computer revolution has morphed into the Internet revolution. This time round Seely-Brown and PARC are looking to make their own splash. Says Seely-Brown:

> "At Xerox PARC our job is to hit home runs. We do not do incremental research. We do not tinker with improving products."[1]

He is interested in business models as well. Under Seely-Brown, the PARC's new business strategy mirrors a phenomenon of the moment, the incubator. When PARC produces an innovative technology or model, the systems are in place to build a business around the idea if at all possible. Seed funding is obtained, a business plan put together, the market evaluated and a new company incorporated. PARC retains equity, and recognizing the importance of talent retention and employee motivation, gives the workforce equity, hopefully enough to prevent defections. There is also a more commercial attitude towards intellectual property issues. A separate division deals with patents and licensing.

Research at PARC goes beyond the boundaries of mere product research. With a BS in mathematics and physics from Brown University, and an MS in mathematics and a PhD in computer and communication sciences from the University of Michigan, Seely-Brown is quite able to talk tech with the best of them. He also has a keen interest in the cognitive sciences. JSB has expanded the horizons of the center to include organizational learning, ethnographies of the workplace and complex adaptive systems alongside the more conventional product

Insight

Reintermediating the channel

Most commentators on the Internet went through a 'disintermediation' phase. Commonly this would involve banging on about efficient markets, cutting the middleman out, channel management and the like. The conclusion would invariably run along the lines of: "the middleman is dead, long live the consumer." The commentators have long since repented, or at least modified their opinions. After all try buying shares without going through a broker, or jam from the jam manufacturers. Consumers don't necessarily want to bury the broker.

Commentators might have been well advised to listen to Seely-Brown's take on disintermediation; what he calls 'reintermediation'. The Internet didn't give us books from the publisher, it gave us Amazon.com, and as Seely-Brown points out, Amazon have reinvented book distribution. They have disintermediated the bookstore, the link between the consumer and wholesaler, and 'reintermediated' through the community; that is the reader-recommendation systems and other associated book communities.

Look for a reinvention of channels to market, not necessarily removal of the components.

research such as the development of electronic paper, for example. Seely-Brown himself is particularly interested in ubiquitous computing and human learning. This goes beyond looking at the individual technologies that affect business to looking at the corporation as a whole in a holistic fashion. He believes that: "The most important invention that will come out of the corporate research lab in the future will be the corporation itself."[2]

When Seely-Brown talks about creating the right environment at PARC to foster cutting-edge research, he uses the phrase "a knowledge ecology." By this he means an interactive environment where people are encouraged to stray out of their area of expertise into, what is for them, uncharted territory. It demands a positive view of risk-taking and the physical space to encourage intellectual intermingling. Within this environment Seely-Brown seeks to foster a well-established group of individuals who are comfortable, and familiar enough with each other, to allow the free flow of ideas. He calls this type of group a "community of practice."

Regardless of whether PARC manages to reignite Xerox Corporation, it is this kind of work on the mechanisms behind innovation that is likely to prove a long-lasting testimony to Seely-Brown's tenure. He has also published countless articles and papers on life in the Information Age. He has authored and co-authored over 95 papers in scientific journals and was awarded the *Harvard Business Review*'s 1991 McKinsey Award for his article, "Research that Reinvents the Corporation." In 1998 he was awarded the Industrial Research Institute Medal for outstanding accomplishments in technological innovation and in 1999 the Holland Award in recognition of the best paper published in *Research Technology Management*.

In his latest book *The Social Life of Information* co-authored with Paul Duguid (HBS Press, 2000), Seely-Brown explores many of the claims that have been made for the Information Age. He looks at what has happened to the virtual firm. The assumption was that the Internet would create a level playing field where small companies could compete with larger ones – so why the trend for mega-mergers? He also considers the notion of a global village, asking why in the digital world where distance and location is supposed to be irrelevant, the talent still heads out to Silicon Valley.

If anyone has the answers to how technological change will shape the way corporations conduct business in the future it could well be Seely-Brown and the team at PARC.

Notes

1. An Interview with John Seely-Brown, *Strategy & Business Online*, Booz·Allen & Hamilton, 1999.
2. *Harvard Business Review*, 1999.

WILLIAM SHOCKLEY

– *Fairchild Semiconductors*

I n the new economy, the need to attract and keep the best and brightest employees has become more vital than ever. In truth, though, had it not been for a famous staff retention failure in the 1950s there might have been no e-business revolution. The story of "the Traitorous Eight" is a defining event from the etiology of the information revolution.

William Shockley was a British-born research scientist who worked at the Bell Labs during the post-war period developing the transistor. In 1947, Shockley was recognized as the co-inventor of the transistor, and in 1956 he was awarded a Nobel Prize for his efforts. In 1955, he left the Bell Labs to found his own company Shockley Semiconductor Laboratory, situated in Palo Alto, Santa Clara County, California. His academic reputation attracted some of the finest minds in electronics to his company. These included: Robert Noyce and Gordon Moore (of Moore's Law fame), who went on to co-found Intel; Julius Blank, Victor Grinich; Eugene Kleiner; Jean Hoerni; Jay Last; and Sheldon Roberts.

Shockley was blessed with a brilliant mind. He was described by Bob Noyce as a "marvelous intuitive problem solver." And by Gordon Moore as having "phenomenal physical intuition." But unfortunately for Shockley his management skills fell far short of his academic brilliance. His personality is best described as somewhat erratic. Moore describes him rather kindly as "an unusual fellow" and "extremely competitive and controversial." When on one occasion he was asked whether his wife liked life in California, he replied: "She didn't like it, so I had to get a new wife."

His eccentric approach extended beyond social encounters to the management of his brilliant team of research scientists. "He had some peculiar ideas on how to motivate people," one colleague observed. "This was the first time he really took on a major management responsibility. At Bell Laboratories, he had run a relatively small research group. But here he was trying to set up a new enterprise and some of his ideas, frankly, didn't work out too well for the success of that enterprise."[1] Robert Noyce found Shockley as "hard as hell to work with"; he "didn't have trust and faith in other individuals."

Typical of Shockley's methods of motivation is an incident when he asked some of his younger employees what he could do to help enthuse them. Several expressed a wish to publish research papers. So Shockley went home, wrote a paper and returned the next day offering to let them publish the paper in their own names. Another famous story of mismanagement at the company relates to the introduction of a lie-detector machine. When a woman cut her hand on a small pin stuck in a door, Shockley was convinced that someone had put the pin there deliberately. Determined to out the malicious prankster, Shockley proposed subjecting his staff to a polygraph test. Staff, however, had other ideas and rebelled, forcing Shockley to backtrack.

In yet another example of poor management Shockley instituted a secret "project within a project" at the company. Although there were only 50 or so people working at Shockley Labs, when some of the group were employed to work on Shockley's new idea – which according to Shockley had the potential to rival that of the transistor– they were not allowed to discuss the project with other colleagues.

It wasn't long before sparks of discontent at Shockley's management style were fanned into the flames of mutiny. The situation deteriorated when Shockley seemed to be heading in a different research direction from his colleagues. Gordon Moore and others became involved in secret talks with Arnold Beckman, who had financed the company. The hope was that Beckman might persuade Shockley to relinquish day-to-day management. They hoped to persuade him to take up a professorship at Stanford or somewhere similar and continue to act as a consultant at the company. After some promising preliminary discussions, however, Beckman got cold feet and backed Shockley.

Moore and the other disaffected staff felt they had been placed in an impossible situation. Shockley was unlikely to look favorably on a bunch of his employees lobbying behind his back for his removal as manager. Eugene Kleiner, one of the group who had been involved in the discussions with Beckman, wrote a letter to a friend of his father who worked at Hayden Stone, a firm of investment bankers. The gist of the letter was that there was a group of scientists at Shockley Semiconductors who wanted to move *en masse* to another company.

Insight

If ever there was a case study of how not to retain talent, this is it. Talented staff who possess special skills are particularly difficult to manage. In the Internet age, people with key skills are only too aware of their market value – it's posted all over the Net. A few clicks of the mouse and anyone can find out what kind of salary their talents might command. Another issue is that talented people often have a low boredom threshold. Fail to challenge them intellectually, or to inspire them with an organizational purpose and, in an era of employee mobility, they will walk out the door.

Shockley was one of the first to fall victim to this new trend of tech mercenaries. It was a tough lesson to learn. His management techniques divided his workforce, disenfranchised them and created an atmosphere of paranoia. In an earlier era the scientists at Shockley's labs would probably have stuck it out. But on the crest of the entrepreneurial wave that was about to cascade across California, they upped and left. Fortunately many entrepreneurs learnt a lesson from the Shockley Labs tale: engage the minds of the best talent – or lose them.

Arthur Rock, a Harvard MBA at the firm, read the letter and persuaded one of the partners Bud Coyle to fly out to California and meet the group. Rock and Coyle suggested the seven should leave to start up their own company. Rock drew up a list of potential investors and, after a lot of disappointment, eventually secured funding from inventor and entrepreneur Sherman Fairchild. Adding Bob Noyce to their number, the group started Fairchild Semiconductors in 1957.

Fairchild Semiconductors went on to revolutionize the world of computing through its work on the silicon transistor. Equally importantly, it threw off a slew of talent who went on to start up some of the best-known companies in Silicon Valley. Intel (Bob Noyce and Gordon Moore), Advanced Micro Devices (Jerry Sanders), and National Semiconductor (Charlie Sporck) were all spin-offs from Fairchild. The defection of the so-called "Traitorous Eight" also played a major part in spawning the professional venture capital industry as a by-product. Arthur Rock and Eugene Kleiner became two of the most respected VCs.

Shockley had inadvertently lain the cornerstone of Silicon Valley. First he had brought together a group of the best scientists in the field of electronics, many of whom might not have otherwise remained in the San Francisco area. Secondly he had created the conditions necessary to provoke his brilliant employees to leave and start up on their own. If Shockley Semiconductor Laboratory had been better managed, who knows what might have happened. Although unlikely, the US might have ended up at the rear of the high-speed computing industry rather than in the engine room. Certainly if Shockley had listened more to his *protégés*, Shockley Labs could have been the semiconductor giant Intel has since become.

As it was, Shockley sold his company to Cevite in 1960: it was subsequently resold to ITT in 1965 and closed in 1968. The departure of 'the Traitorous Eight' affected Shockley for the rest of his life. Some of the eight he never spoke to again. In 1963, Shockley abandoned electronics research devoting his working life instead to the study of human intelligence. He formulated a number of distinctly racist theories about the relationship between intelligence and ethnicity. Many of his former colleagues dissociated themselves from Shockley and his views. Right up to his death at the age of 79 in 1989, Shockley regarded his research into genetics as more important than his earlier accomplishments in the field of electronics. In this he singularly failed to understand that in many ways he was the father of the semiconductor industry – an industry worth in excess of $130 billion.

MASAYOSHI SON

– *Softbank*

Many teenagers have pictures up on their bedroom walls; some take them to school. The latest pop stars, sports personalities, pets, family and friends; these are all candidates for the remaining space on the school locker door. But not Masayoshi Son. When he was 19, he saw a picture in a magazine that captivated him. In fact it changed his life. Reverently cutting the picture out, he placed it in clear plastic wrapper and put it in his bag, carrying it wherever he went. He even slept with it. The picture that captured the heart and imagination of this economics undergraduate was of a microchip.

Son is Japan's Internet emperor. While others stood on the sidelines arguing for caution, Son, founder president and CEO of Softbank Corp, has pursued an aggressive investment strategy, building stakes in companies like Yahoo!, buy.com, E*Trade, E-LOAN and Webvan. He calls it his "cluster strategy." Today he presides over the largest collection of Internet companies controlled by any single company.

Because of the nature of Softbank's business – investing in the Internet – the company's share price is inextricably bound up with the fortunes of the NASDAQ. This creates a roller-coaster ride for the shareholders. When the market plunged early in 2000, Son saw his own personal wealth fall by over $40 million.

Yet Softbank continues to invest. Its venture capital arm Softbank Venture Capital, based in Mountain View, California, continues to inject hundreds of millions of dollars into the Internet industry. This is big money – $1.5 billion investment funds, half of which comes from the company's own coffers. Son is talking of investing $30 billion in new ventures over a five-year period, growing the portfolio of companies under the Softbank banner from 250 to 2000. It's a bold strategy by any standards.

Son is an ethnic Korean. He grew up on Kyushu where his father ran a small business. A bright child, Son was accepted at a prestigious high school in Fukuoka. At an early age he showed a keen interest in business. Spurning film, music or sports stars as role models, one of his early heroes was Den Fujita, who masterminded the success of McDonalds in Japan. Son called Fujita's office and arranged a meeting with him in Tokyo. It was a meeting that reinforced the youngster's interest in the US. In 1973, Son headed to California to study English. As he recalls:

> "I came to the States from Japan when I was 16, and at that time I made up my mind that some day I would start my own business, although I didn't know what kind of business I would start. As a young boy in Japan I wanted to be one of four things: an artist – a painter, a grammar school teacher, a politician, or a businessman. As I grew up I realized that being a businessman, starting my own company, was probably most suitable to my own character."[1]

In California, he transferred to Berkeley high school and from there to the University of California where he majored in economics while pursuing an interest in computers on the side. It turned out to be a profitable interest. To further his business ambitions he determined to raise money by inventing something – anything. Coming up with an idea a day, the anything turned out to be a personal organizer. He offered it to a number of companies and several showed an interest, particularly the Japanese companies. In the end, the electronics giant Sharp bought the patent for what was to become, the Sharp Wizard – handing over the princely sum of $1 million. Son's fund-raising activities were off to a good start.

His next venture was importing cheap video games machines from Japan – Space Invaders. At the time, the craze had yet to catch on in the US. The move into video games was partly driven by the need to smooth the cash flow in his company – he was sinking R&D money into developing small computer devices. He also sensed a major market opportunity. It took just six months to import 300 machines and make Son's company the top games vendor in the area. Shortly afterwards, he returned to Japan fulfilling a promise to his mother. The video game business he gave to a fellow Berkeley student – the first person he had hired – on the condition that when the company turned in a profit, Son

Insight

The client–server organization

After completing his stint at Berkeley, Son returned to Japan just as he had promised his mother he would. He left behind a business. In fact he gave his computer-games business to his colleague and friend. Being forced to relinquish the reins of a business was a good learning experience. A lot of Son's success at Softbank is down to his innovative management style. He is at the hub of the Softbank organization, and from there he hands out responsibility for the day-to-day running of the portfolio of companies to their respective CEOs. It requires a good deal of trust, but it leaves Son free to do the strategic thinking that had made him so successful.

would get paid. By accident he had stumbled on the business model that would eventually lead to the *kereitsu* of Softbank's Internet empire.

After returning to Japan, Son started a software distribution company – Softbank – in 1981. He was 23. To fund it he used $80,000 from his Sharp $1 million. He also raised money from the Japanese Bank Dai-Ichi Kangyo, a reflection of his considerable powers of persuasion. Japan in the early 1980s was not an entrepreneur-friendly environment. It's easy to understand potential investors balking at funding the grand visions of a young man who at the time had only a short track record of success.

To make things more difficult, shortly after Softbank was founded, he became critically ill with hepatitis – an illness that was dog him for several years. By 1994, however, things were looking up. Softbank went public, and Son had shaken off his illness and discovered the Internet. There was no Damascene conversion; the Internet was a revelation. In the same way that he had innately understood how the microchip would change the business world, he once again recognized a technology that would have a profound impact on people's lives. In the mid-1990s the Internet was still in its infancy with e-commerce revenues below $500 million (they are well over $100 billion now).

Son put his money where his vision was, and accumulated stakes in nascent Internet companies. Luck or insight led him to invest over $100 million for a 30 percent stake in an Internet company called Yahoo! There was already a buzz about Yahoo!, hence the valuation.

The investment paid off handsomely when Yahoo! went to the market in 1996. At that time Softbank was saddled with companies that Son had added to his collection over the years. These included companies such as Ziff-Davis, which he'd acquired when pursuing a media-conglomerate building strategy.

But once Son had caught Internet fever, he decided to rationalize Softbank's portfolio of businesses. The company would concentrate its efforts on investing in Internet businesses. Son set up Softbank Technology as the venture capital arm of Softbank's operations. Ex-Cisco and Intel man Gary Rieschel headed the outfit, and ran the limited partnership from San José, California. For its first fund the firm raised $170 million from Japan with $60 million from its parent company Softbank.

While continuing to invest in start-ups and other promising US Internet companies, towards the end of 1999 Son shifted his attention and his person to Japan. He adopted a different approach for Softbank's assault on the Japanese market. In Japan, Son is creating a vertical Internet giant by taking majority stakes in companies and building others from the ground up. In Japan e-business took some time to gather momentum. So when Son relocated his operations, there was still a good opportunity to claim a substantial slice of the Japanese Internet industry. His strategy is to make the Softbank network of companies unavoidable in Japanese cyberspace. The key to Son's plan is the acquisition of a majority stake in Yahoo! Japan. Yahoo! Japan is one of the country's most popular Internet destinations. But just as important is the access it provides to other Websites controlled by Softbank.

Softbank, for example, has controlling stakes in the Japanese versions of NASDAQ, E*Trade, GeoCities, Broadcast.com, CarPoint and E-shopping Toys. Using Yahoo! as the funnel, Son can channel surfers to Softbank's online businesses. It's a clever strategy and Son has stolen a march on his rivals.

Critics say it is a different game, with different rules to the one Son played in the US. They say it's a game that requires skilful management of the companies under the Softbank umbrella – something the impulsive Son may not be ideally suited to. And while Son has shown a knack for investing in companies for the cyber future, until now he has been investing in the management skills of others. The critics may be missing the point. The key to the success of Softbank lies in the vision of its founder. Son has always allowed the individual companies within the Softbank group a high degree of autonomy. The viability and progress of ventures requires monitoring, but the hands-on management skills reside in the people running the portfolio companies

Investors in Softbank are backing Son's vision of the future – an Internet-dependent society. And they are backing his judgment – picking the best companies to succeed in his vision of the future.

"For the next ten years, we do nothing but Internet," he has said. "That's where the whole society is going to have a big revolution."[2]

It's a marathon rather than a sprint. Investors may get twitchy when the company posts losses as it did at the beginning of 2000 (a pre-tax loss of $525 million). But with some $2 billion already invested and another $28 billion to come, if Son gets it right the investors will be very rich indeed. And Son will truly be emperor of the Internet.

Links

www.softbank.com

Notes

1. Interview, *Red Herring*, 1997.
2. *Ibid.*

DON TAPSCOTT

A mid the headline-grabbing activities of dot-coms, the rise of a new generation of management thinkers is easily overlooked. After all, who needs theorists when a revolution is happening? But every revolution needs a theoretical underpinning. The new generation of gurus includes people like Chris Meyer, co-author of *Blur,* Kevin Kelly of *Wired* (the magazine which sounded the clarion call for the new economy), and the Canadian, Don Tapscott. Tapscott is author of *The Digital Economy, Growing Up Digital* and, newly published, *Digital Capital.* For better or worse, he can lay claim to bringing the world much of the language of the New Economy – he coined "prosumers" as a combination of production and consumers; was the first to use the terms "the digital economy" and "paradigm shift"; gave birth to the "Net generation" and was the originator of "e-business communities." His growing influence clearly outweighs his commitment to linguistic purity.

In his most recent book *Digital Capital,* Tapscott celebrates the arrival of "a new business form" which is made up of "fluid congregations of businesses – sometimes highly structured, sometimes amorphous – that come together on the Internet to create value for customers and wealth for their shareholders." This new organizational form is labelled by Tapscott and his co-authors David Ticoll and Alex Lowy a "business web" or "b-web." Business webs, as described by the trio, are a "universal business platform" made up of "a distinct system of suppliers, distributors, commerce services providers, infrastructure providers and customers."

Tapscott and his co-authors bridle at any notion that b-webs are simply the latest reincarnation of the conventional industrial conglomerate. "Business webs are as different from conglomerates as they are from traditional craft shops," says David Ticoll. "Because of the Internet, the cost of communications and transactions between companies and people outside is dropping to create fundamentally new business models. Conglomerates want to do everything. But no company can be a world-class provider of everything. A car company can't be a world-class provider of seats and software. There is always an economic rationale to work with partners. The question is how best to exercise control. It is far easier to motivate a business partner than someone who is simply a supplier."

Adding fuel to the argument, Don Tapscott says: "The last thing in the world a company needs is a great Web site. You need a great business web. The site, the technology, is the easy part. It is harder to cut a deal with a partner than to get a new piece of software running."

If you are looking for business-Web role models, Tapscott and his co-authors suggest you look no further than big names like Microsoft and Cisco Systems. "Microsoft is one of the pioneers of the business-web," he says. "And Cisco has very strong enduring relationships with its business partners and customers. It has developed a feeling of common self-interest."

Digital Capital is the fruit of a $3 million research project – research which generated so much material that the original manuscript was twice the length of the final version. The original inspiration for this research was the Nobel Laureate, Ronald Coase, to whose work Don Tapscott was introduced in 1993. Coase wrote: "A firm will tend to expand until the costs of organizing an extra transaction within the firm become equal to the costs of a carrying out the same transaction on the open market." And this is the basis for Tapscott's current theorizing – "Coase defined transaction costs broadly including the cost of co-ordination, collaboration, and of finding the right people. We have been systematically extending his ideas to the New Economy," he explains. And, in the New Economy, the Internet provides low-cost markets outside the firm for an array of services.

"The big thing about the Internet is not that it's ubiquitous or high bandwidth, moving from a garden path to a highway a mile wide, but that it is growing in function," says Tapscott. "All the things Coase wrote about are being built right into the Net whether it is auction tools, payment systems or collaboration tools like Lotus Notes. As the Internet is a public infrastructure, you can deconstruct the firm and then reconstruct it on the web as a business web."

The business web is regarded by Tapscott as the first significant challenge to the traditional hierarchically and functionally-based organization. The corporation is dead; long live the b-web. "While management fads have been regarded as good medicine, the corporation remained largely sacrosanct and unchanged. The business web provides a new model for the corporation," he says. It is not simply another take on the virtual organization, which he regards as a transactional system rather than a true business system. Initiatives such as outsourcing, virtual organizations, eco-nets, and *keritsu* are regarded by Tapscott as interpretations of business webs: variations on a theme, but lacking a grasp of the bigger organizational picture.

To some extent the b-web concept has already been developed in Asia where partnerships and webs of connections are central to the business world.

"The Asian mindset is one form of what we're talking about but it is undisciplined," says Tapscott, before going on to warn against the perils of lapsing into old command-and-control models, "There is a stronger belief in Europe – where business models are lagging behind – that in order to control you must own. This is stronger still in Japan and Korea."

In traditional guru manner, Tapscott is seeking to create his own b-web. His corporate incarnation is entitled Digital 4Sight, a combination of think tank, research organization and strategy company. In the digital age he christened, the chairman does not spend much time in the office. Indeed, Don Tapscott is the ultimate digital nomad. He calculates he calls in at 120 cities a year, spending 75 percent of time on the road. Tapscott counts his relentless program of seminar appearances as education and learning – "brain rewiring."

While he is racking up the air miles, the company gathers material. Its research projects are broad ranging. Works in progress include one involving 20 countries looking at how the digital economy will change the very nature of governance. The company is also looking at mobile commerce. Its projects usually involve consortia of large companies providing funding usually starting in the region of $100,000. Tapscott explains:

"Typically we identify emergent best practice and take the ideas into the heart of our client organizations. In 1999 the company had 20 people. By mid-2000 this figure was around 100 with its Toronto HQ supplemented by offices in San José, Washington, London and Singapore. What differentiates us is our thought leadership in e-business. E-business is not just one of the things that we do, like many consulting firms. Rather, it is our exclusive focus. We promise our clients that we will remain ahead of the learning curve in e-business."

As the learning curve heads into the intellectual stratosphere, this is a promise only a handful of thinkers will be able to keep. Don Tapscott is likely to be one of them.

Links

www.digital-4sight.com

LINUS TORVALDS

– *Linux*

I f you ask a group of computer enthusiasts today to name their favorite operating system, the chances are it will be Linux. Linux is the open-source operating system that has prompted an outbreak of Linuxmania in the computing world, where it is touted as a potential competitor to Microsoft's all-powerful Windows. Torvalds didn't invent the open-source movement, (much of the credit for that is given to Eric Raymond and Brian Behlendorf) but he did turn the spotlight on it as never before. In doing so he has highlighted how the Internet has made it possible to rethink the organization and the process of product development

Torvalds (born 1969) was barely out of diapers when he started programming computers. Aged 10, he was writing computer games for a Commodore VIC-20 that his grandfather had bought him. At Helsinki University, he graduated from computer games to operating systems. He didn't like his PC's pre-installed operating system (Microsoft's DOS), preferring the University's UNIX system. The problem was that there was no UNIX version for PCs. So he wrote one:

> "When I was 21, I was very self-assured when it came to pro-gramming and not very self-assured when it came to anything else. But I knew I was the best programmer in the world. So I just decided 'Hey, why couldn't I do this myself?' And so I did."[1]

He called the new OS "Linux". And then, astonishingly, instead of making millions of dollars from his new program, he gave away the source code. This instantly made him a hero of the open-source move-ment.

Insight

The penguin story

So where did the penguin come from? The Linux mascot, possibly the most famous penguin ever, came out of a painful encounter Torvalds had in the southern hemisphere. When he came across a fairy penguin on a trip to Australia he just couldn't resist giving it a friendly pat. In turn the penguin couldn't resist taking a chunk out of Torvalds' hand. Luckily Torvalds has a sense of humor. Others wanted a sensible, but dull logo for Linux, Torvalds plumped for the penguin. His reasons are unclear. But the moral of the story, if you live in Redmond, might be that penguins bite.

One of the remarkable things about the development of Linux is the contribution made by hackers (people who write computer code – as opposed to crackers – who break into it). It wasn't that long ago that nerdy kids with an interest in computers spent hours locked away in the darkness of their bedrooms shunned by their non-geek friends. Today it's sexy to be a nerd – almost. Nerds have come out of the closet in their hundreds of thousands. No longer confined to their bedrooms they use the Internet to patrol the cyberway looking for code to mess around with and other programmers to communicate with. This is how Linux became so famous. Above all things what these cyber free spirits hate is proprietary software that they can't get to grips with – like the Microsoft OS for example.

So, when Torvalds decided to post the source code for Linux on the Internet, there was much rejoicing among the programming community. A hundred or so programmers from all over the world downloaded Linux – and started to tweak it and improve it. They tasted victory in the air.

It is a perfect example of what the Internet is best at, and where the future of business may be heading. Linux galvanized a pool of highly talented, focused, motivated individuals geographically dislocated yet all working for a common cause. They started sharing knowledge in a way predicted by futurists, and only possible because of the World Wide Web and the Internet. The fact that just Torvalds and a few others were able to successfully manage the process provides some indication of the potential. In the words of Torvalds:

"It's a chaos that has some external constraints put on it. For example, the pure kernel has a copyright that says that whoever does Linux development doesn't need to go through me. If Microsoft wanted to, they could take Linux tomorrow, start development on it, and do it completely on their own. There's nothing to stop anybody from doing that. However, they are required to make all the changes available to everybody else."

To a degree, the development process was self-regulated by the Linux community. Could this, then, be the organizational model of the future? Possibly, if organizations can fire up individuals sufficiently in a common cause – in the way that making Linux the No. 1 OS and defeating the Microsoft empire united the Linux community. A slight problem with the Linux model, from the business perspective, is that it was a non-commercial enterprise. No one was making money out of the improvements to Linux or the Linux OS itself. At least they weren't at the time. This may explain the free flow of ideas – there was no reason to be protective of knowledge as no one profited.

Wherever there is a demand, however, there will always be someone with a business model to capitalize on it. Linux has now become a commercial product. It's difficult to understand how it is possible to build a business around a product that is available free, but VA Linux, Red Hat and many others have done just that. Typically, they provide added-value services on top of the Linux OS. Linux might be simple enough to install and set up for experienced programmers but the majority of businesses do not have the time to wrestle with the software. By offering a package of services that includes back up, detailed tutorials, set-up and easy installation and configuration programs, the Linux companies can charge for supporting the open-source software. Surprisingly, the open-source community don't feel sold-out. But then a lot of them have stock in Red Hat, VA Linux, Caldera and other Linux companies. But it still seems contrary to the spirit of the open-source movement. Indeed Linux is still a developing OS and the Linux community are still improving the product, the majority unrewarded, while the improved product is making money for a small number of companies.

It could be argued, however, that had it not been for the commercialization of Linux it would never have stood a chance of gaining meaningful market share, let alone usurping Microsoft's Windows.

And Red Hat, VA Linux and some of the bigger companies selling various flavors of Linux do support the community and invest in its development.

Regardless of the debate about the "corporate Linux," Torvalds' OS, along with another program, Solaris, has become one of the most popular versions of Unix. Unlike UNIX, Linux is making the transition from large scale computing applications to the PC market. Computer games are a good example – both Doom and Quake ran in a Linux window before they were ported to Windows.

Torvalds, meanwhile, has moved from his native Finland to Silicon Valley. He still continues to have an input into the development of the Linux OS but is also involved in an exciting new project at Transmeta. Transmeta is threatening to shake up the cozy coterie of chip manufacturers, Intel and AMD. Headed up by CEO David Ditzel, Transmeta has come up with a revolutionary approach to micro processing. After five years shrouded in secrecy Transmeta finally came clean and confirmed the rumors about the hottest project in computing. In its new Crusoe microprocessor, Transmeta's developers have managed to combine the silicon chip with a microchip instruction set executed entirely in software. This means the processor can "learn" and be modified over time, it also means high speeds with little power drain. In other words it's a mobile computer manufacturer's dream.

Torvalds' task in all this was to design an OS based on Linux to run on the mobile. Torvalds has delivered; he calls the new version Mobile Linux. In a shrewd positioning move, the Transmeta has already negotiated deals with Gateway and AOL to supply the Crusoe chip and Mobile Linux for use in jointly branded legacy-free Internet appliances (IAs). It's a small step along the road to defeating the Wintel hegemony, but it's a real and significant one. And for a change it's not just a labor of love for Torvalds – he gets paid.

Links

www.transmeta.com

Notes

1. Linux Torvalds interview, *Linux Manifesto*.
2. Ibid.

JAY WALKER

– *Priceline.com*

For many Americans the first real clue that the Internet was going to change their lives came with the 1998 $15 million radio blitz advertising of Priceline.com Inc. The ads, starring William Shatner, of *Star Trek* fame, invited consumers to log on and name their price for airline tickets. Disbelief rapidly turned to amazement as Priceline became a household name. In its first year, the company generated revenues of $35 million. Its IPO in March 1999, valued the company at $13 billion. (Shatner wisely agreed to take his $500,000 fee mostly in stock – 100,000 shares, recently valued at about $7.5 million.)

Few of those hearing the commercials realized that what Jay Walker, the man behind Priceline, was doing was stripping the previously hidden economics of airline yield management naked.[1] Few cared. Cheaper airline tickets were enough to get their attention. The business model that the company was predicated on was of limited interest. But to Walker, the business model was all. Whilst studying at Cornell University, he dedicated himself to the game of Monopoly, and went on to become world champion. He later co-authored a book *1000 Ways to Win Monopoly Games*.

Today, Jay Walker is one of the most famous sons of the new economy. *Forbes* magazine featured him on its cover, pictured with a light bulb and the headline "New Age Edison." More than just an Internet entrepreneur, Walker has made a business out of patenting business models. He is a serial entrepreneur from an entrepreneurial family. His parents combined the qualities that have made him success. His father was a property developer – a self-made man – and his mother was in sales.

On his way to Priceline fame, Walker, a native of Queens NY, launched more than 10 companies. The businesses tended to be based in marketing and advertising – from mail-order catalogues to schemes to sell magazine subscriptions using frequent-flier miles. Many of these businesses failed or were only a moderate success. But they gave Walker a taste for running his own company. "I was always looking for new ideas, different avenues to try," he says. "Some of them even succeeded."

What fascinated him was the business model: the initial idea itself, and how it could be applied to create a revenue-generating machine. The Internet he quickly realized had the power to make new business models viable. Walker bet his personal fortune – made from an earlier foray into an automated magazine subscription-renewal service – on the power of ideas. Having stumbled on the fact that business models on the Internet could be patented as readily as industrial processes, he founded Walker Digital – a laboratory for developing business strategy. Priceline.com was one of the first businesses to emerge from that lab.

It was based on a system that allows companies to dispose of excess inventory at optimal prices. The key was a "double blind" methodology, allowing both parties to the transaction to make anonymous bids. This ensures that the provider – initially the airlines – do not undermine their brands or ability to charge the full fare elsewhere.

Walker saw an opportunity in the 500,000 airline tickets that go unsold daily. Using the Internet as the interface between airlines' unsold inventory and the traveler seems obvious. Unfortunately for Walker, the concept wasn't as immediately obvious to the airlines. They required some persuading that the Priceline Website would not steal traffic from their own Websites and break the traditional distribution link between the travel agencies and the airlines.

In the event only TWA and America West signed up but that proved enough to set the wheels rolling. After that famous advertising campaign, over a million people logged on trying to buy tickets – too many for an overwhelmed Priceline that was forced to buy tickets in the open market to satisfy customer demand. The company often ended up paying more than it was selling the same tickets on for.

Things took a turn for the better when Walker hired Richard Braddock, ex-Citicorp president, as chairman and CEO. Walker assumed a lower profile as vice-chairman. The company added to its airline partners, including the major carrier Delta. This was a much-needed boost to Priceline's credibility and inventory. The deal came at a price, however, with Delta extracting various concessions from Priceline. These included agreements to allow Delta to veto potential partners in the Priceline ticket scheme; retain all gross profits exceeding 12 percent on the Delta seats; and warrants for the stock amounting to around 12 percent of Priceline's equity exercisable at 93 cents a piece.

Despite the concessions the Delta deal made good sense, if only because it encouraged other airlines to join up, which they soon did. Names like Continental and Northwest attracted high-profile investors like Microsoft co-founder Paul Allen and George Soros the Hungarian-born financier.

The company went public in 1999. It was one of the biggest offerings that year – the stock shot up from an opening of $16 dollars to $69 dollars at the close of the market and $162 a month later. They have since fallen back.

Heady talk followed the IPO. Priceline, it was suggested, would break even by 2001 and roll out the business model to other markets. It was a point of distinction that Walker was an Internet entrepreneur. He was not driven by the technology but by the business model – which he had patented. Walker notes:

> "Priceline was never about the airline industry, we are about excess supply and pricing. The patent does not speak to airlines at all. The patent speaks to commerce, to a whole pricing system. We are not an airline-specific solution – it was just the first thing we chose to price. We have made no secret of the fact that if we can price travel, mortgages and cars, we can probably price anything, and we will. What I am is a marketer. Most people who are in the Internet market are technologists. But as marketers, we ask what are the problems and how can we solve them. We like to think of ourselves as firmly focused on the fundamentals of the marketplace as opposed to the superficiality of the latest technology."[2]

What then of Walker's business model: does it stand up to closer scrutiny? Great marketing cannot disguise Priceline's limitations. Its clarion call is "name your own price," but can you actually name your own price? Well, kind of. While customers may be flexible in their pricing model, the airlines are not. On its Website Priceline states:

> "We collect consumer demand (in the form of individual customer offers guaranteed by a credit card) for a particular product or service at a price set by the customer and communicate that demand directly to participating sellers or to their private databases."

Insight

Patent it, market it

Jay Walker is an Internet entrepreneur with a difference. He discovered that it is possible to patent a business method, provided it satisfies the basic tests of patentability. It must be unique and non-obvious. Once patented, in theory, the originator owns the business model, providing he or she has the money to enforce it in law. Through his company Walker Digital, Jay Walker has filed for over 200 patents, including the "name-your-price" concept.

Then, once a company has patented the model, it has to market it. Where the Internet is concerned, this usually – although not necessarily – means spending a lot of money. That can be the difference between a market value of billions or mere millions. As one of Priceline's rivals said in a 1999 interview: " He [Jay Walker] has created a national brand in a very short period. I think I could've done the same if I spent the money he did on advertising. But then, we've got a policy here at CheapTickets: We need to make money."

In return consumers are required to be: "flexible with respect to brands, sellers and/or product features." What this means in practice, is that the airlines submit details of their unsold tickets to Priceline through a database. The details change frequently throughout the day. When a customer places a bid, Priceline can then scour the database to see if there is flight offered that matches the customer's criteria. True the customer may get a flight at the price they offered, subject to Priceline's conditions. They may however pay more for the flight than the airline's lowest indicated price, and there is no way of knowing. It is a deal with the odds stacked in the airline's favor.

There are also conditions attached. Consumers' flexibility must extend to the time of flying – Priceline can only guarantee the flight will be between 6 a.m. and 10 p.m. Neither can it assure non-stop flights, or what airline you will be flying. Travelers do not get frequent flyer miles or upgrades either. In September 2000, the company issued its first profits warning since flotation – shares fell 42 percent to $10. Angry investors threatened legal action, alleging Priceline had misled them in previous financial statements.

Despite these setbacks, consumers still flock to the Priceline Website. Priceline extended its price distribution system beyond transportation into hard goods. The company started Priceline Webhouse Club, a grocery-purchasing service that allowed customers to name their own prices, and followed it, in February 2000, with a service selling gasoline using the same system. Both have now been withdrawn. Whether Priceline can ride out its current woes remains to be seen.

Notes

1. Rothenburg, Randall (2000) The thought leader interview, *Strategy and Business*, Issue 19, second quarter.
2. *FT Online*, July 2000.

ALAN WEBBER

– Fast Company

T here's an anecdote that Alan Webber, co-founder of the business-cum-lifestyle magazine *Fast Company* likes to relate. Webber was attending a meeting, held by a major US packaged-goods organization, when a speaker caught his attention. When renowned archaeologist Heinrich Schielmann, discovered Troy, said the speaker, he found that the city had for centuries been built and rebuilt, over and over, on the same spot. Why, asked the speaker, did no one ever say: "let's move it over there?"

Fast Company has broken the mold, and more importantly the mindset, of the traditional business magazine. It asks questions relevant to life in the new world of work. In doing so, it's become a totem of the new business tribe. Ancient Troy continues to crumble, while the new Troy goes from strength to strength.

Prior to launching the magazine, in November 1995, Alan Webber spent six years at the *Harvard Business Review,* the bastion of old economy theorizing. He had arrived at Harvard Business School in 1981 as a senior research assistant. He was working on a project related to the auto industry after a spell as Special Assistant to the US Secretary of Transportation in Washington, DC. At HBS, he got to know Bill Taylor, then editor of the flagship journal *HBR.* Webber's interest soon shifted from automobiles to writing and magazine publishing. He eventually became editorial director of *HBR.* While he was there, the prestigious business magazine was a finalist three times for the National Magazine Awards.

From their vantage point in Boston, Webber and Taylor could see the world was changing – quickly. A global revolution, they concluded, was sweeping business. A new magazine was needed to highlight how companies were transforming to compete in the new business world.

One night while working late, Webber tripped on an old shoebox, or so the story goes, and banged his head on an open drawer. On the offending desk there were copies of three magazines: the *Harvard Business Review*, *Rolling Stone* and the *US News & World Report*. This, thought Webber, was the perfect mix:

> "No existing magazine was doing it [the new business revolution] justice, writing about it with energy, insight, utility, and color. The shift in technology, globalization and a new generation called for a business magazine that was fun and informative, so we decided to try to create it."[1]

Webber produced a dummy copy of the magazine: this was well received. (It can still be seen online). Webber and Taylor, *Fast Company's* co-editor and co-founder, concentrated on the editorial, while partners Mort Zuckerman and Fred Drasner of *U.S. News & World Report*, looked after the business side of the venture (they also publish the *New York Daily News*).

Cleverly marketed from the start, *Fast Company's* first issue's print order of 300,000 was strategically distributed to key business contacts drawn from Webber and Taylor's *HBR* days. These included such luminaries as Tom Peters, Regis McKenna and Michael Porter. More copies went to McKinsey executives and think-tank conference attendees. The feedback was positive.

Unit of one

The magazine had a new look – and a new slant. *Fast Company* is what Taylor likes to call a "workstyle" magazine. A business magazine with "a highly-caffeinated personality." In issue number 1 the co-founders outlined their manifesto: "*Fast Company* aims to be the handbook of the business revolution. We will chronicle the changes under way in how companies create and compete, highlight the new practices shaping how work gets done, showcase teams who are inventing the future and reinventing business."

Fast Company set out not only to report the business revolution, but also to play a part in shaping it by creating a vocabulary for the new economy. One of the magazines key contributions to the discussion about the new economy is the "unit of one." In the old world, argues Webber, analysis used to be framed in terms of the corporation. In the new world the unit of analysis is the individual. With a connection to the Internet, one person can transact business across the globe: one individual, one world.

It's a convincing enough argument to persuade the University of Toronto Business School to remodel its curriculum incorporating the concept. In the words of Webber:

> "It's hard to miss the fundamental shifts going on in the world of business. Speed, global reach, blurring boundaries, more women in positions of power, instantaneous technology, the power of good ideas, the importance of great implementation, the high stakes for success or failure, the thrill of the game, the need for some reflection to think about what it all means, the shift of power from the big company to the individual."[2]

Webber believes *Fast Company* offers a new perspective on the world. The underlying premise is that the world is changing. So, *Fast Company* asks 'how is it changing?" When Webber talks about the subjects that fill the magazine's pages he divides them broadly into three categories, the three "G"s. These are: generation, the transfer of power from the old generation to the new; globalization, a collision of different perspectives on business; and gender, the rise of women in the workplace. These then are the key themes underpinning editorial content. *Fast Company* asks fundamental questions about life in the new economy. What is a fast company? How do you become a fast company?

Webber has identified several defining characteristics of a fast company. At its heart he says is innovation:

> "The first thing that a fast company has to be is really driven by ideas. It is an economy where innovation and creativity is the starting point. And the organization that can't figure out how to solve the pendulum problem because this is the way we always do things around here is dead meat. They're simply not going to be able to compete effectively."[3]

Unsurprisingly, too, a fast company should also be fast. It should be "a relentless implementer" says Webber. Startling speed is a must-have in a world that allows the reengineering of a product almost before it hits the stores. Teamwork is also essential, as is a clear identity. Companies must know what they stand for and what they are good at. Stock-options attract talent, but to the new generation of free agents and contract workers, values are just as important. Then throw the killer application

---

Insight

America is not the world

It may be difficult for *Fast Company* to maintain its momentum. It's a magazine that has made a name for daring to be different, for its *élan*, panache, wit and style. It stands out from the competition in both content and design. Its great weakness, however, is a US-centric view of the business world. This seems oddly out of kilter with a publication espousing a global business revolution, but international stories are few and far between.

---

into the pot – or the Web according to Webber – stir and you get an idea of where Fast Company is coming from.

Change agents

This heady mix of ingredients is packaged in a distinctive style and pitched at a target audience of "change agents." These are the "guerrillas in the hills." Mavericks maybe, or dissidents within organizations that become the focus for change within a company. Webber admits that fast company perfection is a fantasy rather than a reality. But, he says, even a few steps along the road to becoming a fast company are better than settling for the status quo. There is a new generation of "free agents" working for new companies playing by the *Fast Company* rules. And there are some *agents provocateurs* at old companies, fomenting the revolution from within. *Fast Company* speaks to both these constituencies. What they have in common is a desire to learn about new ideas and new ways of working.

Fast sales

A stack of issues down the line, Webber and Taylor can justifiably claim a spectacular success. The magazine has tapped into the psyche of a generation. They are the movers and shakers of the new world; the power brokers of tomorrow. A swathe of entrepreneurs has grown up on a diet of *Fast Company*'s cutting-edge informative reporting. It has won its fair share of awards on the way. In 1999 it was named Magazine of the Year by *Advertising Age* and came top of *Adweek*'s hotlist.

Revolutionary fervor, however, tends to fizzle out like the thrill of a new relationship. *Fast Company* could be heading for a steady friendship with its readers, slipping on its post-revolutionary comfy slippers. Many magazines would settle for less: Webber, one suspects, would not. For now *Fast Company* continues to ask some important questions in the modern world of business. It remains an essential read and, possibly the greatest measure of its success, it can be found on the shelves and desktops of the major players in the new business revolution.

Notes

1. natmags.co. magfocus – American Originals, March/April 1998.
2. Ibid.
3. Alan Webber at the New York Ad Club, February, 1998.

DAVID WETHERELL

– CMGI

"**I**f you're well positioned, have a good business model, and can't make a living in an industry growing at five percent a month, you oughta go pick oranges," says David Wetherell. In recent years, CMGI, the Internet holding company Wetherell founded, has been picking more exotic fruit.

One of the big US incubators, CMGI (which started life as College Marketing Group) floated in 1994, and now has a stake in a network of around 65 Internet businesses. With Wetherell as CEO, the Andover, Massachusetts-company has pioneered the so-called EcoNet model – or network of companies. It backs companies that offer synergies with other businesses in the group.

CMGI is a hybrid. It has been described as an "opervesting" company, part operating company and part venture capitalist. The VC arm is CMG@Ventures, and manages a number of investment funds. In Europe, CMGI has established its European headquarters – or "campus" – in Maidenhead, UK, which also act as a European base for other companies in the CMGI group, including AltaVista Europe and Engage.

CMGI is an eclectic collection of operating companies that has spread its tentacles throughout the Internet. Through CMGI and @Venture, the company invests in and incubates promising start-ups. The beauty of the operation, however, is the next stage. CMGI takes the fledgling companies public, retaining a significant share and incorporating them into the CMGI network of companies. So a $6 million investment in GeoCities brought in $1 billion when GeoCities was sold to Yahoo! And $2 million sunk into Lycos is now worth over $700 million. As business models go, it has its attractions.

Wetherell is the man at the center of the CMGI network. A math major from Ohio, Wetherell came to Wall Street's attention when he scuppered the Lycos/USA Networks merger deal, engineered by Barry Diller. As far as the Wall Street pundits were concerned, the deal was done and dusted. Wetherell, however, had other ideas. CMGI had purchased an 80 percent stake in the Lycos portal in 1995. When the USA Networks deal was proposed, he feared the traditional media company would put a brake on the Internet company and resigned from the board. The decision went to the shareholders and the deal fell apart.

Wetherell is currently pursuing a number of different strategies at CMGI. It's all part of his grand design – to build a loose network of Internet companies modeled on the Japanese *keiretsu*. Companies within the CMGI universe profit from dealing with both each other and the outside world. The first part of CMGI's strategy is investing in companies that it can plug into the network. CMGI buys controlling interests in businesses that fit in well with its own core business. Wetherell looks for criteria such as scalability, first-mover advantage and top-class technology. It can then incubate the company, leveraging it within its network and cultivating it to IPO.

Employees in the majority-owned company receive not only stock in their own company but stock in CMGI. This gives them both immediate rewards as well as the promise of further riches when the company goes to market.

Through its VC arm @Venture, started in 1995, CMGI is able to take smaller minority stakes in start-ups. It was the first venture-capital company dedicated to the Internet. Through @Venture, CMGI can acquire a stake in a company that wishes to retain its independence but still requires a cash injection. That way the company can retain an exposure to innovative start-ups at the cutting edge of the Internet. It's a part of CMGI's business that's growing in importance. The first two venture funds were $35 million in size. The third was $282 million. Future funds are likely to be between half a billion to a billion dollars.

In its early life, CMGI was not in a position to acquire companies outright. However, as its market cap increased and it leveraged the companies in the network, Wetherell has been able to make key acquisitions, purchasing for example a majority stake in AltaVista from Compaq for $2.3 billion.

The majority-owned companies are then plugged into the CMGI network, creating synergies that benefit the group. At the center of this maze of assorted companies is the AltaVista portal. CMGI companies like CarParts.com add e-commerce value to the AltaVista proposition.

Insight

Network effects

Several companies such as CMGI and Softbank have established networks and offer a growing array of services. Their progeny can outsource tasks such as finance and accounting and network infra-structure to their ready and willing parents. The result is a spiral of networks and links, spreading virus-like through the corporate world. Some might suggest that incubators are the result of the cur-rent e-business hyperbole. This may be true in some cases, but the incubator as organizational model may prove to be as significant and long lasting as the very concept of the corporation.

AdSmart, specializing in advertising management technology, and Engage, an Internet profiling company, enhance ad targeting and lever-age ad revenue through the portal and CMGI's other Websites.

Ultimately, Wetherell takes the companies in the network to IPO. This generates value, which can then be recycled through more pur-chases. If market conditions are favourable, then the CMGI's growth should continue to accelerate. CMGI has sold GeoCities to Yahoo! for $4.35 billion. It has also taken many companies public, including Chemdex, Engage, Critical Path and Silknet.

Critical to the business model is the state of the markets. CMGI has already accumulated sizeable amounts of cash to fund purchases. However if the climate is hostile to dot-com IPOs, CMGI could stagnate. Similarly, with the stack of networked companies finely balanced on AltaVista, the fortunes of CMGI are closely bound to the fortunes of the portal. It is only possible to leverage the value of companies in the network through AltaVista if the portal gets enough "eyeballs" and in a fragmenting market this might prove an issue.

By building other smaller clusters of specialist companies within CMGI, Wetherell has to some extent defrayed the possible effects of a bear market or a downturn in traffic from one of CMGI's portals. The acquisition of the ad network AdForce coupled with Flycast, the permission marketer Yesmail.com, together with the technologies of Engage, gives CMGI a formidable advertising, targeting and user profiling capability. Wetherell has put together a suite of ad companies to take on the might of the market leader in online advertising – Double-Click.

DoubleClick provides a one-stop-shop for companies that want to advertise online. It plans the advertising strategy, sells the ads, and serves the ads to a targeted market. Taking on DoubleClick at its own game is, however, a tough proposition for CMGI. DoubleClick not only has a substantial head start but online advertising has always been its core business and it has grown in a consistent, streamlined and focused way.

Don't bet against Wetherell pulling it off though. He is not a man to be dismissed lightly. Wetherell also has plans to build the largest entertainment company in the world – through the online netcasting vehicle iCast.

Regardless of operating losses, CMGI looks certain to be a major Internet player for some time to come. With 1500 plus business plans passing across its virtual desk a month, CMGI is expected to add 50 to 60 new companies to its portfolio in 2000, as well as 9 or 10 IPOs, adding a possible $10 billion or so tradable securities to its existing collection. That's in addition to the 40-plus investments and 12 majority-owned companies it already has.

Wetherell has bet on the Internet big-time – don't expect to find him picking oranges any time soon.

Links

www.cmgi.com

BOB YOUNG

– Red Hat

Linux is an open-source operating system developed by Linus Torvalds (see *Linus Torvalds*). Open-source software is free. Giving stuff away may not appear a sensible, or profitable, business model. But Red Hat, Linux specialists, and one of the leading companies in open-source Internet infrastructure, had a successful IPO in October 1999 and reported revenues of $13.1 million for the quarter ending February 29, 2000. This is how it works.

When Linus Torvalds invented the software program Linux, based on the UNIX kernel, he was motivated not by a desire to make money, but to build a tool that did exactly what he wanted it to. When he was satisfied with the results, instead of patenting it, and in keeping with the tradition of the open-source movement he released the source code to the wider programming community. The open-source movement (OSS) has been around since the early days of commercial computing. It has long campaigned against proprietary software, arguing instead that an open approach to building software results in better products. When the Internet became mainstream it created the perfect medium for the dissemination of source code. Consequently the movement flourished and products like Apache – a Web-server – and the Linux operating system (OS) have become widespread.

Companies began to recognize the commercial value of releasing source code into the community. Netscape, for example, released its source code for the Netscape Internet browser in order to establish it as the Internet standard.

Ironically, if it had not been for the open-source movement then Red Hat would not exist. The company's founders took one look at Linux and saw their future. By the time Bob Young founded Red Hat, he was on his fourth start-up. A modern-history graduate of the University of Toronto, he teamed up with Marc Ewing to start a company that commercialized Linux. Possibly the motivation was an evangelical desire to spread the Linux gospel and vanquish the arch-enemy Microsoft. If it was, it would have struck a chord with devotees of the open-source movement. Or maybe it was a glimmer of the large amounts of money to be made if even a fraction of Microsoft market share could be achieved. Or maybe a mixture of both. Either way, the pair determined to exploit the commercial opportunities that Linux presented.

Linux may hail from the non-commercial traditions of the open-source software movement, but there's still money to be made from the OS, as Red Hat has patently demonstrated. Based in the Research Triangle, in North Carolina, Red Hat makes its money from bundling its version of the Linux OS – Red Hat Linux 6.0 etc. – with a full range of services such as telephone support, on-site consulting, training, certification and priority updates. The company distributes Linux and Apache on Intel, DEC Alpha and Sun SPARC platforms. Linux may be available free over the net, but it takes time to download and then you have to know what to do with it. When you buy the software CDs from Red Hat you get product literature and tutorials that help you realize the full potential of Linux as as well as back-up support. Because Linux and therefore Red Hat's products are open-source, they offer a completely customizable software solution.

Red Hat customers also get access to the world's largest help-desk – a global bank of software programmers to call upon for advice and assistance. Because of the nature of the open-source movement – which is a community – thousands of programmers are happy to offer the benefit of their expertise online free of charge.

You might expect the corporatization and commercialization of an open-source technology to upset a few people – not least the multitude of developers in the Linux community who helped improve the Linux OS. But then maybe not – after all, over 8000 members of the open-source community attending Linuxworld voted Red Hat their "LinuxWorld Favorite."

The company had its IPO in October 1999, narrowly avoiding a minor fiasco and some negative publicity along the way. Due to the regulations governing IPOs it looked for a while as if members of the open-source community weren't going to be able to buy shares in the IPO. This would have not have pleased the community. Young and Ewing stepped in to make sure they could. There was no shortage of takers.

Many would argue that the kind of commercial clout Red Hat has is exactly what Linux needs if it is to compete with the likes of Microsoft. It

Insight

Seeing opportunities where none exist

The natural route to making money from the Linux OS would have been to patent the software and sell it as a proprietary brand. This, however, went contrary to inventor Linus Torvalds' philosophy on software development.

Torvalds deliberately and cleverly structured the general copyright and licensing to make it almost impossible to manufacture a copy of Linux that doesn't have to be given away free of charge. Anyone can work on the kernel of Linux, but the copyright requires them to make any code they produce freely available to everyone. This might deter most people from trying to build a business around Linux. Not Young and Ewing, however, who thought of charging not for the software but for the added value – thus avoiding litigation over the copyright, yet profiting from the invention of the open-source software. It's a canny strategy, but one that risks alienating the open-source movement.

would be a shame to develop a great product, never to see it established outside the geek community. Red Hat isn't the only company to jump on the Linux bandwagon; VA Linux has also listed.

The future for the Linux OS seems secure as it gains a firm foothold in the Internet software market. The future for Red Hat, however, is less certain. Success depends on critical factors, such as early acquisition of market share.

With Linux being an open-source program, there are few other barriers to entry other than the size of the competition. So if Red Hat is able to establish itself in the minds of consumers as inextricably associated with Linux, competitors may find it impossible to muscle their way in. But don't write off Microsoft, the software Goliath has come from behind too often for comfort. In theory, there is nothing to prevent the mighty Microsoft from hedging its bets and packaging its own Linux software product. The number of companies joining the Linux fray is likely to grow. This could mean that every computer user will get to benefit from Linus Torvalds' invention.

Links

www.redhat.com

Index